JOHN DAVID BOSCH

JOHN DAVID BOSCH

IN THE VANGUARD OF HEROES, MARTYRS, AND SAINTS

ANGELINA DILIBERTO ALLEN

Baháʼí Publishing
WILMETTE, ILLINOIS

Bahá'í Publishing, Wilmette, Illinois

401 Greenleaf Ave, Wilmette, Illinois 60091
Copyright © 2019 by the National Spiritual Assembly
of the Bahá'ís of the United States

All rights reserved. Published 2019

Printed in the United States of America ∞
22 21 20 19   1 2 3 4

ISBN 978-1-61851-150-8

Cover design by Carlos Esparza
Book design by Patrick Falso
Photos courtesy of National Bahá'í Archives, United States

"Someday, when the 'spirit moves,' I may write all my experiences with 'Abdu'l-Bahá in New York, Chicago, San Francisco and Haifa. With love from both of us, John."

Dedicated to the memory of Mrs. Molly S. King, program director at Bosch Bahá'í School and Mr. James S. Kelly, administrator of Bosch Bahá'í School.

With gratitude to Martha Schweitz and Brent Poirier for their careful review; Christopher Martin for his fine editing; Margie and Gary Bulkin for their thoughtful ideas; Edward and Evelyn Diliberto for their clear guidance; and Andy Allen for his family's long legacy with John and Louise Bosch.

Also, a special thanks to the U.S. National Spiritual Assembly's precious archivists Mr. Edward Sevcik, Mr. Roger Dahl, and Mr. Lewis Walker, whose generous assistance made this biography possible.

Contents

Note to the Reader xi
Introduction xv
1 / On a Train 1
2 / Become as True Brethren 19
3 / I Have Traveled 8,000 Miles to See You 63
4 / Louise 81
5 / Awakened by the Tablets of the Divine Plan 97
6 / Tahiti 113
7 / 'Abdu'l-Bahá is in the Utmost Longing to See You 145
8 / An Indefatigable Trio 183
9 / Not Alone of the Mind, but of the Depths of the Heart 221
10 / Your Milly 275
11 / Saints 293
Notes 331
Bibliography 353
Index 359
Photos of John Bosch 367

Note to the Reader

The Tablets from 'Abdu'l-Bahá to individual believers cited in this biography are obtained from the U.S. Bahá'í Archives. While some of the translations of the Tablets may have been revised in later years, in most cases throughout this biography, the original translations of the Tablets have been used. This is for historical purposes and for the purpose of understanding the events in the life of John Bosch. The English translations made at the time of the original Tablet and sent to the recipient with the original are published here as historical documents, not as authorized translations.

Furthermore, Shoghi Effendi on numerous occasions cautioned against attributing too great an importance to "pilgrims' notes" or the personal impression of 'Abdu'l-Bahá's words from an individual believer: "It was chiefly in view of the misleading nature of the reports of the informal conversations of 'Abdu'l-Bahá with visiting pilgrims, that I have insistently urged the believers of the West to regard such statements as merely personal impressions of the sayings of their Master, and to quote and consider as authentic only such translations as are based upon the authenticated text of His recorded utterances in the original tongue."*

Further guidance regarding the use of "pilgrims' notes" can be found

---

* Shoghi Effendi, *The World Order of Bahá'u'lláh*, 5.

NOTE TO THE READER

in a letter dated October 2, 1935, written on behalf of Shoghi Effendi to the National Spiritual Assembly of the United States and Canada: "He would also urge you to attach no importance to the stories told about 'Abdu'l-Bahá or to those attributed to Him by the Friends. These should be regarded in the same light as the notes and impressions of visiting pilgrims. They need not be suppressed, but they also should not be given prominence or official recognition."

The Universal House of Justice has made clear that the Bahá'í Faith has two sources of authoritative interpretation: 'Abdu'l-Bahá, Whose authority is derived from His appointment in the Kitáb-i-Aqdas and the Kitáb-i-'Ahd (Book of the Covenant) as the Center of Bahá'u'lláh's Covenant; and the Guardian, whose authority is derived from 'Abdu'l-Bahá's Will and Testament:

> A clear distinction is made in our Faith between authoritative interpretation and the interpretation or understanding that each individual arrives at for himself from his study of its teachings. While the former is confined to the Guardian, the latter, according to the guidance given to us by the Guardian himself, should by no means be suppressed. In fact such individual interpretation is considered the fruit of man's rational power and conducive to a better understanding of the teachings, provided that no disputes or arguments arise among the friends and the individual himself understands and makes it clear that his views are merely his own. Individual interpretations continually change as one grows in comprehension of the teachings. As Shoghi Effendi explained: "To deepen in the Cause means to read the writings of Bahá'u'lláh and the Master so thoroughly as to be able to give it to others in its pure form. There are many who have some superficial idea of what the Cause stands for. They, therefore, present it together with all sorts of ideas that are their own. As the Cause is still in its early days we must be most careful lest we fall under this error and injure the Movement we so much adore. There is no limit to

the study of the Cause. The more we read the Writings the more truths we can find in them and the more we will see that our previous notions were erroneous."

So, although individual insights can be enlightening and helpful, they can also be misleading. The friends must therefore learn to listen to the views of others without being over-awed or allowing their faith to be shaken, and to express their own views without pressing them on their fellow Bahá'ís.*

A final note should be added about the transliteration of Bahá'í terms and the names *Bahá'u'lláh*, *'Abdu'l-Bahá*, and spellings of the salutation *Alláh'u'Abhá*. In a letter dated April 8, 1923, the Guardian established a universal standard for transliteration of Bahá'í terms: "[The Guardian] has given the list of the best known and most current Bahá'í terms, and other Oriental names and expressions, all properly and accurately transliterated, the faithful spelling of which by all the Western friends will avoid confusion in [the] future, and insure in the matter a uniformity which is greatly needed in all Bahá'í literature."**

For historical purposes in this biography, the majority of Bahá'í terms and names mentioned in documents prior to 1923 have been kept in their original transliterated form; nevertheless, some of these spellings have been changed to the spelling outlined by the Guardian in order to avoid confusion.

---

* The Universal House of Justice, letter dated May 27, 1966, cited in *Messages from the Universal House of Justice, 1965–1986*, no. 35.13.
** Shoghi Effendi, *Bahá'í Administration*, 43.

Introduction

Marzieh Gail, outstanding scholar and author, began an early manuscript of John Bosch's life just before his passing in 1946. In that manuscript, Marzieh wrote, "The material we give here consists of conversations with John at Geyserville, written down as he spoke, and of documented information supplied by him and Louise, often copied in their presence, in preparation for a biographical account which they desired me to write and which is currently on file in the archives of the National Spiritual Assembly of Switzerland." Marzieh never published a full biography, although excerpts of her early manuscript were published in *Bahá'í News* in 1974. Her wish that the manuscript be in the care of the Swiss Bahá'í Archives was her way of ensuring that John's memory be associated with Switzerland, the land of his birth. In fact, at the end of John's life, Rúhíyyih Khánum wrote on behalf of the Guardian to Mrs. E. C. Newell (John Bosch's home-nurse during the final days of his life): "'No doubt, when the Cause spreads more throughout Switzerland, this fatherland of his will grow to be proud of this heroic and noble soul it produced; even though the best days of his life were spent in America. The influence of such a pure spirit grows as time goes by and he wishes you to assure Mrs. Bosch that the services she and her husband have rendered the Faith are very great and very deeply valued by him.'"*

---

* Rúhíyyih Khánum, quoted in Marzieh Gail, "For John, With Love," Bahá'í News (July 1974): 9–21.

INTRODUCTION

Marzieh Gail's original manuscript is the foundation of this biography. To describe Marzieh as a remarkable person is an understatement. She was the child of Dr. Alí Kulí Khán and Florence Breed, and she saw herself as neither Persian nor American but as a citizen of the world. She was highly educated and has been characterized as the "patron saint of women Bahá'í scholars, always conscious of her audience, unveiling the Cause in her books and essays, lectures and talks."* Her early research on the life of John Bosch is aimed at unveiling a wide range of Bahá'í subjects that would be of interest to someone learning about the Bahá'í Faith. Furthermore, reading the story of John Bosch's life is an illustration of how teaching the Cause of Bahá'u'lláh can become "the dominating passion"** of one's life.

Although it is difficult to separate the story of John Bosch from that of his wife Louise, Marzieh places John at the center of the narrative, and I have approached this biography in the same fashion. In learning about John Bosch, one also learns about Louise and the remarkable Bahá'ís associated with them. They were ordinary people who achieved extraordinary things in their desire to be of service to humanity.

The central aim of John Bosch's life was to put into form and action the high standards of the teachings of Bahá'u'lláh, and one way to accomplish this was through Bahá'í summer schools. John and Louise donated their Geyserville property to be used as a place for the training of teachers for the Cause. The Geyserville Bahá'í School's first season began in 1927 and continued until 1971, when it had to be closed in order to make way for the State of California's expansion of the Redwood Highway, which ran across the Geyserville property.

When the Geyserville Bahá'í School was relocated to its new campus of sixty-eight acres of redwood forest in Santa Cruz, California, more

---

* Constance M. Chen, "Obituary: Marzieh Nabil Carpenter Gail (1908–1993)," *Bahá'í Studies Review*, vol. 6 (1994). http://bahai-library.com/chen_marzieh_gail_obituary (accessed April 23, 2014).

** The Universal House of Justice, letter dated January 9, 2011 to the Continental Board of Counselors.

xvi

INTRODUCTION

than four hundred people attended the dedication of the new campus on July 13, 1974, and it was renamed the *John and Louise Bosch Bahá'í School*. The keynote speakers were Hand of the Cause of God Mr. William Sears, member of the Universal House of Justice Amos Gibson, and members of the National Spiritual Assembly of the Bahá'ís of the United States Miss Charlotte Linfoot and Dr. Firuz Kazemzadeh. Marzieh Gail was there, and she noted Professor Kazemzadeh's observation about the history of the John and Louise Bosch Bahá'í School and the early expansion of the Bahá'í Faith in America:

> This Bahá'í sense of history is an important element in the way Bahá'ís see the world. We talk about progressive revelation, which is actually an historic view of revelation. We believe in newness, in progress; but we also believe in continuity. We do not believe that the new Faith abolishes the Faith of the past; we believe that it fulfills the Faith of the past. We believe that in order to succeed today, one must have laid a firm foundation yesterday. We know that all time is a chain stretching from yesterday until tomorrow. And so today is appropriate for us to take a look back at the origins of the John and Louise Bosch Bahá'í School.*

When John Bosch was forty-eight years old, he learned of Bahá'u'lláh and His teachings of the oneness of God, the oneness of religion, and the oneness of the human race. The year was 1903, and Bahá'u'lláh had ascended more than a decade before, but His son 'Abdu'l-Bahá was alive in the world, and John Bosch was determined to meet Him. This is the story of John Bosch's spiritual life which began with how he came to meet 'Abdu'l-Bahá.

---

* Marzieh Gail, "For John, With Love," *Bahá'í News*, (July 1974): 9–21.

1 / On a Train

It was an autumn sunset in October of 1903, and John Bosch was heading home after a business trip to the city. He boarded the train from San Francisco to Cloverdale, a town in Sonoma County eighty-five miles north of San Francisco. As he made his way to an open seat, he spotted a friend he knew from a Theosophical Society meeting he attended and took the seat next to her. Little did he know that this chance encounter would change the course of his life.

John David Bosch was a successful winery superintendent living in Sonoma County. Born in 1855, he was now forty-eight years old, and having apprenticed as a wine-maker in Germany and in Spain, his experience was valuable to the California wine industry at the turn of the century. An immigrant from Switzerland in 1879, he had moved to Nebraska with his sister's family, the Zuberbuhlers. Some years later he traveled west to California and became a U.S. citizen in Los Angeles in 1887. Shortly after, he moved to Sonoma County, where grapes ripened well in the California sun. In October of 1901, John purchased forty-five acres of land in Geyserville, California that would not only be his home until his death in 1946, but would feel like home to hundreds and hundreds of Bahá'ís in the future.

In that same autumn of 1903, a book called *The Life and Teachings of Abbas Effendi* was first published in the United States. The author of the book, Myron H. Phelps, was an American who had traveled to

Palestine to meet 'Abbás Effendi, known as 'Abdu'l-Bahá, the son and appointed successor of Bahá'u'lláh, the founder of the Bahá'í Faith. Myron Phelps was one of the first Americans to meet 'Abdu'l-Bahá and was one of the first of the early Western observers to publish impressions of Him.[1]

When John Bosch took his seat on the train, his friend was reading Phelps's book. John Bosch recounted the meeting in this way:

> In 1903, October, on the train from San Francisco to Cloverdale, a Mrs. Beckwith had a book with her called "Abbas Effendi" and I asked her if I could look over it and she permitted it and after reading a few pages I asked her where I could obtain one as I felt strongly that I should read the whole book.
>
> It was the early Edition of "Abbas Effendi" by Phelps. Mrs. Beckwith said that you go and call on Mrs. Goodall in Oakland and that I could buy a book from her. Mrs. Beckwith said to me before going into this, that to hear of this is the greatest privilege, but it will be followed up by the greatest obligations and better <u>not</u> know it if you cannot follow it.
>
> I called on Mrs. Helen Goodall early in 1904 on Jackson Street in Oakland and she gave me the first inspiring words and explanations of the Bab, Baha'u'llah, and Abdul Baha.[2]

John Bosch's initial response to the book *Abbas Effendi* is telling of his spiritual receptivity to Bahá'u'lláh's teachings of the oneness of God, the oneness of religion, and the oneness of humanity. John described his new understanding of how religious truth is given to humanity through progressive revelation from God: "In this book I found that in reality we have only one God and one truth. Why all the differences then? I learned that most of the present creeds were made up by the minds of some men. Statesmen and Ministers have tried to give us a new concept of the Books of the prophecies, forgetting to tell us that the foundation of all religion is one."[3]

Mrs. Helen Goodall's guidance would have the greatest influence on John Bosch's consecration as a Bahá'í; therefore, a brief survey of her Bahá'í life is helpful in understanding her importance. When John Bosch met Mrs. Goodall, she was fifty-six years old. She had only been a Bahá'í for five years, but she had a profound grasp of the central principle of Bahá'u'lláh's teaching about the covenant between God and His creation. It is a covenant that promises the progressive flow of God's revelation to humanity through a succession of divine Manifestations. The divine religions founded by these divine Messengers of God are fundamentally one Faith. Therefore, God's covenant with His creation is a promise of progressive revelation of God's will.* In his survey of Bahá'í history, Shoghi Effendi wrote that Mrs. Helen Goodall was among those "whose names will ever remain associated with the first stirrings of the Faith of Bahá'u'lláh in the North American continent, [and will] stand out as the most prominent among those who, in those early years, awakened to the call of the New Day, and consecrated their lives to the service of the newly proclaimed Covenant."⁴

In the early 1930s, Shoghi Effendi named Helen Goodall as a "Disciple of 'Abdu'l-Bahá," describing those who held that title as "Heralds of the Covenant." During his ministry, Shoghi Effendi designated nineteen Western believers as Disciples of 'Abdu'l-Bahá. In addition to Helen Goodall, three more Disciples of 'Abdu'l-Bahá bear mentioning here in order to appreciate the company with whom Helen Goodall shared the honor of such a distinction.⁵

---

* See Helen Hornby, *Lights of Guidance*, no. 593. In a letter written on his behalf, Shoghi Effendi describes the Greater and Lesser covenants: "First is the covenant that every Prophet makes with humanity, or, more definitely, with His people that they will accept and follow the coming Manifestation Who will be the reappearance of His reality. The second form of covenant is such as the one Bahá'u'lláh made with His people that they should accept the Master. This is merely to establish and strengthen the succession of the series of Lights that appear after every Manifestation."

First and foremost of the Disciples of 'Abdu'l-Bahá was Dr. John Esslemont, whose early drafts of the book on the Bahá'í Faith, *Bahá'u'lláh and the New Era,* was not only requested by 'Abdu'l-Bahá but was also partially reviewed by Him. Another Disciple of 'Abdu'l-Bahá was the beloved Robert Turner, the first African-American believer, who was so consecrated in his firmness in the Covenant that the Master said to him that if he remained firm he would be the door through which untold members of his race would enter the Cause. Another is Lua Getsinger, who traveled throughout America and to various countries to promote the Bahá'í principle that the foundation of all religions is one and that God's purpose for humanity today is to unite under the banner of the Covenant of Bahá'u'lláh.

As John Bosch's first Bahá'í teacher, Helen Goodall was a uniquely informed spiritual guide. She met 'Abdu'l-Bahá when she and her daughter Ella Cooper made a pilgrimage to Haifa together in 1908. They wrote about their pilgrimage in a book titled *Daily Lessons Received in 'Akká, 1908.* It is a survey of fundamental principles of Bahá'í belief—principles upon which Helen Goodall would base her approach when deepening new adherents of the Faith of Bahá'u'lláh. Through Helen Goodall, 'Abdu'l-Bahá addressed letters to believers in the West and would mail to her address in San Francisco one of the Tablets of the Divine Plan.* During World War I, the Ottoman government did not allow the delivery of letters sealed in envelopes, so the Master wrote the Tablets on postcards in order to ensure their delivery during the war. The following is an excerpt from a Tablet that was written on a postcard dated April 1, 1916 and addressed to the Western States. The Master concludes the Tablet with these words: "Travel ye throughout the world and call ye the people to the Kingdom

---

* The Tablets of the Divine Plan are a series of letters written during World War I and addressed to the believers in America and Canada; the letters outline a global teaching campaign to spread the teachings of Bahá'u'lláh to all of humanity.

of God. Now this is the time that you may arise and perform this most great service and become the cause of the guidance of innumerable souls. Thus through this superhuman service the rays of peace and conciliation may illumine and enlighten all the regions and the world of humanity may find peace and composure."[6]

The word *superhuman* suggests the power of the Bahá'í teachings to raise one to serve at a level beyond one's human capacity, and Helen Goodall would arise to this calling. She had a keen perception of the fundamental truths of the Faith she espoused, and those seekers who were under her care became quickened with the love of the Ancient Beauty and His Covenant.

Although John Bosch was one such seeker, his immediate questions did not concern the verity and truth of this Cause, for he had already accepted the fundamental oneness of God and His Revelation. Instead, he wanted to know how to practice this new Faith, and naturally, his questions were framed by his Christian background—a background wherein one's Faith is consecrated by partaking of "communion" as a way of receiving the holy sacrament of one's faith. After attending meetings at the home of Mrs. Goodall in 1904, John Bosch received the following letter from her wherein she answered his questions with her characteristic wisdom, and perhaps as someone who had had the same questions herself when she first learned of the Cause. While there is no such ritual in the Bahá'í Faith called "First Communion," it is likely that Mrs. Goodall's word choice in the following letter is in the interest of explaining "communion" as synonymous with a prayer offered by a soul in supplication to God:

Dear Mr. Bosch,

The "First Communion" is the first prayer given to Believers to memorize and use. Then the morning Tablet is for use every morning. There are many of these prayers and communes. We can readily see the wisdom of giving out these forms—one is that all are using the same words thereby uniting in spirit more than they would otherwise. Then, the utterances of Baha 'Ullah are full of meaning and instruction.

We will have the references printed on the mimeograph very soon. Then I can send you the complete list.

I have not been able, in all this time, to send for the Phelps book, but will do so very soon. It will be better not to study the philosophical side of the Instructions until one is fully established spiritually, for it is more important in this matter to educate the heart.

Very Sincerely Yours,
In His Name,
Helen S. Goodall
February 1, 1905[7]

It is endearing to read how she was in no hurry to send to John Bosch the Phelps book—as Phelps's book is simply the impressions of the personage of 'Abdu'l-Bahá from the point of view of a distant observer. Helen Goodall knew that John Bosch's attachment to the Covenant of Bahá'u'lláh must come foremost through the Creative Word of the Manifestation of God Himself.

John asked questions regarding the reality of man, progressive revelation, and God's purpose for Creation. Like many early seekers, he wondered about the station of 'Abdu'l-Bahá in relation to the station of Jesus Christ. Shoghi Effendi explains that while 'Abdu'l-Bahá was not a Manifestation of God, His station was higher than that of a normal human being: "He ['Abdu'l-Bahá] is . . . the *'Mystery of God'*—an expression by which Bahá'u'lláh Himself has chosen to designate Him and which, while it does not by any means justify us to assign to Him the station of Prophethood, indicates how in the person of 'Abdu'l-Bahá the incompatible characteristics of a human nature and superhuman knowledge and perfection have been blended and are completely harmonized."[8]

Similarly, John the Baptist—who heralded Christ's coming—was an ordinary man, while the Báb and Bahá'u'lláh were both Manifestations of God. Helen Goodall's guidance to John in the following letter reveals that although her explanation of some of these spiritual concepts was imperfect, she was attempting to lead John as best as she could to a greater understanding of the unity of God:

Allaho'Abha!
My dear Mr. Bosch:
While we know you cannot attend all the meetings, we always miss an absent Believer. How are you getting on? Do you understand the idea of all the manifestations being of the One Spirit? God, the One, manifests in different stations. As the Forerunner (John the Baptist, and the Bab); as the Sons (Jesus and Abbas Effendi); as the Father, the Lord of the Vineyard, the Shepherd (Baha 'Ullah).

All these Manifestors were Mirrors, reflecting God. That is, His Effulgence, qualities, etc. but not the Essence, which is forever back [sic] of His Expression of Himself. No one will ever comprehend the Essence. If this were to be given to man then he would be a God also and this would never do for of Gods there would be no end and unity would cease.

The material sun typifies the spiritual Sun. If the sun be reflected in a clear mirror, and we look in the mirror we see the sun in it. If a Messenger reflects the attributes, qualities, and effulgences of God we can look to Him for the expression of these qualities and say we see the Father. It was not the bodily appearance of Baha 'Ullah that showed forth God but the spirit in Him and His <u>utterances</u>. The utterances of all the messengers have been their proofs of their mission, for they were words of God inspired. Without God nothing can be done spiritual nor material. He inspires the poet, the singer, the inventor, for he sets others to thinking, until, finally, the thing was figured out in the true way and knowledge of its shape and movements correctly established.

It was better for man that this worked out this way than that the truth of it be given him without effort. So it is with everything. The shape of the world was one of the many problems and new ones are springing up all the time that humanity may not sink into apathy.

Spiritual problems have appeared from the beginning until the present time when all things are to be made clear. The Master says there is nothing man cannot find out, but of course he must first become attuned to Spirit.

I will send more Tablets soon.

Very sincerely yours,
Helen S. Goodall
February 26, 1905[9]

It is likely that Helen Goodall is alluding to the Bahá'í principle of the independent investigation of reality when she writes to John about how "there is nothing man cannot find out."

The Bahá'í teachings on equality, oneness, and the independent investigation of truth attracted many fair-minded seekers, including John Bosch, who sought to create a link between Socialism and the teachings of Bahá'u'lláh. In several of His public addresses in the United States, 'Abdu'l-Bahá made clear that the teachings of Bahá'u'lláh are not an assimilation of any manmade doctrine; nor are they to be thought of as having any affinity with material philosophy. Rather, the teachings of Bahá'u'lláh are divinely proclaimed from God to His Creation. In one address, the Master said,

> The principles of socialism are outstripped in the religions of God. [. . .] That is, the believers spend of their substance and share their possessions and prefer others to themselves willingly

and with utmost spirituality. Socialists, however, desire to enforce equality and associations by compulsion. Although the preference for others, which is the exhortation of God, is more difficult because the rich are enjoined to prefer others to themselves, this will become common and will be the cause of tranquility and an aid to the order of the world, because it depends upon the inclination and willingness of the giver. But socialism and egalitarianism, although easier, as those who have are made equal with others, yet such a system will not become widespread and is the cause of disturbance and tumult because it rests on compulsion and coercion.[10]

John Bosch's evident interest in Socialism must have been sincere and his questions about it in relation to the Revelation of Bahá'u'lláh must have been equally sincere. Helen Goodall was firm yet loving in her explanation of how Socialism can only pretend to affect social change and that only the divine power of God has the power to transform the human heart. Her gentle persuasion resonated loud and clear in the following letter to John Bosch. In it, she referred to Mrs. Anna Reed, who was editor and owner of the *Sonoma County Independent* newspaper:

Dear Believer,

I was interested in reading Mrs. Reed's editorial; thank you for sending it. You see she is connecting socialism with Bahaism. In reality, socialism, as preached today, tears down but it has no power to reconstruct. It is a movement that will do some good—when it has adopted Bahaism and not before. It pretends to be a civilizer, but true civilization follows only after a special Revelation from God. Just watch the spirit of a socialist. He thinks he wishes to better conditions, but how about the spirit in which he attacks the people?

The Bahai religion is the great reforming influence and when the socialists become imbued with this spiritual influence, they will get their balance. The spirit of contention prompted the first socialist movement, but it is not now so pronounced.

Should Mrs. Reed wish, from her heart, to put before the people the right information, it would be best that she be rightly instructed, as you suggest. The first and most important thing for her to learn is that civilization depends entirely upon Spirit and not upon the effort of man apart from Its influence. A great lesson is learned from the instruction regarding Mohammad's appearance amongst the barbarous Arabians.

I believe it would be best for you to correspond with Mrs. Reed a while before giving her things to publish; however, your intuition is keen so you can judge. She is evidently a (rampant?) [sic] socialist. It would not be at all well for this spirit to be mixed with the heavenly spirit of the Bahai movement [. . .].

Greetings in His Name,
Helen S. Goodall
December 8, 1910[11]

In his correspondence with Helen Goodall, John Bosch's questions gradually returned to where he began: on a train headed for home and thinking about the person of 'Abdu'l-Bahá. John felt a spiritual attraction to 'Abdu'l-Bahá, and it compelled him to seek a better understanding of the relationship between the station of Bahá'u'lláh and the station of 'Abdu'l-Bahá. In those early days, as Helen Goodall's February 26, 1905 letter to John demonstrated, there was some confusion on the part of the American believers regarding the station of 'Abdu'l-Bahá. It would not be until 1938 that the Guardian would write this unequivocal clarification of the station of 'Abdu'l-Bahá:

An attempt I strongly feel should now be made to clarify our minds regarding the station occupied by 'Abdu'l-Bahá and the significance of His position in this holy Dispensation. It would be indeed difficult for us, who stand so close to such a tremendous figure and are drawn by the mysterious power of so magnetic a personality, to obtain a clear and exact understanding of the role and character of One Who, not only in the Dispensation of Bahá'u'lláh but in the entire field of religious history, fulfills a unique function. Though moving in a sphere of His own and holding a rank radically different from that of the Author and the Forerunner of the Bahá'í Revelation, He ['Abdu'l-Bahá], by virtue of the station ordained for Him through the Covenant of Bahá'u'lláh, forms together with them what may be termed the Three Central Figures of a Faith that stands unapproached in the world's spiritual history. He towers, in conjunction with them, above the destinies of this infant Faith of God from a level to which no individual or body ministering to its needs after Him, and for no less a period than a full thousand years, can ever hope to rise. To degrade His lofty rank by identifying His station with or by regarding it as roughly equivalent to, the position of those on whom the mantle of His authority has fallen would be an act of impiety as grave as the no less heretical belief that inclines to exalt Him to a state of absolute equality with either the central Figure or Forerunner of our Faith. For wide as is the gulf that separates 'Abdu'l-Bahá from Him Who is the Source of an independent Revelation, it can never be regarded as commensurate with the greater distance that stands between Him Who is the Center of the Covenant and His ministers who are to carry on His work, whatever be their name, their rank, their functions or their future achievements. Let those who have known 'Abdu'l-Bahá, who through their contact with His magnetic personality have come to cherish for Him so fervent an admiration, reflect, in the light of this statement, on the greatness of One Who is so far above Him in station.[12]

While the Master traveled throughout America in 1912, He emphasized that He is the Center of Bahá'u'lláh's Covenant and that His station is the servant of Bahá'u'lláh, the Glory of God. Yet so many new believers perceived 'Abdu'l-Bahá as the return of Christ, as a Prophet, and as a Manifestation of God—perhaps because any lesser epithet seemed unworthy of the divine spirit reflected in 'Abdu'l-Bahá. Although 'Abdu'l-Bahá made it very clear that His station was servitude to Bahá'u'lláh, early believers in America framed an understanding of His station in their own words. In a postscript to a letter to John Bosch dated June 20, 1907, Helen Goodall expressed her own understanding of the Master's station:

> The reason I wrote the letter about the Station of Abdul Baha was I had heard that you did not quite understand why we called the Master <u>Lord</u>. Abdul Baha makes His <u>soul</u> evanescent before God [so] that the world may recognize the <u>Spirit</u> that is shining through Him. It is always the One Spirit manifesting so we must arise above personalities.
>
> God, through Baha'u'llah, calls the Master the Greatest Branch that hath branched forth from the Pre-existent Root. The Master has perfected His soul. This is why He is greater than the people of the earth.[13]

In 1905, John Bosch asked Mrs. Goodall how he might write to the Master and express his devotion to the Cause. At that time, it had been only a dozen years since the passing of Bahá'u'lláh, and 'Abdu'l-Bahá's station as Center of the Covenant was very real indeed: new believers wishing to declare their Faith had to communicate directly to 'Abdu'l-Bahá. Therefore, writing such a communication to the Master meant learning how to convey one's feelings in a manner worthy of such a declaration of Faith while at the same time allowing for a freedom of expression removed from ritual and unfettered by sanctimony and pretense. Below is Helen Goodall's unambiguous and practical guidance to John Bosch on how to address a letter to the Master. While it is unclear if she intended to make a distinction between the word "Form" as capitalized, and later "form" as uncapitalized, the spirit of her guidance is understood: there is no ritual or "Form" to follow, but one should consider the demeanor or "form" of one's expression when writing to 'Abdu'l-Bahá. Later in this letter, Mrs. Goodall offers guidance about the application of Bahá'í law in the absence of an authorized and complete translation of Bahá'u'lláh's book of laws, the Kitáb-i-Aqdas:

Allaho'Abha!
Dear Believer:

Enclosed is the Form, which is instructive, showing us how to address the Master and also a statement of Faith. No one is obliged to follow the Form and some prefer to write in their own way, although using the form of addressing the Beloved One. These letters are placed on file and it has been requested that we write upon the inside of the sheet. How practical is everything connected with this religion—even the fasts are to be kept under certain conditions only, that is, the sick or very old and feeble ones are not required to fast. The command to fast is in the Kitab-El-Akdas. This book has not yet been given out, but portions have been translated and circulated by some Believers for information. Until the book is given out we feel that no one is compelled to fast but some have already begun to follow this and some other commands. The fast takes place in March then afterward there is the feasting time when the people are to visit one another and have a season of rejoicing. When all this is established, there will be a great stride onward.

It will give me great happiness to forward your letter to the Master. For political reasons, His mail is sent under cover.
With Bahai Greetings,
Helen S. Goodall
May 17, 1905[14]

Although Mrs. Goodall's letter speaks of "a great stride onward" that would come when the Law of God is established, John Bosch was not about to wait for a future season of rejoicing. Over the next week he prepared himself to write to the Master and, in doing so, took the great stride onward to seize his chance to join the Cause—a Cause he referred to as "this universal life."

Bahá'u'lláh taught that every human being is endowed with a soul capable of recognizing God. He wrote, "I have perfected in every one of you My creation, so that the excellence of My handiwork may be fully revealed unto men. It follows, therefore, that every man hath been, and will continue to be, able of himself to appreciate the Beauty of God, the Glorified." Therefore, Bahá'u'lláh concludes in this passage, "the faith of no man can be conditioned by anyone except himself."[15]

Mysterious, indeed, is the understanding of one's own soul, let alone the soul of another. How precious it is to imagine the stirrings of John Bosch's soul the morning he arose early and went to the winery office to sit down to write a letter to 'Abdu'l-Bahá. Shoghi Effendi wrote that "when a person becomes a Bahá'í, he gives up the past only in the sense that he is a part of this new and living Faith of God, and must seek to pattern himself, in act and thought, along the lines laid down by Bahá'u'lláh."[16] Upon becoming a Bahá'í, John Bosch would try to pattern himself in accordance with the high standards of the Bahá'í teachings, and this meant he would have to change his profession as a vintner. He would have to give up one occupation and acquire a new one, in the spiritual sense, as a vintner of the wine of spiritual enchantment.

In the morning hours of May 29, 1905, a Holy Day marking the eighteenth year since the passing of Bahá'u'lláh, John Bosch wrote to the Master on stationery from his home vineyard from which he made non-alcoholic grape juice. The letter is brief, no longer than a single page. It is handwritten in elegant strokes, the ink pressed gently on the paper, each letter shaped like a mistral leaning eastward, each word bearing the appearance of a light breeze flowing over a landscape.

John's words demonstrate a poetic economy of language that is austere and without pretense, yet fully expressive of his soul's desire—his words belong to that spiritual world above rather than the material world below:

BOSCH'S California Grape Juice
Absolutely Pure and Non-Alcoholic
Bottled at Vineyard
Geyserville, California
Allah'o Abha
In God's Name,
To the Greatest Branch:

I believe in the existence of an Almighty Power, of which we all are created and descendants.

By degree and choices we had manifestations and I sincerely believe that Thou art one of this higher exalted manifestations of the Universal Power.

Thy teachings are proof of the continuance of the spiritual evolution and may my name be entered in the Great Book of this Universal Life is my earnest request.

My watchword will be "Justice."
Humbly Thy servant,
John D. Bosch
May 29, 1905[17]

In less than a fortnight, the Master replied to John Bosch. The Master's original letter—written in Persian and in the traditional calligraphic style—appears more like verse-poetry than linear prose. Both the Persian Tablet and its English translation were sent to John Bosch, care of Helen Goodall.

Convey longing greetings from me to Mr. John D. Bosch and say:
"O thou John D. Bosch!

Raise the Call of the Kingdom and give the glad tidings to the people. Guide them to the Tree of Life, so that they may gather the fruits from that Tree and attain the great Bounty."
Signed: Abdul-Baha Abbas
Acca June 11, 1905
Translated by Mirza Ameen Ullah Fareed,
Chicago, December 23, 1906[18]

Although the Master's first letter to John Bosch was written in June 1905, John Bosch did not receive the letter until sometime after December 1906. So, it was not until April 1907, nearly two years since his first letter to 'Abdu'l-Bahá, that John Bosch wrote again to the Master, and, as always, on his home-vineyard letterhead:

BOSCH'S CALIFORNIA GRAPE JUICE
Absolutely Pure and Non-Alcoholic
BOTTLED AT VINEYARD
Geyserville, California
April 30, 1907
Allah-o-Abha!
Longing greeting to Abdul Baha Abbas!
 . . . Your message to me of June 11, 1905 has given me great joy and I have a great desire to make the trip and meet you at Acca. However my business and financial conditions are not fully settled to make that long trip. Have been unfortunate in several of my personal undertakings and I wonder why I should not have the harvest of all my material efforts as long my desire is to live right and make use only for the advancement of others. My desire is to be helped by your powerful influence and to teach freedom and justice.
 I hope that conditions will shape itself that I may be ready with the freedom of my heart, that when you call on me to make the trip, the way will be opened and all matters firmly settled.

Humbly thy servant,
John D. Bosch[19]

Little did he know that in five years, the Master would journey to the West. John Bosch's meeting with the Master in the United States would come only after John had developed a deep friendship with Thornton Chase—the man whom 'Abdu'l-Bahá named as the first American believer and whom the Master called "Thabit" for his steadfastness in the Covenant.[20] Thornton Chase and John Bosch were true brothers in the Cause; theirs was a friendship of spiritual dimensions, with each finding in the other a soul drawn as if by a magnet to the Center of the Covenant. One of them would not live to meet the Master on His visit to America, and the other would be forever changed by it.

2 / Become as True Brethren

In describing the meaning of true fellowship, the Báb* wrote, "Become as true brethren in the one and indivisible religion of God, free from distinction, for verily God desireth that your hearts should become mirrors unto your brethren in the Faith, so that ye find yourselves reflected in them, and they in you."[1]

Thornton Chase was this kind of brother to John Bosch. Both men embraced the Cause of God with an earnest commitment to help others understand that the universal teachings of Bahá'u'lláh were more than simply a metaphysical pastime. In his last public talk given in Chicago before moving to Los Angeles, Thornton Chase spoke about how the "'Bahá'í Revelation does not spring out of the human concept of God. It is not a mystical cult, not a psychological problem, not an Oriental philosophy, not a religious fad.'"[2] Rather, the Bahá'í religion is a Cause with spiritual laws destined to transform human behavior and advance human civilization. Naturally, Thornton Chase would have been interested in finding other Bahá'ís who could assist in clarifying this distinction between the Bahá'í Faith and popular beliefs prevalent at the time.

---

* *The Báb* means *The Gate* in Persian and in Arabic. The Báb is recognized in the Bahá'í Faith as a Manifestation of God and is the forerunner of the Promised One, Bahá'u'lláh.

It must have been a happy meeting of illumined souls when John Bosch met Thornton Chase at the Bahá'í Temple Convention in March of 1909. Later that year, in September of 1909, Thornton Chase would leave his home community of Chicago and relocate to Los Angeles for professional reasons beyond his control. He had ambivalent feelings about leaving Chicago. Although he had lived in California a decade before, in Chicago he was more spiritually at home, for it was in Chicago that he found the teachings of Bahá'u'lláh.

A coincidence of circumstances led to John Bosch meeting Thornton Chase at the Temple Unity Convention. Six years prior, in 1903, around the same time that John Bosch first learned of 'Abdu'l-Bahá, the Bahá'ís of Chicago had petitioned 'Abdu'l-Bahá for permission to build a House of Worship in the United States. Having received the Master's "ready and enthusiastic approval," a convention was organized in Chicago on the day of the Bahá'í New Year in 1909—coinciding with a most holy occasion on Mount Carmel, in Haifa, Israel. Shoghi Effendi, in *God Passes By*, explains the significance of the Temple Unity Convention coinciding with the interment of the sacred remains of the Báb by the Master on Mount Carmel on March 21:

> . . . in March 1909, a convention representative of various Bahá'í centers was called, in pursuance of instructions received from 'Abdu'l-Bahá. The thirty-nine delegates, representing thirty-six cities, who had assembled in Chicago, on the very day the remains of the Báb were laid to rest by 'Abdu'l-Bahá in the specially erected mausoleum on Mt. Carmel, established a permanent national organization, known as the Bahá'í Temple Unity, which was incorporated as a religious corporation, functioning under the laws of the State of Illinois, and invested with full authority to hold title to the property of the Temple and to provide ways and means for its construction. At this same convention a constitution was framed, the Executive Board of the Bahá'í Temple Unity

was elected, and was authorized by the delegates to complete the purchase of the land. . . .³

John Bosch was a delegate to that convention, and he counted it as one of the most significant experiences of his life. Although today no alternate delegates are chosen for the Bahá'í National Convention, in the early days of the Cause in the United States, alternate delegates were selected in case the primary delegate could not attend the National Convention. How surprised John Bosch must have been upon reading the following telegram dated Friday, March 13, 1909, sent from Oakland from Helen Goodall and addressed to John D Bosch:

D'EVELYN CANNOT GO AS DELEGATE WILL YOU SERVE LEAVING TUESDAY FUNDS HERE FOR TRIP ANSWER IMMEDIATELY MRS GOODALL⁴

Receiving the telegram on a Friday in Geyserville, California and leaving by train for Chicago the following Tuesday, March 17, must have made John Bosch feel the air beneath his wings. It meant traveling to Chicago and meeting Bahá'ís from all over North America, many of whom would become his lifelong coworkers in the Cause.

Among the delegates were Thornton Chase and Charles Greenleaf, both of whom would later be named by Shoghi Effendi as Disciples of 'Abdu'l-Bahá. There was Edward Getsinger, whose wife Lua would be named by the Guardian as the mother-teacher of the American Bahá'í community. Also present was Albert Hall, a lawyer, who defended Fred Mortensen in juvenile court and then introduced Mortensen to the Cause and changed the course of Fred Mortensen's life forever. There was Howard MacNutt, who would later compile all of the talks given by the Master in America in the compilation called *The Promulgation of Universal Peace*. Also attending was Mountfort Mills, who was an international lawyer and would later be called upon by the Guardian to represent the interests of the Faith to the League of Nations Commission regarding the defense of the property of Bahá'u'lláh against the Covenant-breakers.* There was Susan Moody, who would later pioneer to Persia to advance the education of girls in that country. Also present was Corinne True, who would later be named a Hand of the Cause of God and whose tireless efforts to establish a Mashriqu'l-Adhkár in the West would win for her the personal gratitude of the Master when He named her the "Mother of the Temple."[5]

The Convention began on Saturday night, March 20th, with the Feast of Naw-Rúz, followed by a Bahá'í New Year devotional the next morning and a visit to the Temple Site in the afternoon. The spiritual significance of the Convention taking place on Naw-Rúz, 1909 bears further explanation here as it was an occasion that coincided with 'Abdu'l-Bahá's interment of the holy remains of the Báb on Mount Carmel. It is humbling to note that the following description of events is an eyewitness account of the Guardian—who would have been a boy of twelve years of age in March of 1909—recounting it thirty-five years later and associating the interment of the Báb's remains with the raising of the Mother Temple of the West:

> . . . at the time of the opening of the first American Bahá'í Convention, convened in Chicago for the purpose of creating a permanent national organization for the construction of the Mashriqu'l-Adhkár, 'Abdu'l-Bahá brought His undertaking to a successful conclusion, in spite of the incessant machinations of enemies both within and without. On the 28th of the month of Safar 1327 A.H., the day of the first Naw-Rúz (1909), which He celebrated after His release from His confinement, 'Abdu'l-Bahá had the marble sarcophagus transported with great labor to the vault prepared for it, and in the evening, by the light of a single

---

* Someone who initially declared his or her belief in Bahá'u'lláh but then refused to acknowledge the authority of 'Abdu'l-Bahá, Shoghi Effendi, or the Universal House of Justice.

lamp, He laid within it, with His own hands—in the presence of believers from the East and from the West and in circumstances at once solemn and moving—the wooden casket containing the sacred remains of the Báb and His companion.

When all was finished, and the earthly remains of the Martyr-Prophet of Shiraz were, at long last, safely deposited for their everlasting rest in the bosom of God's holy mountain, 'Abdu'l-Bahá, Who had cast aside His turban, removed His shoes and thrown off His cloak, bent low over the still open sarcophagus, His silver hair waving about His head and His face transfigured and luminous, rested His forehead on the border of the wooden casket, and, sobbing aloud, wept with such a weeping that all those who were present wept with Him. That night He could not sleep, so overwhelmed was He with emotion.

"The most joyful tidings is this," He wrote later in a Tablet announcing to His followers the news of this glorious victory, "that the holy, the luminous body of the Báb [. . .] after having for sixty years been transferred from place to place, by reason of the ascendancy of the enemy, and from fear of the malevolent, and having known neither rest nor tranquility has, through the mercy of the Abhá Beauty, been ceremoniously deposited, on the day of Naw-Rúz, within the sacred casket, in the exalted Shrine on Mt. Carmel . . . By a strange coincidence, on that same day of Naw-Ruz, a cablegram was received from Chicago, announcing that the believers in each of the American centers had elected a delegate and sent to that city . . . and definitely decided on the site and construction of the Mashriqu'l-Adhkár."[6]

At the close of the Convention on March 23, 1909, Corinne True wrote to the Master to report to Him of the great success of the Convention. In His reply to her, He emphasized the "wonderful coincidence" of the Temple Unity Convention taking place at the same time that the holy remains of the Báb were interred on Mount Carmel. Here is the Tablet, in part:

To the maidservant of God, Mrs. True (Upon her be Baha'o'llah!)
HE IS GOD!
O daughter of the Kingdom!

Thy epistle was received and the Convention of the delegates of the Mashrek-el-Azkar on the day of Naurooz, at Chicago proved a cause of joy and gladness. In reality, a wonderful coincidence has taken place. In that blessed day Abdul Baha hastened to Haifa and with the divine friends was present at the Supreme Station (The Tomb of the Báb). The pure body of His Holiness, the Supreme (The Báb), after sixty years of homeless wandering and placelessness, was established on Mt. Carmel, the mountain of the Lord, in the Supreme Station, and in Chicago there was held (at the same time) the Convention of the delegates of the Mashrek-el-Azkar. [. . .]

I beg of God that that radiant Assembly may become aided in pure, truthful intentions and confirmed in the service of the Kingdom, so that it may be a sample of the Assemblages of the Supreme Concourse. . . .

Upon thee be Baha-el-ABHA!
(signed) Abdul Baha Abbas
Translated by: Dr Ameen U Fareed
Haifa, Syria, July 29, 1909[7]

In a small notebook kept by John Bosch throughout his life, he wrote the following entry. Whether he wrote it at the time of the Convention is not known, but it demonstrates the sum of John Bosch's sentiments about the building of a Mashriqu'l-Adhkár and the significance of the Temple Unity Convention of 1909: "The miracle of the Mashreq'ul Adzkar lies in the uniting together of the Baha'is of the different nations and races of the world. In the effort of building the Temple of the Lord, the believers throughout the world have striven to gather the funds to build this Temple, just as though they were the members of <u>one</u> family, and the children of <u>one</u> father. There is no other Church that will do this or has done this. This is <u>one</u> of the results of the Unity and Oneness of mankind. This is the <u>first</u> fruit of the principle of the oneness and unity of mankind. No other church has this record behind it."[8]

When John Bosch was on his return home from the Convention, he wrote to Helen Goodall from Kansas City on March 24, 1909:

Dear Mrs. Goodall,
Convention closed March 23rd 4pm with the greatest success. Mrs. True requests we send the California contributions to her until a new treasurer is elected.
   With Bahai greetings,
   John D. Bosch[9]

The planning, the fundraising, and the construction of the Mother Temple of the West would take another forty-four years until its official dedication in May of 1953. John Bosch would not live to see its final completion, but because building it was the wish of the Master, he lived to support it by every material means possible and by educating the Bahá'ís on the importance of the House of Worship.

John Bosch knew of the challenges that the American Bahá'í community would face in carrying out such an undertaking. Helen Goodall, who was already working toward its progress in the years preceding the 1909 Convention, wrote the following letter to John Bosch in December of 1908. Her letter includes financial details of the purchase of the land at the Temple site; then, she harmonizes those details by calling attention to the true purpose of the undertaking: that the real Temple is the unity of the body of believers who share in bringing about the Dawning-place of the mention of God:

Dear Believer,

The great benefit to the believers in this undertaking, by working together for a common Cause, is the blessing of Spirit that has been promised to all who arise to obey the Command. As Abdul-Baha says, the real Temple is the united hearts of the believers that the effect of the buildings of this second* Bahai Temple will be great not only upon those who build it, but upon the whole world. <u>United</u> obedience and <u>united</u> effort combined will surely affect the people.

Not having talked with you on the subject, I do not know how you feel about the Temple. Most of the friends respond heartily, but one or two asked us "What benefit would a Temple in Chicago be to us in California?"—(thinking of the <u>building</u> and the <u>letter</u> of the thing) we have to respond to this query as above. The more the friends unite on any proposition, the stronger we will all become.

To grow in Grace together and not apart is the thing that will prepare us for the coming tests and trials.

While wonderful things are transpiring spiritually and materially, we Bahais must remember that a time of confusion has to come and that we are expected to meet it—<u>together</u>.

Regarding the tract of land the believers would like to secure, it borders on the lake and is surrounded by a park-site with well-laid roads. The corner secured is inland. If we could secure the whole

---

* The first Bahá'í House of Worship was begun in Ashkhabad, ('Ishqábád) Turkmenistan and completed by 1906. In 1928, it was expropriated by the Soviet State. In 1948, it was damaged by an earthquake and rendered unsafe. It was demolished by the State in 1963, and the land is currently used as a public park. See Julie Badiee, "Ma<u>sh</u>riqu'l-A<u>dh</u>kár," *The Bahá'í Encyclopedia Project*. http://www.bahai-encyclopedia-project.org (accessed Feb 19, 2017).

tract a small, temporary building could be placed on the corner and plenty of time allowed for the building of the permanent Temple.

The idea is to have the Mashrak-El-Askar always open and to have reading there every morning, of the Words of Baha'o'llah. Will you kindly let us know what you think about the believers of California and Honolulu joining hearts and hands in buying a portion of this tract of land, assuming, say, the payment of $2,000? I believe the payments are to be made easy. The price of the whole is $34,000. Mr. Woodcock asked the New York Assembly if they could assume $9,000 of this. We have not heard any reports as yet, but shall write for further information. We have collected about $200, which we were going to send on when we heard of this new idea. It pleased a number of us. We shall need some more money, so, if you would like to join us will you kindly let us know. [. . .]

Greetings in His Name,
Helen S. Goodall
December 12, 1908[10]

When the Master made His historic visit to America in 1912, the plans for the Mashriqu'l-Adhkár were foremost on the minds of the believers in the United States. In a talk given by 'Abdu'l-Bahá in New York in 1912, the Master addressed this preoccupation and cautioned the Bahá'ís against unrealistic expectations and reminded them to be practical in achieving their objective: "The attainment of any object is conditioned upon knowledge, volition and action. Unless these three conditions are forthcoming, there is no execution or accomplishment. In the erection of a house it is first necessary to know the ground, and design the house suitable for it; second, to obtain the means or funds necessary for the construction; third, actually to build it."[11]

An endeavor such as the one envisioned by the delegates at the Temple Unity Convention of 1909 would bring about a series of crises and victories, in the path to completing the Mother Temple of the West, resulting in a unity of purpose shared by the Bahá'ís the world over.

As always, John Bosch was inspired to do more. He himself had been attracted to the Cause by reading about it, so naturally he sought ways in which to increase the supply of literature on the Bahá'í Faith so that others would be led to the teachings of Bahá'u'lláh in the same way that he had when he found the book titled *Abbas Effendi*. The dissemination of literature required knowledge, volition, and action, and seeking help from his spiritual brother Thornton Chase was a good place to start.

Of the correspondence between Thornton Chase and John Bosch, the earliest communication on record in the United States Bahá'í Archives is dated January 16, 1910. John Bosch and Thornton Chase had known each other for less than a year and were already deeply united in the work of the Cause. They were relatively close in age, as Mr. Chase had been born in 1847 and John Bosch in 1855. They came from similar life-experiences even though one was American and the other Swiss. One might say that they shared a "unity of thought in world undertakings"—even if that "world" was merely the sphere of their own practical experience.[12] The formality with which they addressed one another is endearing, and the brotherly tone of their correspondence is a clue to the deep love and respect they had for one another. Most of their letters are handwritten; Thornton Chase's handwriting is a hurried scrawl of broad-sweeping strokes, and John Bosch's handwriting is careful and deliberate, with each stroke elegant and graceful.

Often the discussion between the two friends had to do with their interest in the accuracy of Bahá'í literature. The following letter, for instance, concerns the translation of Thornton Chase's book *The Bahá'í Revelation*. In the biography *Thornton Chase: First American Bahá'í*, Robert H. Stockman gives an eloquent review of the significance of this book describing it as "arguably the most profound work produced by an American Bahá'í to date. Written to be an introduction to the Bahá'í Faith, it is also a meditation on love, for Thornton

Chase considered love to be the basic Bahá'í teaching. In his mind love represented the essence of religion and living; hence he believed love had to be the central theme of any book that sought to explain the basics of the Bahá'í Faith."[13]

The Bahá'í Revelation was widely read when it was published, and Thornton Chase oversaw translations of it to ensure accuracy. For example, in the following letter there is mention of Dr. Wilhelm Herrigel, a Bahá'í in Stuttgart, Germany, who acted as translator during the Master's visit to Stuttgart in 1913, but who, years later in 1930, became a Covenant-breaker because he could not accept the administrative order as directed by the Master in His *Will and Testament*.[14] John Bosch and Thornton Chase's communication with Dr. Herrigel took place twenty years before Herrigel's departure from the haven of the Covenant. Nevertheless, the mention of Herrigel in the following letter demonstrates Thornton Chase's vigilance in verifying that Herrigel's translation of the Bahá'í teachings into German accurately conveyed the spiritual nature of the teachings:

Los Angeles
May 13, 1910
Dear Brother in El-Baha:

I was glad to get your letter and remembrance. I sent a portion of the German letter to our friends in Chicago, and presume they will use it at some time in the Bahai News. I also had a letter from Mrs. Cooper of Oakland, in which she said that Mr. Herrigel had asked permission to translate the book "The Bahai Revelation" and I wrote a letter to him at once, to Stuttgart, expressing my pleasure at his request, and also telling him how I enjoyed his letter to you, which you had showed me when I was in San Francisco. I asked him to write to me also [. . .].

Mrs. Goodall and Mrs. Shuey were here for some days, and we had the great pleasure to entertain them at our home one evening. They returned to Oakland this week. They said the Chicago Convention was delightful. Of course you will see them and hear all about it. There is no especial Bahai news here. This is the most quiet place on the Coast in these matters, because the friends are so scattered and some of them in very delicate health, so that it is difficult for them to gather in meetings. But their hearts are warm, and they do all they can to spread the Glad Tidings of the Bounty of God. I had a fine long letter from my "chum" and dear friend Carl Scheffler of Chicago, who was with me on my trip abroad. He left me at Naples and visited Stuttgart and many places in Germany. He will be interested in the Herrigel letter, of which I wrote him. I think he will come out here after a while and visit me. I want very much to keep him here, and he will try if he can find some work whereby to live here. He is a pure hearted, kind reliable young fellow.

I hope to hear from you again.

Greetings to the friends,

Sincerely Yours,

(signed) Thornton Chase[15]

Neither Thornton Chase nor John Bosch attended the Chicago Convention in 1910. John Bosch's absence from the convention was due to events beyond his control. He wrote to the Master to apologize for his absence from the Convention, to ask a question about the use of Esperanto as a universal language, and to ask about the Bahá'í law prohibiting the use of alcohol. John's profession was in the wine-making industry, but on his private property, he grew grapes from which he made his own grape juice. His personal stationery letterhead read: "BOSCH'S CALIFORNIA GRAPE JUICE, ABSOLUTELY PURE AND NON-ALCHOLIC, BOTTLED AT VINEYARD, GEYSERVILLE, CALIFORNIA." Therefore, John Bosch's concern about the law against alcohol was a professional one, not a personal one. The Master's reply was sent by way of Thornton Chase, who included his own note as a preface to the Tablet from the Master. Here is Thornton Chase's note, in part:

Los Angeles, California
June 3rd, 1910
Mr. John D. Bosch
Geyserville, California
 My dear Friend,
 I am happy to enclose to you herewith a Tablet and translation from Abdul Baha. Will you please acknowledge the receipt of it right away to me, as I want to send on the acknowledgement to Mirza Ahmad. I congratulate you on getting this Tablet, even though it emphasizes the fact that spirituous liquors will not be used in the new Kingdom on earth. Of course the change will come gradually, as all great changes do, but we can each use what influence we can wisely toward its consummation [. . .].
 I am writing in haste, but with a burst of good wishes to you!
 Yours sincerely in His Name,
 (signed) Thornton Chase
 May I use a copy of the instructions in your Tablet? T.C.

Tablet of 'Abdu'l-Bahá addressed to "John D Bosch, Geyserville, California":

O Thou who art attracted to the Kingdom of God!
 Although means were not provided so that thou mayest present thyself at the general Convention for consultation in Chicago, still thou art excused and thy apology is accepted. I beg of God, that the means of thy composure may be brought about, that thou mayest be released from the fetters of this world, become a nightingale, be freed from the cage of the attachment of this earth and soar heavenward in the atmosphere of joy [. . .].

The language of Esperanto is not yet perfected so that it may become useful in travel. In the course of time it will be spread in various countries and will become a universal language.

Regarding the use of liquors: According to the texts of the Book of Akdas both light and strong drinks are prohibited. The reason for this prohibition is that it leads the mind astray and is the cause of weakening the body. If alcohol were beneficial it would have been brought into the world by the divine creation and not by the effort of man. Whatever is beneficial for man exists in creation. Now it has been proved and is established medically and scientifically that liquors are harmful. Therefore the meaning of that which is written in the Tablets "I have chosen for thee whatsoever is in the heaven and earth" are those things which are according to the Divine Creation, and not the things which are harmful.

For instance, poison is one of the things. Now can we say that poisons are to be used habitually because God has created them for man? However spirituous liquors, if prescribed by a Physician for the patient and their use is necessary, then they may be used as directed.

In brief: I hope that thou mayest become exhilarated with the wine of the love of God, that thou mayest find Eternal Bliss and receive inexhaustible joy and happiness. The after effect of drinking is depression, but the wine of the love of God bestows exaltation of the spirit.

Upon thee be Baha El Abha

(signed) Abdul Baha Abbas

Translated by Mirza Ahmad Sohrab, Washington D.C., May 1910[16]

After receiving this Tablet, John Bosch wrote to Thornton Chase to ask if he thought the Tablet should be disseminated for the education of the Bahá'í friends via the newsletter called the *Bahá'í News*. In Thornton Chase's reply to John, Thornton asks if he may use the Tablet as a source of guidance for others who may have similar questions about the law prohibiting the drinking of alcohol:

Los Angeles
June 15, 1910
Mr. John D. Bosch
Geyserville, California
My dear Friend:

Your welcome letter of 9th is received and noted. I kept a copy of the instructive portion of your Tablet as I thought you would permit me to have it. Yes, I thought of sending it to the Bahai News, unless you wish to do so yourself. They may be able to use it, and maybe not. Just according to the space they have, but at any rate it will go into the records and be spread among the people as an instruction from Abdul Baha. I was touched by your suggestion that we may visit Acca together. I wish it might be so, but it is now impossible for me to know whether I can go next year or the year after. It will be a question of means.

As to writing for permission for the visit, I would suggest that it would be well to defer doing so until within 3 or possibly 4 months of the time when you could go. Permission depends much upon the political conditions at the time and it is better to bring the permission and the going as nearly together as possible on that account.

I note your suggestion of the word "competent" before "physician," but I would not wish to introduce the word. In fact he who is not competent is not "a physician"—and again—if one sought to dodge the issue by getting a prescription to use liquor from one not competent, or just as an excuse for drinking, he would not be an obedient soul in the Kingdom. The meaning and purpose of the instruction is plain and it is for those who will receive it, not for others. It is a matter of will in the heart. Who seeks to obey will do so; who wishes otherwise, will not do so, no matter how strong or definite the words.

With love,
Your brother,
Thornton Chase[17]

The brotherly affection between Thornton Chase and John Bosch deepened through their letters to one another rather than by actually meeting face-to-face, as they were separated by nearly 450 miles between Geyserville and Los Angeles. Thornton Chase's position with the Union Mutual Life Insurance Company included frequent travel from the Los Angeles offices to the San Francisco offices. John wrote to Thornton Chase on September 7th, 1910, inviting Thornton out to Geyserville the next time his business brought him to San Francisco. Here is Thornton Chase's response, in part:

Los Angeles, California
September 10, 1910
Dear Brother in El Baha,
I am pleased to receive your kind letter of the 7th [. . .]. I do not now know when I shall be able to go north again, but I presume it will be some time this Fall or early winter. It depends upon business affairs. I should like much to visit you at Geyserville, and shall make an effort to do so when I am in S.F.

I think you will like the little "Bahai News." It is, as you say, a good medium to be posted as to what is going on. Now that the Persian side of it is being used, I think it will be of keen interest in Persia and elsewhere.

I am always glad to hear from you. I well know what it is to be busy, and how difficult it is to write under such circumstances, but writing or no writing, I know that we are bound closely in the bonds of Bahai affection.

There is little here in the way of news. A certain Madame Bethlin is a very enthusiastic individual and is holding some public meetings to tell of the Message, but sometimes enthusiasm is not as well balanced by wisdom as it should be, and I am not sure that real good will result. Still I think her heart is right, and it may be that some of the "seed" will fall on ground that shall mature it.

I have not heard from my letter to Mr Herrigel in Germany. I wonder if you have again heard from him.

With Bahai greetings and good wishes,

Your brother in His Service,

(signed) Thornton Chase[18]

Most of the letters and personal papers of Thornton Chase were destroyed by Mr Chase's second wife after Chase's death.[19] Although the letters that John Bosch sent to Thornton Chase are lost, the subjects of those letters may be pieced together from the replies he received from Thornton. Their correspondence concerned the interests they shared; most prominent are topics related to Tablets received from the Master, discussions regarding the application of Bahá'í law, the sharing of Bahá'í literature, and about how one's professional work often interfered with the real work for the Cause:

Los Angeles
September 21, 1910
Dear Bahai Friend:

I have received a good letter from Mr. Wilhelm Herrigel of Stuttgart and it gives one pleasure. It is dated Sept. 1st. He tells me about the translations they are making and he has sent me copies of three of the printed ones. One is Mrs. Brittingham's *Revelation of Baha'o'llah*, one Sydney Sprague's book, and one *The Universal Religion* by Mr. Herrigel [. . .].

I suppose you are very busy now, and so am I.

> Good wishes in His Name,
> (signed) Thornton Chase[20]

Insight into the books that interested both men is telling of their interest in the history of the Cause. A study of the heroic sacrifices made by the early adherents of one's Faith can be a source of profound inspiration, but these histories of the heroes of the Bábí and Bahá'í dispensation were either scarcely available in English or were unauthorized accounts. *Nabil's Narrative*, also known as *The Dawn-Breakers*, would not be published for another twenty-three years.[21] Despite the scarcity of history books on the Cause, John Bosch and Thornton Chase's first concern was authenticity and accuracy, no matter how scarce the literature.

Two books on Bahá'í history, in particular, interested John Bosch, and both had been published in 1910. They were *The Oriental Rose* by Mary Hanford Ford and *God's Heroes: A Drama in Five Acts* by Laura Clifford Barney.[22] The latter might be more accurately described as "God's Heroine" because the action revolves around the magnificent Persian poetess and heroine, Táhirih. The author, Laura Clifford Barney, was well-versed in her material, having spent some years in the household of 'Abdu'l-Bahá. It was an experience that led her to compile the book now known as *Some Answered Questions*. Thornton Chase was a shrewd judge of Bahá'í literature, and Laura Clifford Barney's history must have proven worthy and reliable because he recommended the book to John.

In the introduction to *God's Heroes: A Drama in Five Acts*, Laura Clifford Barney gave a brief history of the central figures of the Cause, then concluded her introduction with these words of guidance to any reader of Bahá'í history:

> I have thought it preferable not to have the Bab or Baha'u'llah appear on the scene, for certain beings cannot be adequately impersonated; their influence, nevertheless, will be felt through-

out the play, and especially in the life of the splendid Qurratu'l-Ain, who stands forth in history as an example of what the disciple of truth can accomplish despite hampering custom, and violent persecution.

Indulgent reader, I am aware that the only merit of my play is its subject; yet I hope, notwithstanding to give you a glimpse of Eastern glory, and to awaken your interest in this great movement, the universal religion—Bahaism, which is today bringing peace and hope to expectant humanity.[23]

Thornton Chase told John Bosch about Laura Clifford Barney's *God's Heroes* and remarked on the beauty of its appearance. Indeed, the book was beautifully presented, with each of the five dramatic acts illustrated in a calligraphic style with intricate and colorful patterns of birds, flowers, and cypress trees surrounding the borders of each page.* In return John Bosch told Thornton Chase about Mary Hanford Ford's *The Oriental Rose*, which was an early history of the Bábí Faith told through the story of Táhirih, the Persian poetess whose spiritual courage in recognizing the Báb as the Forerunner of the Ancient Beauty, Bahá'u'lláh, was marked by her dramatic removal of the veil that covered her face. This single act of Táhirih's courage was regarded as a symbolic trumpet call for the emancipation of women.

The following are a series of letters from Thornton Chase to John Bosch wherein he discussed the books they had been studying. Reading Thornton's correspondence gives one the sense of being in a room with him as he conversed with John about their love of good books, their love of teaching, and their love for the Cause of God:

---

* A color printing of *God's Heroes* is available for viewing at the Stanford University Library.

Seattle, Washington
October 30, 1910

My dear Mr. Bosch:

I am glad to receive your letter of the 21st. I start back from here tomorrow and shall be in S.F. Wednesday and Thursday and then on to Los Angeles. Possibly there may be a meeting at Mrs. Bell's while I am there. A letter from Hyde Dunne says he and Dr. D'Evelyn want to have a meeting with some others while I am there. I wish it might happen that you would be there too.

Been having a constant succession of meetings in Portland and here—much interest manifested by many here. Two meetings today: afternoon and evening. I just got the new book "God's Heroes" by Laura Clifford Barney. It is a very beautiful book and will make fine present to give at Christmas. Have not read it yet, but it's <u>beautiful</u>.

Yours in love,
Thornton Chase[24]

Los Angeles
November 29, 1910

Dear Mr. Bosch:

Yours of 21st was duly received. I got your note just as I was leaving S.F. but could not stay there longer. I am glad for your letter. Have been busy and could not answer sooner.

[At this part of the letter, Chase changes from handwriting to typewriting].

I can't write very well with a pen, so must use the machine. I think you can find the new book, "God's Heroes," at the Book store in S.F. where you took me, or at one of the other good stores. It is issued by Lippincott and Co. Publishers, Philadelphia, Penn.

If you don't find it at the stores in S.F., any one of them can get it for you. The price is $3.00 and it is a handsome book: one of the nicest Christmas presents you could give to any one. You mention a book I have never heard of, "The Oriental Rose." I must get one. I suppose that is Mrs. Hanford Ford, whom I know.

What is the price of it? And do you know the number on Broadway of the Broadway Publishing Company?

I am delighted that you have succeeded in giving the message to Mrs. Cunningham and Mrs. Pearce. What a pleasure it is when one will listen with an open heart to these beautiful things! I was entirely out of the book "In Galilee," but ordered some, and have just received four at this minute, while I am writing to you. I will send one to each of these new friends, and two to you. I note what you say about finding a good many "searching souls" in the country. I think it is far better and easier to find them there than in the city. The city has so many attractions, so many things to attract the mind and prevent the serious attention and thought that is needed by this great truth; but in the country, people have more time; and then there is something about the living closer to nature which opens the hearts of people with more willingness to listen to the real things of life.

I have heard nothing from anyone in San Francisco. I am sure that men are needed there to spread the Message. I wish you might meet Mr. Hyde Dunn there. He is a beautiful soul and ever trying to guide people to the Truth. But his wife rather opposes him in it, and so it makes it hard for him.*

I am not much better physically, but am all right, and only wish I could do more work in the Cause.

Ever yours in His Name,
(signed) Thornton Chase[25]

---

* This is in reference to Hyde Dunn's first wife, Fannie, who died in 1916. In the following year, Hyde Dunn married Clara Davis and together they pioneered to Australia in response to the Tablets of the Divine Plan. See Barron Harper, *Lights of Fortitude*, 62.

Los Angeles, California
December 3rd, 1910
[At the top of this letter is the Greatest Name hand-written in Arabic.]
My dear Friend,
    Your letter of the 1st is just received. I note what you say about the books of Mrs. Ford, and if you have one to spare, I wish you would send it to me. I enclose a dollar to pay for it, as I understood you that they are a dollar a piece. I mean "The Oriental Rose." I remember when Mrs. Ford first became interested in Bahai matters. She was quite a good lecturer, and began giving lectures on Bahai teachings even before she understood them rightly, and it became necessary for me to correct some of her mistakes, in a friendly way. I think she is a good character, and I shall be very much interested in her book. It is now some ten years or more since she came to the knowledge of these things.

    Mr. Hyde Dunn's address is 1221 Linden St. Oakland, Calif.

    The lady to whom I wrote the letter you mention is Mrs. Augusta W. Bissell. 1412 Bay St. Alameda, Calif.

    The letter I wrote her was simply an endeavor to give her some idea of the meaning of the Bahai Revelation. I am glad if it proved helpful, as she wrote me it did.

    We have our monthly general meeting tomorrow here. How I wish you could be with us.

    I write in haste.

    Yours sincerely,
        (signed) Thornton Chase[26]

Los Angeles, California
December 12, 1910
    My dear Brother Bosch:
    Yours of Dec. 5th was duly received. I thank you for sending for "The Oriental Rose" for me. It will come in due time [. . .].

We had a gathering at my home here yesterday. I did wish you could have been with us. Tonight the Unity Feast is held at Mr. and Mrs. Frankland's in Tropico.*

I thank-you for your kind suggestions concerning my physical annoyance. I know that simple and plain food is always better for any trouble. Mine has been going on so long that it is doubtful if I can get any permanent relief. The Doctors say I cannot [get relief] except through an operation: but I am going to try every possible way to get along without that. For about ten days now, I have been troubled but little with it, and I am almost hoping that I have the trouble under control [. . .].

With all good thoughts and wishes,

Yours sincerely,

(signed) Thornton Chase[27]

Los Angeles
December 24, 1910
A Merry Christmas to you! The "Oriental Rose" has just come. I am surprised that it is such a book. I supposed it to be some booklet or pamphlet. I thank you for getting it for me. Good wishes to you.

Yours sincerely,

(signed) Thornton Chase[28]

Thornton Chase appointed John Bosch as his literary executor, and he entrusted all of his writings to him. When John Bosch arrived in Los Angeles about a month after Chase's passing, it must have been a relief to learn that even though Mrs. Chase had burned a vast majority of her husband's letters, she preserved the Tablets he had received

---

* Tropico, California was an area of Los Angeles County that is now included in the city of Glendale, California.

from 'Abdu'l-Bahá. John Bosch secured the remaining papers and took them to his home in Geyserville. Over time, John sent some of Chase's papers to the National Bahá'í Archives of the United States. Nevertheless, it comes as a great surprise to learn that John destroyed most of the surviving personal letters of Thornton Chase—particularly the letters to individuals. In a letter to Mrs. Scheffler dated June 11, 1936, Louise Bosch explained that she and John destroyed those letters "'by reason of the private nature of their contents [. . .]. We have kept only letters of spiritual import.'"[29]

There is a clue to the nature of these letters of a "private nature," as the following letter—a letter in which John wrote the word "Keep" at the top of the letter—demonstrates. Perhaps John decided to keep this particular letter because it captured, for him, the essence of Thornton Chase's steadfastness. Furthermore, the letter he decided to keep gives a clue as to the delicacy of the subject matter of the papers that John Bosch burned. The contents of those letters must have been of a nature that John felt would be unbefitting to a believer such as Thornton Chase, whom the Master described as a soul whose "sun will be ever shining" and whose "star will ever bestow the light."[30] Here is the letter of Thornton Chase's that John kept, in full:

San Francisco
March 21, 1911

My dear Brother,
A Happy New Year to you on this bright morning of the Nawrooz! Your letter did not reach me in time for me to go up on Sunday, and I could not do so anyway, as I was kept very busy indeed all day. I had expected to stay here for a week or more, but advices from the Company are of such a nature that it is probable I shall have to go back to Los Angeles tonight or tomorrow and then on to Arizona. When I shall be here again I do not know, but I think it will be in about a month or six weeks.

I have your letter from Los Angeles. About the books for the Library, as you suggest, I am sure your judgment is as good or better than mine. I have not the list of publications with me at hand, but I will mention some that seem fitted for such a purpose. The works of Baha'o'llah especially The Hidden Words, The Ighan, The Tarazat, The Ishrakat. (Not the Surat I Hykl, because it is not correctly published). "Some Answered Questions" (Barney). "Unity through Love" (Mac Nutt). Possibly "The Bahai Revelation" (Chase), if you deem it worthy. I should question the use of "Sacred Mysteries" by M. Assadullah, as it is not in good shape for reading or study. I think "Ten Days in the Light of Acca" might be used. It is by Mrs. Grundy, but really was edited by Mr. Mac Nutt. I do not think now of others that would be suitable for such use. Oh Yes! M. Assadullah's "School of the Prophets," would be all right.

I am sorry to hear of the possible division in Stuttgart, but I have been expecting it. It occurs everywhere as soon as some strength is developed in an assembly. I think I see its meaning and purpose. The essence of this Cause is UNITY, and there must be strong testings <u>along that line</u> to prove the sincerity and soul-values of the Friends. The division usually occurs along the lines of differences of opinions concerning the station of Abdul-Baha. The same thing was in Persia concerning the station of the Manifestation, Baha'o'llah, and when two of the disputants traveled all the way from Persia to Palestine to lay their beliefs before Him, you remember his answer, viz: that as long as they disagreed, they were both wrong and disagreement would destroy them, but if they would love each other in unity, they were both right. Thus was shown the supreme value of Unity, or harmony, over all opinions, or stations.

There is a class of people who go to extremes. They are usually not persons of deep perceptions, but are ardent devotees of that which appeals to them, which is usually the outside appearance.

They are strongly inclined to worship personalities, and the letters of the Law, rather than to direct their sight to the Realities and to the Things themselves. This has been one of the errors of the Christian Church, in that it has directed its followers' attention and devotion to the person of Jesus, rather than to the Spirit, which He came to manifest. There is danger of this Cause degenerating into the same lines through the same kind of people.

And such persons are inclined to be quite intolerant of anyone who does not view matters exactly in the same light as themselves, no matter how pure and earnest the others may be. Sometimes this personal devotion and intolerance of the views of others goes to such extremes that it throws such persons "off from their balance," and they then become the bitterest factors in the processes of disunity. They really become insane, and will not tolerate sanity.

Furthermore, this Cause is so vital, so powerful and penetrating, that it reaches to the centers of beings, and brings forth the hidden things, which may have been there unperceived before, both good and evil. Sometimes it arouses all the "devil" in one's nature, and causes it to become manifest where all before was quiet and simple. I think that this is in order that man may see and "know himself," may recognize his weaknesses and distortions, and overcome that which is not for the best. But this bringing of hidden things to light is often a powerful factor in producing separations.

Another thing! The instructive power of this Word is so strong and clear that he who is touched by it soon finds that he knows more about spiritual matters than his neighbor, and he gets a sort of spiritual "swelled head." It is like the youth who passes out from childhood into the period of adolescence: he feels the currents of life within him and thinks he knows more than parents, brothers, sisters, or anyone else. We recognize the source of this, and smile at him, although, for a while, he is an intolerable nuisance. As it is physically, so is it spiritually. We have to arrive and pass through a period of spiritual adolescence, in which similar traits appear, and we become, for a time, spiritual nuisances. This also leads to disunion. If you watch you will see that a very large portion of the troubles come from this class of persons, who have not yet "settled" into the calm assurance and quiet knowledge of maturity. "Outwardly it is a burning fire, inwardly it is calm Light."

I do not know whether a delegate will go to Chicago. I think it doubtful. I wrote Mr Herrigel a little while ago and also George Haigis there. Write me at Los Angeles. Some day we shall meet again.

With hosts of good wishes,

Yours sincerely in His Name,

(signed) Thornton Chase[31]

Thornton Chase's cautionary insights into human nature were motivated by his devotion to the preservation of unity in the Cause of God, a principle central to the Bahá'í Faith and at the heart of both John Bosch's and Thornton Chase's friendship. These letters represent the early years of John's life as a Bahá'í when he was learning from his friend, the steadfast one. In his remarkable book *The Bahá'í Revelation*, Chase writes of what will come from the "spiritual adolescence" referred to in the letter above:

We are entering upon a human period when the motives of man shall be reversed, when his purpose shall be to serve rather than to be served, to benefit others, to conserve the interest of the whole rather than the individual self. Instead of oppression, greed and selfishness, the motive powers of man shall be justice, helpfulness and love. These are the elements of peace and prosperity which are twin brothers born of man's true evolution. Man is emerging from barbarism into civilization, from childhood to manhood, from darkness to light; he is just now passing out of his period of adolescence, of little wisdom and callow pride, into a noble maturity of conscious strength, knowledge and manly stability. A great cycle of past conditions is closing and we stand upon the threshold of a new age, which is beyond all our present conjectures in its values to man. In its reality, it is the Manifestation of God, the Glory of the Lord revealing itself upon the plane of humanity.[32]

The "threshold of that new age" was about to dawn upon the shores of America with the arrival of 'Abdu'l-Bahá as the Perfect Exemplar of how to "serve rather than to be served."

In the years leading up to 'Abdu'l-Bahá's visit to America, the Master received many requests for His visit, and Thornton Chase was one of those who respectfully asked the Master to visit the West. The Master's reply to Chase's plea comes at the end of a lengthy Tablet wherein the Master addresses several biblical questions of Thornton Chase. Here is the Tablet, in part:

Upon him be BAHA'O'LLAH-EL-ABHA!
HE IS GOD!
O thou herald of the Kingdom!

I received thy two letters, an old one and one of recent date, and both of them were read with the utmost attention. Praise be to God! that thou didst not waver before the tests; nay, rather thou didst remain firm and steadfast. When the tree sends down its roots into the bowels of the earth, then, it will bring forth blossoms and fruits. Now, Praise be to God! that in this day of the kingdom thou art firm and steadfast. Rest thou assured that thou wilt become the recipient of confirmation and assistance and the object of infinite bounties.

Thou hast asked about the statement in the Hidden Words, which reads: "O Son of Spirit! Turn thy face so that thou mayest find Me within thee. Powerful, Mighty and Supreme." This is the statement to which His Holiness the Christ, referred His apostles in the Gospel, saying. "The Father is in the Son, and the Son is in you."

This is evident that, when the hearts are purified and through divine education and heavenly teachings become the manifestors of infinite perfections, they are like clear mirrors, and the Sun of Truth will reflect with might, power and omnipotence in such a mirror, and to such an extent that whatever is brought before it is illumined and ignited. This is a brief interpretation because of the lack of time. Therefore, do thou reflect and ponder over it so that the doors of significance may be opened before thine eyes [. . .].

Regarding my coming to America, it depends upon the realization of conditions of which I have already written to that country. If those conditions are brought into fruition, rest thou assured that I will present myself, otherwise, it will be difficult.

Upon thee be the Glory of God!

(Signed) ABDU'L-BAHA ABBAS.

Translated by Mirza Ahmad Sohrab, 8 June 1911. Washington, D.C.[33]

Mr. Chase must have sent news of the Tablet right away to John Bosch, as here is Bosch's letter to Thornton Chase asking if he might study the Tablet from 'Abdu'l-Bahá. Also in this letter, John includes his suggestions regarding Herrigel's translation of Mr. Chase's book *The Bahá'í Revelation*:

Geyserville Winery
Geyserville, California
July 26, 1911
    My Dear Mr. Chase,
    From your letter of July 7th I am very glad to note that you are

getting better and I hope now that your health will be perfectly restored. We need you for a long time to promulgate the teachings of Baha Ullah and Abdul Baha on this coast and I do not know of any resident person who can fulfill this responsible position better than yourself.

Are you going to have the Tablet you have received from Abdul Baha printed in the Star of the West? I certainly would like to read it. Or when you come up on your next trip, kindly bring it along with you so I may read it.

I hope some day that you can finish the book on the views of reincarnation. Many Bahais are still "hung up" on that point. The translation of Mr. George Haigis of Constatt [Germany] is very good, of course there is some in it that sounds like a dictionary translation. One word should be changed on page 3 and should read "Lob" instead of *Preis*. This latter word means a money value and not the praise of God. The dictionary has *Preis* and *Lob*, but the latter should be used for "praise." The blue print is a translation of "To Live the Life." To be no cause of grief to any one. To love each other very much. To be kind to all people and to love them with a pure spirit. It takes in the whole tablet as written on pages 168–169–170 in *The Oriental Rose*.

Enclose you herewith the two translations of Mr Haigis. Trusting you will now enjoy the best of health, with Bahai greetings and in His Name, sincerely yours,

(signed) John Bosch

Postscript:

Have received a letter from Mrs. Goodall in which she writes that Abdul Baha sends me this message: "Give the glad tidings of the Bounties of the Supreme to Mr. John D. Bosch." Isn't that short and impressive: It is more to me than a long letter.

I am going to San Francisco on the 29th, to Alameda on the 30th and extending my trip to Martinez and Knightsen, returning to San Francisco and Geyserville by Aug 4th.[34]

In her book *Dawn Over Mount Hira,* Marzieh Gail retells the story of how John Bosch and Thornton Chase would often meet in San Francisco when Thornton was on business at the Union Mutual Life Insurance office there. Although John and Thornton would stay at separate hotels, they would dine together:

"He was very tall—about six feet two. He always ate two or three ice creams after supper; he always dug a big bite right out of the middle of it to start with. Around eleven o'clock, he used to say, 'Now John, I guess it's about time to take you home.'" Arm in arm, they would go to John's hotel, talking steadily about the Cause. They would sit in the parlour. "About one o'clock I used to say, 'Now, Mr. Chase, I guess it's about time to take you home.' We used to wonder what the policeman on the beat thought about us. One night we brought each other home till four in the morning."[35]

Originally, the Master's visit to America did not include a visit to the state of California. Once this became clear to John, he wasted no time in making efforts to influence the Master's travel itinerary. At the time, John Bosch was teaching the Cause to his business associates—one of whom was Luther Burbank, whose work with hybridizing hundreds of varieties of fruits such as plums, pears, and peaches drew John's interest. Luther Burbank is best known for his 1893 publication of his agricultural research in hybridization called *New Creations in Fruits and Flowers.*[36] He lived near John Bosch in Santa Rosa, California, and while John Bosch's friendship with him originated from their shared work in cultivation of plants, John did his best to help Luther Burbank cultivate the soul. Although Luther Burbank was attracted to the Cause, he never fully embraced it. His interests, albeit high-minded and overall humanitarian, were limited to this material world, while John's sights were set on that heavenly world not bound by the laws of nature. John Bosch and Luther Burbank remained good friends until

Burbank's death in 1926—after all, their friendship will ever remain a spiritual one, as this letter from 'Abdu'l-Bahá attests. This Tablet also hints at the possibility that the Master might come to California. So intent was John Bosch on persuading the Master to come to California that his heart must have skipped a beat upon reading the Master's hint that such a journey might be "What God hath decreed."

To: Mr. John D. Bosch and Mr. Luther Burbank
Upon them be Baha'u'llah El Abha!
He is God!
O ye sons of the Kingdom:

Thy letter was received and from its contents perfect attraction to the Kingdom of Abha became evident. I hope day by day you will draw nearer to God until ye be established in the pole of the Kingdom. Glad Tidings to you for you are of the chosen and not of the called.

The call of praise from Heaven reaches you saying "O ye two roses of the Garden of the Knowledge of God. Rejoice, for the shower of grace arrives from the Cloud of Mercy. Rejoice, for the breezes of favors are wafting from the direction of Clemency so that in the utmost of freshness and beauty ye may become manifest, that is, ye may arise to serve the Kingdom of God. This is the great bestowal.

As to my coming to California it is a little doubtful, for the trip is far and the weather hot, and from the labors of the journey the body of Abdul Baha has not much endurance. Nevertheless we shall see what God hath decreed.

Convey to his honor Mr. Chase the utmost love and longing and kindness. I hope that with a power from the Kingdom he may at every moment add to service to Baha'u'llah.

Write long letters to Mr. Herrigel and lead him to firmness and steadfastness and say, "Miss Knobloch, though a weak woman,

remained firm and steadfast. It is a pity that thou art a man, with power and might, yet thou hast remained behind."
Verily, this is a strange affair!
Upon thee be Baha'u'llah El Abha!
(Signed) 'Abdu'l-Baha Abbas
Translated by Dr. Ameen Fareed
11 Bradford Place, Montclair, N.J.
June 23, 1912[37]

At the end of the Tablet, there is mention of Mr. Herrigel, a Bahá'í in Germany with whom John Bosch corresponded on behalf of Thornton Chase. The reference to Miss Knobloch and Mr. Herrigel together makes clear that the comparison of the two is a lesson in firmness in the Covenant. In a pilgrim's note of one of John Bosch's closest friends, George Latimer, he writes that the Master made a comparison between Miss Knobloch's spiritual strength and Mr. Herrigel's, saying, "Consider the power of God. Such a small Woman! She is confirmed in service. She is greatly assisted. When a person compares her success with her physical body, a hundred people will not be so assisted as she [. . .]." In the Tablets of the Divine Plan the Master praises Miss Knobloch as an example of firmness in the Cause: "Miss Knobloch traveled alone to Germany. To what a great extent she became confirmed! Therefore, know ye of a certainty that whosoever arises in this day to diffuse the divine fragrances, the cohorts of the Kingdom of God shall confirm him and the bestowals and the favors of the Blessed Perfection shall encircle him." It is also important to note that Alma Knobloch is mentioned in the document *Century of Light* wherein she is named among "a galaxy of unforgettable women who became the principal exponents of the Bahá'í message on both sides of the Atlantic" in the first decades of the 20th Century.[38]

John Bosch wrote to Thornton Chase about the Tablet concerning Miss Knobloch and Mr. Herrigel. Bosch's early association with

Thornton Chase explains how John developed deep wisdom in dealing with instances of personality conflicts within the Cause. Thornton Chase would have had many experiences with such personality conflicts, having come into the Faith when Ibrahim Kheiralla's* influence was becoming pernicious. Thornton Chase remained unaffected by Kheiralla's divisive personality. Biographer O. Z. Whitehead wrote that although Kheiralla was "blinded by self-love and ambition" Thornton Chase was impervious to those whose personality contradicted the spirit of the teachings of Bahá'u'lláh.[39] Rather than becoming distracted by the selfish ambition of others, Thornton Chase explained that all he could do was to focus on the sincerity of his own actions, as he explained in this letter to John Bosch:

Los Angeles
July 6th, 1912
   My dear Brother:
   I have not been able to answer your kind letter with the enclosed word from Abdul-Baha. I thank you so much for the copy of your Tablet. It shall not be copied for others. Oh, I think you are greatly blessed in His love and remembrance. It is truly not words that make one of any importance in the Kingdom but that sweet, pure, unselfish, loving, sincere nature which Abdul-Baha perceived at once in you, and which we all perceive with you, to the degree of our enlightenment. Truly you are "of the chosen, not only of the called."
   I do not think the sentence you marked in red pencil belongs to either you or me. If to either, it is to me. But from the context, the mention of Miss Knobloch, a weak woman, as remaining firm and steadfast, I think He refers to Mr. Herrigel. Mr. Herrigel has "remained behind," for he has done all he could to establish an active body in the Cause, but he has shown some anxiety

---

* An early Bahá'í teacher in the United States who became a Covenant-breaker.

and depression because of the fact that Miss Knobloch and her followers would not affiliate with him and his friends. He has been going through experiences similar to those of nearly all the earnest workers in the assemblies in this country and elsewhere. It may be, that in the eyes of Abdul-Baha [Brother] Herrigel has been somewhat shaken by these times of testing, and He wants him to become more firmly rooted, and wants us to help him as far as we can with sympathy and encouragement.

I presume Miss Knobloch has felt keenly the lack of sympathy in her views, but in spite of that has adhered very steadfastly to the faith, and it is probably this to which Abdul-Baha refers.

Pray for me, my brother, that I may receive "power from the kingdom" to "add to service to Baha'o'llah." I thank you much for this word from Him.

My dear brother. I cannot write to Abdul-Baha to tell Him of what I try to do. I do not feel it is fitting or becoming for me to do so. Of course, I wish that He might know, but the information must reach Him, if at all, from another than me. All I can do is to try to serve where opportunity appears. But I feel that most of my effort is without result. Still I will try to do what I can as long as it is permitted [. . .].

Love to you, my Brother.

Greetings to all!

Remembrances to the shoemaker.

Yours sincerely,

(signed) Thornton Chase[40]

Thornton Chase's true name, given to him by 'Abdu'l-Bahá, is *Thabit*, or *Steadfastness*, and indeed that quality protected him from becoming distracted by personalities. In this regard, the Guardian, writing many years later, advised that "one must look upon the perfection of the Faith and not upon the imperfections of the believers."[41] Like Thornton Chase, John Bosch was given a name by 'Abdu'l-Bahá—the name

Nurani, meaning *Luminous.* How fitting that Thornton would refer to John using the epithet "Luminous One" in the following letter:

> Los Angeles, California
> July 26, 1912
> Dear Friend and Brother [. . .]
> I understand that Abdul-Baha will be in this country until some time in September, and everybody is invited from California to go and see Him. But think of the poor ones, the ones who need Him most, and who cannot go to the east to meet him. It is too bad!
> My friend, I appreciate keenly your remembrance of this servant and mention of me to Mr. Burbank. I wish he could meet Abdul-Baha. That would "settle it" as far as he is concerned, for a nature such as his would respond to Abdul-Baha at once. But what could I say or do that would be of any use with a man like that! Nothing I fear. But, if the opportunity should ever come, I can only pray for the Guidance of the Spirit. But you, your own good self, the Luminous One, can do more than to cause Mr. B. to conceive a favorable idea of the Bahai. In fact, you have already done so, as is evident. May God bless you!⁴²

Thornton Chase was reluctant to try to convince the Master to come to California. To John Bosch, Thornton said, "'John, don't you think it's too soon? The Bahá'ís aren't ready for Him.'" John Bosch replied, "'Well I'm ready for Him!'"⁴³ John was unreserved in his efforts to attract 'Abdu'l-Bahá to California. In the following Tablet to John Bosch, the Master acknowledged the effect of Bosch's persuasion:

> To Mr. John D. Bosch (Nurani)
> San Francisco, California
> Upon him be Baha'o'llah El Abha!

HE IS GOD!

O thou who art longing for the visit of Abdul Baha!

Your yearning letter was wonderful and eloquent and its effect upon Abdul Baha was inexpressible. I long very much to fulfill the request of the friends, but I am yet in these parts, until later the requirement of wisdom will be revealed. If the Western cities <u>demonstrate</u> their infinite firmness in the Covenant, this will act as an attractive magnet to draw Abdul Baha and unquestionably the Divine Destiny will <u>assist</u> and make you victorious.

Therefore, strive as much as you can to manifest the Power of the Breaths of the Holy Spirit in the firmness of the Covenant.

I am very much pleased with thee.

Upon thee be Baha El Abha!

(signed) Abdul Baha Abbas

Translated by M. Ahmad Sohrab

August 1, 1912, Dublin, N.H.

Translation signed by Abdul Baha[44]

John Bosch must have sent this Tablet to Thornton Chase immediately after receiving John's correspondence because within a week's time, a meeting was planned in San Francisco—a meeting where a number of the friends there would consult about how to demonstrate firmness in the Covenant in order to attract the Master to come to California. Thornton Chase sent the following to John Bosch from his hotel in San Francisco. It was a Friday, and the meeting was planned for the next night—Saturday, August 10th:

San Francisco, California

August 9, 1912

My dear Brother:

Yours rec'd. Shall meet you Sat. eve. Was intending to ask you to come. The reply to a wire from Southern California Assemblies and a personal one from me. ['Abdu'l-Bahá] has sent two wires to me, rec'd yesterday as follows:

Dublin, N.H. Aug 7

"Greetings to Friends in Tropico, Pasadena, Los Angeles and all California. I hope from the favor of Baha'u'llah that means be brought about so that I may associate with all of you." —Abdul Baha

Dublin, N.H. Aug 7

"I hope that God may answer your request and with perfect happiness meeting be realized." —Abdul Baha

A telegram of similar import and a long Tablet is rec'd by Mrs. Goodall. I think now that He will come. Inshallah!

Yours,

(signed) Thornton Chase[45]

Spiritual opportunities were rarely lost on John Bosch. He was noble and saintly, but he did not hesitate to seize a spiritual opportunity that may never come again. So it was in an attitude of spiritual readiness that he wrote to the Master after the meeting with the Bahá'ís in San Francisco. On August 10th, at 11:00pm, John Bosch sent a telegram to the Master:

Abdul Baha Abbas
Care A. J. Parsons, Dublin, N.H.

I made a special trip to San Francisco today. A great spirit of prayer, thankfulness, joy and hope filled the assembly tonight anticipating the coming of the Center of the Covenant. Unity and firmness are manifest. This supplication begs earnestly for Thy personal presence from D'Evelyn, Lua [Getsinger], [Bijou] Straun, Bozork and [Thornton] Chase.

Signed: John D. Bosch[46]

On August 13, at 11:00pm, the Master sent the following reply to John Bosch:

Mr. John D. Bosch
Care Mrs. Ella Cooper
1357 Jackson St., Oakland, Calif.

Your telegram was the cause of much happiness. God willing I will depart for the Western Part. Give this glad tiding to each and all.

Abdul Baha.[47]

John Bosch forwarded the message to Thornton Chase the next day, with a postscript that read: "If you should see Abdul-Baha before I do, please talk it over with Him to come up to my place and one evening at Mr. Bozork's as Mr. Bozork may interpret for us." Alas, it would not be, as Thornton had to return to Los Angeles and wrote to John to tell him of his disappointment:

San Francisco, California
September 9, 1912
My dear "John D,"

I enclose P.O. Order for the Fifty Dollars with which you last helped me. I thank you very much. I am still trying to get the other to repay you, and will do my utmost to get it as soon as I can.

Wish I could see you. Abdul-Baha will surely be here before very long. I expect to go to Los Angeles on Monday Boat [September 16]. I wish I could stay here until He comes.

Your friend,
(signed) Thornton Chase[48]

Thornton Chase returned to Los Angeles on Monday, September 16. On that day 'Abdu'l-Bahá was giving a talk at the home of Mrs. Corinne True in Chicago. The subject of His talk was how "the source of perfect unity and love in the world of existence is the bond and oneness of reality."[49] From Chicago, the Master would make His journey westward toward California, with a plan of arrival sometime in the first week of October. Thornton Chase took ill on September 23; on that day the Master had arrived in Denver, Colorado. The next day, Chase's secretary wrote to John Bosch:

[On office letterhead]:
Union Mutual Life Insurance Company, Thornton Chase, Manager
Los Angeles, California
September 24, 1912
To: Mr. John D. Bosch, Geyserville, California
Dear Sir:
    Mr. Chase has asked me over the phone to send you $50.00, for which amount you will find Postal Order herewith enclosed.
    Mr. Chase has been at home ill yesterday and today, but hopes to be all right by tomorrow. He says will you please keep him posted.
    Yours very truly,
    Edna R Sedge, Cashier[50]

On September 26, while en route to California, the Master left Denver and stayed in Glenwood Springs. Meanwhile, Thornton Chase wrote the following letter to John Bosch:

[On office letterhead]:
Union Mutual Life Insurance Company, Thornton Chase, Manager
Los Angeles, California
September 26, 1912
Dictated by Mr. Chase.
To: Mr. John D. Bosch, Geyserville, California
Dear Friend:
    They have just brought me to the hospital and are going to operate on me for obstruction of the bowels in about an hour. It

is a very serious operation and will tie me up here for two weeks or more. Please let Abdu'l-Baha know.

Yours in love,
Thornton Chase
Typed by Edna R Sedge, Office Cashier[51]

On the evening of September 30, Thornton Chase passed away. The train upon which 'Abdu'l-Bahá was traveling would have been just hours from crossing the border of Nevada into California. Just before midnight the next day, the first of October, the Master arrived in San Francisco.[52] When He was given the news of Thornton Chase's passing, this was His immediate response:

This revered personage was the first Bahá'í in America. He served the Cause faithfully and his services will ever be remembered throughout future ages and cycles. He has written many books in this Cause and they will be studied carefully by the coming generations. He traveled once to 'Akká and there we associated with each other for several days. Indeed he became free from the troubles of this world. No matter how long he might have remained here, he would have met nothing else but trouble. The purpose of life is to get certain results; that is, the life of man must bring forth certain fruitage. It does not depend upon the length of life. As soon as the life is crowned with fruition then it is completed, although that person may have had a short life. There are certain trees which come to fruition very quickly, but there are other trees which attain to fruition very late; the aim is fruit. If the tree brings forth its fruit young, its life is short; it is praiseworthy. How regretful it is that a man may live a long life and yet his life may not be crowned with success, like unto the cypress tree which does not give any fruitage. Praise be to God! the tree of Mr. Chase's life brought forth fruit. It gave complete fruit, therefore he is free. He attained to eternal rest. He is now in the Presence of Bahá'u'lláh. His Holiness Jesus Christ lived only thirty-three years, but the world is filled with the fruits of his life. Others have lived a hundred years, with no result and no fruitage from their lives. There was a rabbi in Tiberius who lived 120 years, but the tree of his life was fruitless. He had great enmity against Jesus Christ. He often used to argue: "The ephemeral life is subject to many trials and vicissitudes; there is no enjoyment in it." The life of Mr. Chase was spiritual in character; his services will ever he remembered and he has already attained to the desire of his heart.[53]

In contemplating the Master's meaning when He said, "the world is filled with the fruits of his life," one cannot help but think of the man whom Thornton Chase considered his true brother: John Bosch.

It is very likely that John Bosch first heard of Thornton Chase's passing before receiving the following letter; nevertheless, it is the only record of such a communication among the Bosch papers. Earlier that year, John had given financial assistance to Thornton Chase. It is heartbreaking to read in the following letter about Chase's repayment of the balance of a loan from John, as surely John would not have needed the repayment. It is a sign of their friendship and trust—and the way in which the Master described Thornton Chase's soul as one that is free from the fetters of this world. This letter is from Thornton Chase's secretary:

[On office letterhead]:
Union Mutual Life Insurance Company, Thornton Chase, Manager
Los Angeles, California
October 3, 1912
To: Mr. John D. Bosch, Geyserville, California
Dear Mr. Bosch:
  Yours of the 2nd just received and I hasten to reply. I was under the impression that some one of the Bahais had told you about

Mr. Chase, as those in San Francisco all know the sad news. His dear soul passed to its Maker on Monday [30 September] evening at 6:45, after a week of great suffering. I join with those who mourn, as he has been like a father to me these past three years. I would have written you at once, only I thought someone else had done so. They even talked of asking you to come down to conduct the funeral service tomorrow morning at 10 o'clock. I am sorry you have been neglected, as Mr. Chase loved you so much, but then you know that. Please let me know if you got the Money Order I sent you for $50. It was sent after Mr. Chase was taken ill.
Yours very truly,
Edna R Sedge[54]

After visiting Thornton Chase's grave, 'Abdu'l-Bahá intimated something about the liberation of Thornton's soul when He said that he "became free from the troubles of this world. No matter how long he might have remained here, he would have met nothing else but trouble." John Bosch understood the Master's meaning; indeed, the burdens of this world weighed heavy on Thornton Chase. John Bosch explained Thornton Chase's relationship to this material world by simply saying, "It was too much for him," and in the space of six words John Bosch captured the purity of Thornton Chase's heart. That longing of the soul to be detached from the chains that temporarily bind it to this world is reminiscent of the poem "Ode to the West Wind" by Romantic poet Percy Shelley. In that poem, the poet calls out in prayer to the Wind, "Oh! lift me as a wave, a leaf, a cloud! I fall upon the thorns of life! I bleed!"—a sentiment echoed by any soul longing to be free.[55]

3 / I Have Traveled 8,000 Miles to See You

To count the blessings bestowed upon John Bosch is to witness the "Bounties of the Supreme" promised him by 'Abdu'l-Bahá. John's blessings were not only numerous but astounding in their spiritual significance. In a Tablet addressed to Helen Goodall on August 17, 1909, the Master wrote, "Exercise on My behalf the utmost kindness and love to John D. Bosch. With the utmost humility I pray to the Kingdom of Abhá that that soul may become holy, find capacity to receive the outpouring of Eternity and become a luminous star in the West."[1]

While John Bosch is primarily known for his role in establishing a permanent Bahá'í summer school in California for the Pacific Coast region of the United States, one is awestruck by the bounties that preceded that achievement. The significant experiences of Bosch's Bahá'í life coincided with important historical periods in the first century of Bahá'í history. In the preface to the book *God Passes By*, Shoghi Effendi surveyed the first Bahá'í century, spanning from 1844–1944, by dividing the century into four periods. The first period (1844–1853) centered on the "youthful and irresistible person of the Báb." The second period (1853–1892) centered on the "august figure of Bahá'u'lláh." The third period (1892–1921) "revolve[d] around the vibrant personality of 'Abdu'l-Bahá, mysterious in His essence, unique in His station, astoundingly potent in both the charm and strength of His character." The fourth period (1921–1944) centered around the forces of the

Will and Testament of 'Abdu'l-Bahá, "that Charter of Bahá'u'lláh's New World Order." John Bosch was to become deeply linked to both the third and fourth periods of the first Bahá'í century: first through his close association with 'Abdu'l-Bahá during His visit to America; secondly, by being present in Haifa at the time of the ascension of 'Abdu'l-Bahá and, in due course, being asked by the Guardian to carry a copy of a portion of the Will and Testament of 'Abdu'l-Bahá from the Holy Land to the cradle of the administrative order in America.²

John Bosch received at least twelve Tablets from the Master.* Theirs was a correspondence that began in 1905 and lasted until the Master's passing in 1921. Of the Tablets from 'Abdu'l-Bahá addressed to John, the best known is the Tablet dated May 10, 1910, cited in its entirety in the previous chapter. In that Tablet, the Master explained to Bosch that Bahá'í law prohibits the drinking of alcohol, and that "the reason for this is that [liquor] leads the mind astray." The Master concluded the letter with the hope that John Bosch would become "exhilarated with the wine of the love of God." John Bosch must have given this instruction further thought because three months later he wrote to the Master of his plans in the following letter addressed to 'Abdu'l-Bahá through His secretary, Mírzá Ahmad Sohráb:

Geyserville, California
August 10, 1910
 Mr. Ahmad Sohrab, Washington D.C,
 My Dear Spiritual Brother,
 I am enclosing you herewith a letter to our Master Abdul Baha, which letter I wish you kindly send to him. (Stamp and envelope enclosed herewith.)
 Following the instruction of Abdul Baha, I feel inclined to gradually change my occupation and business. For this reason I wish

---

* These Tablets are on record at the U.S. Bahá'í Archives in Wilmette, Illinois.

to find out if any new production plants as vines, grains, figs, nuts could be introduced here from Syria or Persia for good commercial results and going hand in hand with the spirit of Bahaism.

We have a good climate here and possibly plants from the East would mature well here.

Thanking you in advance for the trouble. I am sincerely in His Service,

Yours,

John D. Bosch[3]

John Bosch's anticipation that "plants from the East would mature well" in California was especially fitting when one remembers the words of 'Abdu'l-Bahá in the Tablets of the Divine Plan, which would be written six years later, in 1916:

> The blessed state of California bears the utmost similarity to the Holy Land, that is, the country of Palestine. The air is of the utmost temperance, the plain very spacious, and the fruits of Palestine are seen in that state in the utmost of freshness and delicacy. When 'Abdu'l-Bahá was traveling and journeying through those states, he found himself in Palestine, for from every standpoint there was a perfect likeness between this region and that state. Even the shores of the Pacific Ocean, in some instances, show perfect resemblance to the shores of the Holy Land—even the flora of the Holy Land have grown on those shores—the study of which had led to much speculation and wonder.[4]

Surely the Master's imagery alludes to both the literal and the figurative meanings of the similarities between the spiritual landscapes of California and the Holy Land. The Persian flora may be an allusion to the divine teachings taking root in such western climes. Regardless, the teachings had certainly taken root in John Bosch's soul, and he had a strong desire to do something for the Cause.

By 1910, John Bosch was the superintendent of four wineries that produced two and a quarter of a million tons of wine in one year. The work was time-consuming, to say the least. During this same year, at age fifty-five, Bosch decided to make plans to retire from the winemaking business and devote the remainder of his life—which was to be another thirty-six years—to service to the Cause. Furthermore, it would not be long before the course of his Bahá'í activity would be changed forever by 'Abdu'l-Bahá's visit to America.

John Bosch's correspondence with 'Abdu'l-Bahá included additional correspondence with 'Abdu'l-Bahá's translator, Mírzá Ahmad Sohráb, who was residing in Washington DC and who was serving as a translator of communications between the American believers and the Master. The following letter demonstrates John Bosch's early interest in furthering the various aims of the Cause, particularly his interest in helping girls to obtain an education in places where they would not otherwise be afforded one:

Geyserville Winery
Geyserville, California
July 6th, 1910
Mirza Ahmad Sohrab, Washington D.C.
My Dear Bahai brother,
    Since writing to you on June 23rd, I find in the "Bahai News" that a school for girls will be established in Teheran and my request to use the scholarship fee for a girl may have been inspired at this right time. Should the scholarship fee for one girl be more than for a boy, kindly let me know and I will send the additional amount. I trust and pray that a girl will be chosen with the best of qualities physically, mentally and spiritually, who later on may teach the great truth of Bahaism in all lands. With Bahai greetings and in His Service, sincerely yours,
    John D. Bosch[5]

John's willingness to contribute to meaningful humanitarian efforts reveals important qualities in his character. His charity was not limited to educating future Bahá'í teachers. For instance, in addition to supporting the education of girls in Tehran, John sent contributions toward the relief of Persians suffering from famine in 1912, as noted in the following letter to Mírzá Ahmad Sohráb on March 14, 1912: "Dear friend. Enclose you herewith Post money order $10.00 for the Persian Sufferers. With Bahai greetings, Very truly yours, John D. Bosch."[6] Sohráb's reply follows, which includes information about 'Abdu'l-Bahá's arrival in New York:

March 20, 1912
To Mr. John Bosch, Geyserville, California
My dear Bahai Brother:
   Your kind letter enclosing ten dollars for the Persian sufferers of famine duly received; it just came in time to complete the sum of $600, which I have sent this morning. I had $590 and yours completed the round sum. I was very anxious to make up this $1,000 but I thought it would not be wise to wait any longer and if I get more money in the future I will send it. Abdul Baha will leave Alexandria on the 25th of this month and arrive in New York about the 11th of April. It will be very nice if you send a telegram to greet His arrival. I will go there myself and the address will be 718 West End Avenue. Thanking you again for your contribution towards the famine in Persia, I am,
   Your sincere brother,
   (signed) Mirza Ahmad Sohrab[7]

In the years preceding His visit to America, 'Abdu'l-Bahá wrote Tablets to the Local Spiritual Assemblies of several cities in the United States, guiding and encouraging their efforts and appealing to each Spiritual Assembly to remain steadfast in the Cause so that each

Assembly might become illumined with the love of God. For example, in 1910, the Master wrote Tablets to the Spiritual Assemblies of Baltimore, Cincinnati, and Chicago, to name a few. When the Assembly of the Bahá'ís of San Francisco was organized in January 1911, 'Abdu'l-Bahá sent the following Tablet:

> Through the maid-servant of God, Mrs. Helen S. Goodall, to the Members of the Assembly of Abdul-Baha, San Francisco, California.
> HE IS GOD!
> O ye, faithful friends!
> The maid-servant of the Kingdom of BAHA'O'LLAH has written the joyful news that the friends in that region have established an Assembly, have engaged in the spreading of the teachings of God and have arisen with the utmost endeavor, sincerity of intention, and enkindlement with the fire of the Love of God so that that country may become a main-spring of the signs, and that city become illumined, and a number of souls like stars of the Horizon of Holiness may shine in the assemblage of the Kingdom of man (humanity).
> This Assembly was organized at the right time. It is My hope that it may become a magnet of confirmation. If it remain firm and steadfast this Assembly will become so illumined that it will be a full, refulgent moon in the Horizon of everlasting Glory.
> Report and write to Me the services which are accomplished by this Assembly so that they may become the cause of spiritual happiness and joy to the heart.
> Upon thee be the Glory of God!
> (Signed) ABDUL-BAHA ABBAS.
> Translated by Mirza Ahmad Sohrab, Washington, D. C.
> July 11, 1911[8]

While the Master was strengthening the communities of the West ahead of His visit, those same communities were endeavoring to demonstrate a readiness to receive Him. To John Bosch, the most practical and direct way to report to the Master of an Assembly's spiritual readiness was to say it in a letter.

Most of the letters written by Bosch are characterized by a tone that is humble but not sanctimonious, respectful but not impersonal, dignified but not formal. An opportunity to meet the Master here in America would not come twice; therefore, securing the Master's visit to California required desperate measures: although John Bosch was not a member of the "Assembly of Bahá" of San Francisco, he took it upon himself to write to the Master on the Assembly's behalf.* He signed not only his name to it, but he signed Frederick D'Evelyn's name and Thornton Chase's name as well—and used an uncharacteristically elaborate style of expression:

Geyserville Winery
Geyserville, California
September 20, 1911
Allah o Abha!
O thou Beloved Abdul Baha the Center of the Covenant!
We, Thy humble servants in the Holy Cause, acknowledge with joy and happiness Thy most precious Tablet in which Thou didst address us as the "Assembly of Abdul Baha." Verily, this great, great Favor is from the Boundless Mercy of God, & means that we have the capacity to become such an Assembly if we stand firm & steadfast through all the Divine tests & each one of us is engaged in spreading the Fragrances of the Kingdom, living the life according to Commands, & uniting together in pure spiritual harmony and love. With the help of the Life-giving Breezes blowing from the Rizwan of Favor, we humbly supplicate at the Threshold of Oneness that nothing may prevent us from attain-

---

* The name "Assembly of Bahá" is the name that 'Abdu'l-Bahá used in this Tablet. It is important to note that the Spiritual Assembly of the Bahá'ís of San Francisco was not legally incorporated until 1938.

ing to this station of being, in truth, & reality the "Assembly of Abdul Baha."

Signed [all three names in John Bosch's handwriting, and in this order]:

Frederick W. D'Evelyn
JDB
T. Chase[9]

Even though John succeeded in his efforts to ensure that 'Abdu'l-Bahá would visit California, the Master's specific travel itinerary remained uncertain for several months. John Bosch would not wait on uncertainty; he made plans to meet 'Abdu'l-Bahá upon His arrival in New York.

Among John's personal papers are several handwritten accounts of his meeting with 'Abdu'l-Bahá. Some were written on stationery from the Hotel Ansonia from 1912, and others were written under his old Geyserville Winery letterhead and appear to have been written many years later. In 1931, Ella Cooper wrote to John that she and Mrs. Nellie French of *The Bahá'í World* editorial committee were preparing the history of John's experiences with 'Abdu'l-Bahá and were "trying to get accurate data for all these events which will be important in the future, and according to the desire of Shoghi Effendi." The letter concluded with Ella Cooper writing that she "would appreciate greatly if you could answer quickly. As Mrs. French must have [your] account in hand by the middle of next week." John replied the following day to Ella Cooper: "Your letter just received and I started at once to look over my old papers and find the following [attached papers]. Make use of above pages, whatever you think that may be right. Please return all papers to me and if possible give me a copy of what you are using for your report."[10]

Among John Bosch's papers there is a typed draft of such a report, but it is unclear whether it is Ella Cooper's report. John hand-wrote his notes and there is no record of him ever piecing the various parts of his narrative into one typed memoir. To Ella Cooper he wrote, "Some day, when the 'spirit moves' I may write all my experiences with Abdul Baha, in New York, Chicago—San Francisco, Haifa."[11]

The following narrative of John's experiences with 'Abdu'l-Bahá is comprised of John's detailed handwritten notes. The words are his, but the present writer has combined these accounts to render the narrative chronologically. These are pilgrims' notes, and while they may convey deep spiritual significance, they are not authoritative.

John begins his account by telling of his longing to meet 'Abdu'l-Bahá:

> When I heard that Abdul Baha intended to visit America, and was on the ocean [from Alexandria, Egypt], I felt a strong desire to meet him, not to meet him for curiosity or a novelty, but for a longing to see him.
>
> Informed that he would reach New York on April 11th, I started to make arrangements for over two weeks and tried to make up a round trip ticket for a reasonable rate to the Chicago Convention but could not arrive at conclusions, until April 11th, the arrival of Abdul Baha in New York. Then the thought suddenly came to me, why not try to meet him in Washington or New York and without any further consultation with my own mind I just walked into the Union Pacific office and purchased a ticket on the shortest and fastest route, the Overland Limited and Pennsylvania Rail, and departed on April 12th Friday at 10:00 am. On account of the snow storms in the Rocky Mountains the train was three hours late and I had to take a later train out of Chicago on the 15th at 5:30 pm. Arriving at Washington on the 16th at 5:00 pm I made arrangements at the hotel and believing that Abdul Baha might be in Washington I telephoned to Mr. Remey for information. In an hour he called at the hotel and said all quiet in Washington and no news about the movements of Abdul Baha.
>
> So, I thought best to continue my trip to New York on the next train at 9:00 pm arriving there at 3:50 am, Wednesday, April

17th. The passengers had to remain on the train until 5:00 am, at which time I made myself ready to walk to the Hotel Ansonia, which was about 30 blocks from the Pennsylvania Depot. I arrived at the Hotel Ansonia by 6:00 am and after engaging my room there I requested the Clerk to find out for me if Dr. Fareed is up at this early hour and the Bell Boy reported that he is up and the door open. Without further formalities I started for the 5th Floor and found Dr. Getsinger and the door was open to Abdul Baha's apartments. Dr. Fareed introduced me to Mr. Getsinger, Sayed Assad 'Ullah and Mirza Mahmud and said that Abdul Baha would be in the room shortly. In a few minutes I was called into his Parlor. I had in mind to enter cool and resigned as into a business office.

Dr. Fareed introduced me as John D. Bosch of California. With a warm wholesome handshake Abdul Baha greeted me and said "I have been longing to see you." He offered me a chair and to be seated close where he was seated. I said that I am greatly pleased and fortunate to have the opportunity and privilege to meet him so early in New York and that I travelled 3,000 miles to see him. To which he answered that he has come 8,000 miles to see me and the American Believers.

Abdul Baha ordered the tea served (of the most delicious brew.) I had a pocketful of questions from the West, but never gave them to Abdul Baha, for he told me all that I wanted to know.

I said to Abdul Baha: I regret very much that I have not the capacity as a teacher and by nature am rather reserved in talking and that the work I have been doing in the cause was mostly in the line of Universal Peace and by circulating books and pamphlets.

Abdul Baha looked directly at me, put his hand on my shoulder and said: "You are doing well, you are doing better than talking. It is not always the elaborate talking, the movement of the lips, that would accomplish results. It is the heart that is powerful. With you it is not words. Your heart talks. Wherever you go your heart radiates, which is even more than the movements of the lips. With you often silence talks and radiates. You are doing very well, to live, to act is the real true response. Your station, your name is Nurani, illumined, enlightened, light, radiant."

I looked, watched, and listened, words rolling through my mind. This the Son of Baha Ullah. This the man, who suffered 40 years in Prison for doing no harm,—only good,—working for the freedom of all people. His expressions, the illumined calm eyes shown at different movements, his acts, the immense simplicity and the grandeur at the same time, impressed me absolutely.

We then had tea and after an hour he said to me: "You are now one of the family, you may come and go as you please." So, I remained in the apartment as much as I could while he received his callers. Between times, I walked with Mirza Mahmood around the square, returning to the hotel about 1 o'clock. I was amazed to see the people, numbering about 200, in the lobby, arise in respect to Abdul Baha as he was just passing [through the lobby]. There were three taxis awaiting him and his party. Abdul Baha stepped into the first, with Mirza Mahmood, and Sayed Assad 'Ullah, and there being a seat vacant, Sayed Assad 'Ullah motioned me to come, and as I neared the taxi Abdul Baha put out his hand and pulled me right in. He seemed very tired, and he immediately put his arm around my waist, put his head on my left shoulder, and with a big sigh, fell asleep. We were bound for the home of Mr. and Mrs. Edward Kinney for dinner, and the believers expected that the drive would afford Abdul Baha an opportunity to see the streets and public buildings of New York, but instead of looking at all the big buildings, to our surprise he had a restful nap.

We reached the Kinney's after a half an hour's ride. I was an uninvited guest, but having been taken there by Abdul Baha I felt quite safe to attend the dinner. During dinner, Abdul Baha spoke briefly on different subjects to the guests, but afterward he gave a general address to the friends who had assembled to the number of about 150.*

When the meeting was finished, Dr. Getsinger put a large chair in the center of the room and asked Abdul Baha to be seated, so as to make it easy for him, and then [Dr. Getsinger] asked the people to come up to speak with him. But instead of accepting the chair, Abdul Baha had his own way of meeting the friends and saying goodbye to them, and he walked about among them shaking hands with each in turn. When he came to me he said nothing and just passed by, and I wondered why he did not say goodbye to me too, and I felt rather hurt that he had overlooked me. But when I remembered that in the morning he had told me I was one of the family, I knew then that there had been no need to say goodbye to me.

I attended nearly all the meetings in New York, and was privileged to accompany the party in the same car to Washington D.C. in which city there were many well-attended meetings in halls, Churches, and University, to both white and colored people. I attended most of the meetings in Washington DC and I was at the reception at Mrs. Parson's home where foreign diplomats came to meet Abdul Baha [. . .].**

I remained in Washington DC eight days and also attended most of the meetings there. Departing from Washington DC, again I had the privilege to travel with Abdul Baha in the same railway car with him to Chicago. We traveled the Pullman car called "Marvelous" over the Baltimore & Ohio Railroad. The party in Pullman included Abdul Baha, Dr. Fareed, Dr. Getsinger, Sayed

---

* This address is published in *The Promulgation of Universal Peace*, pp. 31–33.

** All of the talks given by 'Abdu'l-Bahá in Washington, DC are published in *The Promulgation of Universal Peace*. Most notable are the meetings wherein 'Abdu'l-Bahá spoke about the oneness of mankind at His talk at the Orient-Occident-Unity Conference on April 20, 1912, and at Howard University on April 23, 1912.

Assad 'Ullah, Mrs. Moss, Miss Matthews who became the wife of Louis Gregory, J.D. Bosch, and Mirza Mahmood.

While on this trip I took occasion to say to Abdul Baha that if he should have time to visit Geyserville, I would be highly honored though I could not offer him a palace like Mrs. Parsons'. He quickly responded, "With you," and repeated, "With you I would sleep in the basement." It just happened that I had recently raised my house and had a comfortable basement in which there were several beds that could readily be occupied during warm weather, when sleeping upstairs in the heat would have been quite uncomfortable.

It was also at this time (April 29th) that Abdul Baha handed me a ring stone, saying nothing that I could understand, as the interpreters were mostly asleep around the car.

While on the train to Chicago I asked Abdul Baha to write for me the name "Nurani" he had given me in New York that I might keep it in memory of him, and he wrote it for me in Persian.

When we arrived in Chicago about five o'clock in the afternoon where the sun was shining brilliantly, we found the friends awaiting us at the Plaza Hotel. Among them were some Westerners—Miss Muther of Honolulu, Dr. D'Evelyn, Mrs. Cordie Cline, Mrs. Getsinger, Mrs. Ralston, Mrs. Wagner, and others. (Mrs. Goodall and her party came on the same train from Washington, DC).

At 7 in the morning, the first of May, the California believers had a special audience with Abdul Baha in his apartment, and at 11 o'clock we all went to the Temple grounds for the dedication. It was a frightfully cold day, very raw weather, and Abdul Baha unfortunately caught a terrible cold. It was part of the program for a representative of every nation to turn over a shovelful of earth, and so I was called upon to represent Switzerland.

The next afternoon Dr. D'Evelyn and I called by appointment at Abdul Baha's apartment, as we were leaving that night for home. It was but a short interview. Later in the afternoon I was in the lobby talking to the hotel proprietor when I suddenly noticed everyone rising, and then I saw Abdul Baha coming into the hotel. He had been out for a walk in Lincoln Park. On his way through the lobby he greeted all with a hand shake. However he passed by me, apparently not noticed, and I thought he would not repeat the telling of good bye. It was a greeting hand for the guests and not a departing one for me.

But before Abdul Baha reached the elevator, he looked around and said Ka--i and seemingly looked at me. I paid no attention and did not understand what it meant. He turned again, saying Ka--i and at the same time Sayed Assad 'Ullah who followed him motioned with his hand and even that didn't move me as his motioning was the reverse of ours. They repeated again and the proprietor said he is motioning for me to come.

I followed and when I reached the elevator Abdul Baha took my hand and held it firm until we reached the 5th floor and to his apartments and private room for nearly an hour. In the meantime I had several guests awaiting me downstairs for dinner, and they finally began their dinner without me, thinking that I had gone earlier than I anticipated. Dr. Nutt was waiting in the apartment with me and Abdul Baha requested Sayed Assad 'Ullah to make tea. In ten minutes it was brought in and Abdul Baha served it. Dr. Bagdadi interpreted for us, as Abdul Baha rested in the large bay window overlooking Lincoln Park. In his smiling way and with great simplicity he said, "I am going to tell you all about the meeting I addressed this afternoon, the Federation of Women's Clubs, arranged by Miss Jane Addams." It was at the La Salle Hotel. He said the women were highly pleased but the men were disappointed. He spoke in a most happy way, at the same time, laughing, saying, "Men are not perpetuating the race alone. The women are the bearers of the children for both male and female, and therefore there should be no superiority of one over the other, but equality for all. Look at the monuments erected by the races and nations, are they not equally or even more in commemoration of women than men? Look at the statues of Venus equal with Jupiter. Look at the myriad statues of Madonna. Look at the great Statue of Liberty. Do animals show any differences between sexes, male and female? No, they are at peace. Look at the birds, how peaceful they are. They show no superiority one over the other. Why should we?" I told Abdul Baha that many of my friends in San Francisco by the Golden Gate had criticized me sharply for being in favor of equality for men and women, but when 55,000 women in Los Angeles voted for the Progressive Movement, the men had nothing to say. Abdul Baha said he would protect me, that criticism would not affect me.

To Dr. Nutt, in answer to a question about the House of Justice in Chicago, Abdul Baha said, "I have brought the stones, the bricks, the mortar, the material, to build the house for you. Now build it. I will crush the stones that come in your way and you will walk over them. I did not come to mend, I came to teach."

I then thanked Abdul Baha for the privilege of traveling with him from New York to Washington, and thence from Washington to Chicago. He replied, "I wanted you to come," and then he rose and took from the table a big cake 12 or 14 inches in diameter, which he handed to me. Also, some bananas, apples, and oranges until my arms were packed full to overflowing. That was goodbye.

All these gifts I then hastily took downstairs where my guests were supposed to be waiting, but found they had at last gone into dinner without me. At 10:30 Dr. D'Evelyn and I took the train for home.

One apple and the bananas Dr. D'Evelyn and I enjoyed on the train when we crossed the highest altitude in the Rocky

Mountains thinking of partaking of spiritual food at the highest elevation. The cake was carefully preserved until we reached our destination; then shared with the believers at the meeting of the Assembly of Abdul Baha in San Francisco on May 11th. Some of it was taken to the absent ones also, and thus the far-away friends, about forty in all, partook of this bounty of spiritual fellowship.[12]

Five months after John's return from meeting 'Abdu'l-Bahá on the east coast, the friends in California succeeded in attracting the Master to visit the west coast of the United States. His arrival, having coincided with the passing of Thornton Chase, certainly must have had an effect on John's spirits—how bittersweet his feelings must have been. The Master's words about the station of Thornton Chase's soul becoming "free from the fetters of this world" came to characterize the themes of His talks given in California. For instance, in His address to the students at Stanford University, 'Abdu'l-Bahá said that "a claim and title to territory or native land is but a claim and attachment to the dust of earth" and that "We live upon this earth for a few days and then rest beneath it forever." The Master spoke at the University by invitation of Stanford's president, David Starr Jordan; there were 1,800 students and 180 professors in attendance to hear the person whom their university president introduced as "one of the great religious teachers of the world." 'Abdu'l-Bahá concluded His talk at Stanford with the hope that the students "may never be called upon to fight for the dust of earth which is the tomb and sepulcher of all mankind" but that they may, instead, "enjoy the most perfect companionship one with another [. . .] associating together in peace and true fellowship."[13]

Meanwhile, as it was October and harvest season in Geyserville, the demands of the harvest kept John Bosch from attending all of 'Abdu'l-Bahá's talks in California. In the following account, written in John's pensive and elegant handwriting, his tone is resigned, and there seems to be a lingering sadness for the absence of his closest coworker in the Cause, Thornton Chase. John wrote:

When Abdul Baha came to California it was the busy harvest season in Geyserville and I could not remain in San Francisco during his entire visit. I came to the city whenever I could for some of the public meetings. I attended a dinner that Mr. and Mrs. William Grosse gave him at their home after the address at the Theosophical Society. I also attended the big feast at Mrs. Goodall's home in Oakland, but I did not have any further private talks with him, other than in Oakland a few days before he left for the East. As there were no interpreters present, there was nothing said. Abdul Baha was very tired, lying on the bed, resting, and we merely had a silent greeting and parting."[14]

It would not be the last time that John Bosch would see 'Abdu'l-Bahá; all the same, the parting must have felt like a deep emptiness. Without the Master and without Thornton Chase, John was alone, but not for long.

Among the personal papers of John Bosch, there are various sheets of paper upon which he made a list of the significant events in his life. Here is a portion of one of those brief chronologies wherein he measured the years of his life based on the year he first learned of the teachings of Bahá'u'lláh:

1903, I read a book called Abbas Effendi.
1909, in my 6th year, Convention.
1910, in my 7th year, Mr. Chase
1912, in my 9th year, 'Abdu'l-Bahá in NY, Washington, Chicago, S.F.
1913, in my 10th year, Louise came to my rescue.[15]

4 / Louise

Among the numerous Bosch papers from the United States Baháʼí Archives, there are only a few personal papers of Louise Sophie Stapfer that are dated prior to her marriage to John Bosch. A perusal of those papers reveals that the three most significant experiences in her life before marrying John were her meeting with ʻAbduʼl-Bahá in 1909, her intimate friendship with May Bolles Maxwell, and her close friendship with Lua Getsinger. Reading the letters she received from May and from Lua gives one a glimpse into Louise Stapfer's personality. Reading the Tablets she received from the Master gives one a glimpse into her soul.

Like John Bosch, Louise Stapfer was from Switzerland, but she did not meet John until many years after her immigration to the United States. Louise was born in Zurich on July 11, 1870. When she was nineteen years old, in 1889, she came to New York to study homeopathic medicine. In her own words, she says that upon her arrival in New York, she was "full of Swiss determination and industry, and brimming with hope and the idealism of youth. Homeopathy was my field of interest and I longed to be a source of healing and comfort to the distressed."[1]

Two years later, in 1901, she met Miss Fanny Montague of Dobbs Ferry, New York, who introduced her to the Baháʼí Faith; subsequently, Louise met Sarah Farmer and Agnes Alexander, with whom she studied the Baháʼí teachings at Green Acre. Later in her life, Louise reflects on that moment of becoming a Bahá'í, saying, "How fortunate I was to find the Faith of Bahá'u'lláh in 1901, just as I entered my 30's. It filled me with a zeal to serve and a recognition of how privileged one is to be part of the beginning of a New Order."[2] Louise must have written to 'Abdu'l-Bahá regarding her acceptance of the Teachings because among her personal papers is this Tablet from the Master, addressed to her, dated 1904.

> The Maid Servant of God, Louise
> O thou who art advancing towards God!
> Verily the Cause is great and the Lord is Merciful and Clement. Trust in the Grace of Thy Lord, and be firm in love for Him who has created thee and made thee. The veils shall be removed, the shining lamp shall beam, the clouds shall be dispelled, the lights of the Sun of love shall appear on the horizons and God shall grant thy wishes and give thee the power of deeds.
> It is incumbent upon thee to depend wholly upon the Center of Lights, and call out for love, universal peace and harmony amongst the people in the East of the earth and its West, so that the foundation of rancor may be destroyed and the edifice of love and faithfulness be set up, and that the heavenly powers may govern the mortal sentiments and the merciful feelings may become manifest in the human realities.
> This is becoming of those maidservants of God, who are attracted to that Beauty which is shining from the Horizon of the Kingdom of God upon the world.
> Upon thee be greeting and praise.[3]

In many respects, this Tablet is an outline for her future happiness. The Master acknowledges that Louise is "advancing towards God"; He reassures her to "trust and be firm." He promises her that the "veils shall be removed." He grants that her life shall be characterized by "the power of deeds." He advises her to be the cause of love between the

"East of the earth and its West." He instructs her that these attributes and deeds are "becoming of those maidservants of God." Most importantly, He extols her with "greeting and praise." Surely, this Tablet was sustenance to her soul and a protection from insurmountable personal tests.

Sometime in 1905 Louise became engaged to Lua Getsinger's brother, Dr. William Moore, and they planned a life devoted to administering homeopathic remedies. In 1906, before the marriage could take place, William died of yellow fever—a tragedy that resulted in a close, sisterly bond between Louise and Lua Getsinger.[4]

Four years later, when Louise Stapfer had the bounty of coming into the presence of 'Abdu'l-Bahá on her pilgrimage in 1909, she expressed to 'Abdu'l-Bahá her great desire to "rise to the heights of spiritual knowledge." She asked, "'Abdu'l-Bahá, what can I do to attain this?" and He replied, "Give me thy heart."[5] By giving her heart to 'Abdu'l-Bahá, she was giving her heart to the Center of the Covenant, fulfilling the Master's earlier admonition wherein He wrote to Louise that "it is incumbent to depend wholly on the Center of Lights."

Her pilgrimage was uniquely special because she made the pilgrimage as the traveling companion of the newly married May Ellis Bolles and William Sutherland Maxwell. Louise and May were the same age, both born in 1870. They had met in New York where Louise was living at the time and where May Bolles spent much of her time consolidating the Bahá'ís there between the years 1903 and 1905. Of their first encounter, Louise wrote, "My meeting and acquaintance with May Bolles Maxwell brought to me a complete transformation and a wholly new existence. I was a young believer in New York and not yet understanding very well the Message that I had received. In my love and friendship for May Maxwell I found a complete transformation and a wholly new existence."[6]

May Bolles Maxwell was an effective teacher of the Cause because she had an ability to establish true bonds of friendship, and much of her teaching work was overseen and guided by 'Abdu'l-Bahá Himself.

On one occasion, He wrote to May saying that she must never neglect her attentions to Louise, intimating that Louise's future contributions to the work of the Cause were dependent upon her becoming firmly rooted in the Bahá'í teachings and the Covenant.[7]

Louise's intimate spiritual association with May began with Lua Getsinger's spiritual influence in the lives of both women. Lua was the first teacher of May Maxwell, and she was also one of the first teachers of Louise Stapfer. Many of the early believers in America were deepened and nurtured by Lua Getsinger; it is no wonder that the Guardian would later call Lua "the Mother Teacher of the West." Virtually every believer in the West would have known of Lua Getsinger. Of all the Bahá'ís with whom Lua kept close contact, Lua claimed that there was a "special five" of them with whom she felt the deepest spiritual connection, and she referred to them as "a glorious collection of souls": Mary Lucas, Juliet Thompson, Mariam Haney, May Maxwell, and Louise Stapfer (Bosch). Lua Getsinger wrote a most spiritually revealing letter to Louise regarding the happy news of May Maxwell's pregnancy in 1910. The letter, written six years before Lua Getsinger's premature death, takes the reader into Lua's private thoughts and into the depths of her spirit, so endearingly exhibited by her generous use of exclamation marks. The letter also reveals a clear portrait of the spiritual susceptibilities of its recipient, Louise Stapfer—or "Lysa":[8]

> My dear Lysa
> Your long looked for letter was indeed very welcome! I have so often wondered why I have never heard from you! Yes, I was in Acca last Winter and it is true that the Master now lives in Haifa—Acca is no longer a prison! They were all well and enquired after you! Have you heard from May recently? I saw her in New York in June and she was expecting to be confined in July and very happy over the prospect of having a baby. She looked so well and, as I have never seen her before! I have not heard anything since and am so anxious to know about her if

you have any news please let me know! My dear Lysa there is a great reason why you love me so—and feel as you do when you mention me! Abdul Baha knows and so do I! In this world you may never know, but dear—if you die before I do just know that when I come to you everything will be right—and if I go <u>first</u> when you come, just ask for Lua and then you shall understand. I love you dear "Lysa of the Lilies" with all my heart and you are always with me—you—May and Mariam are the stars of my existence with one other whose name you do not know now—but you <u>five</u> together are a glorious collection of souls & you are mine. Now and always—God only knows how much I love you! Dear the love for Abdul Baha will come as you go on and obey the commands of Baha'u'llah—for His words are creative and have the power to give <u>life</u> even—to say nothing of <u>love</u>, and <u>faith</u>. Aunt Charlotte Colt passed on [to] the heavenly Kingdom last Friday—dear old angel soul she was! Oh Lysa, what a joy to leave this dark and gloomy sphere! May my release soon come! I am so weary of <u>clay</u>! [. . .] Edward is with me in Washington for the present—I don't know where we will live in the future. I gave all my furniture away so I have nothing but my love for God and "<u>My Five</u>" left of this world's goods.

Write me again soon
Always your devoted
and tender
<u>Lua</u>
August 10th, 1910[9]

Further insight into Louise's character can be drawn from her close friendship with May Maxwell. Their friendship was the most meaningful of Louise's early Bahá'í life, and it was a friendship that defied words, as noted by Louise herself: "I cannot speak of the great benefits to my life and the transformation I experienced through the association of May Maxwell."[10]

Although May's first pilgrimage was ten years earlier in 1899—a pilgrimage from which she documents her experience in *An Early Pilgrimage*—May associates Louise with that earlier pilgrimage in the following letter, likely written in 1932 when May Maxwell had finished a series of radio broadcasts that summer in New York. It also marks the year of the passing of the Greatest Holy Leaf, who passed away on July 15, 1932. Rúhíyyih Khánum explained that two days after the passing of the Greatest Holy Leaf, the Guardian "wrote to the American and Canadian believers a letter that provides a glimpse of what was passing in the surging sea of his heart and in which he eulogizes the life, station and deeds of 'Abdu'l-Bahá's sister pouring forth his love in an unforgettable torrent of words." The letter had a profound impact on May Maxwell, and she wrote to Louise Stapfer about it. One cannot read the Guardian's tribute to the Greatest Holy Leaf without swooning away with the spiritual power it holds. At one point in the letter the Guardian interrupts his address to the believers, and, instead, addresses the Greatest Holy Leaf directly, supplicating that she intercede to 'Abdu'l-Bahá on his behalf: "Dearly-loved Greatest Holy Leaf! [. . .] Bear thou this my message to 'Abdu'l-Bahá, thine exalted and divinely-appointed Brother: If the Cause for which Bahá'u'lláh toiled and labored, for which Thou didst suffer years of agonizing sorrow, for the sake of which streams of sacred blood have flowed, should in the days to come, encounter storms more severe than those it has already weathered, do Thou continue to overshadow, with Thine all-encompassing care and wisdom, Thy frail, Thy unworthy appointed child."[11]

In the following letter from May Maxwell to Louise, May wrote of the Guardian's supplication to the Greatest Holy Leaf and the spiritual effect it has had on her:

Dearest Louise,
    Your dear letter has just come and I had met you last night in the inner world of dreams. We had held a unity Feast in which some paragraphs of the Guardian's divine letter regarding the

Greatest Holy Leaf had been read, and his beloved sacred spirit had diffused Itself as an Essence in our hearts. How strange and wonderful that when these mortal veils, beneath which we all suffer captivity, lift, we find ourselves, without search or effort, in the eternal world of oneness, wherein we all abide in reality, all the time. It is like opening a door and finding the dear one there, waiting. If we could only have gone to Geyserville, our summer would have been happy and blest. Instead we went to Green Acre late in August. When I had finished broadcasting in New York, and Mary got scarlet fever and was ill for weeks, my strength gave out nursing her, then I had a nurse for a while, and finally brought her home. She is recovering her strength slowly and writes with me in dearest love to you and John. I am sending under separate cover a copy of the *Early Pilgrimage,* which you can forward to Mrs. [Schwarz]. Inscribed your name and mine, my own beloved Louise. Tell John too I'm sorry I missed the ripe figs! How we long for such a paradise, darling.

Tender love to you and John,
Maylie
1548 Pine Avenue, October 18th [1932] [12]

May's spiritual exuberance complemented Louise's more subdued expression of that same spirituality. Reflecting upon the life of May Maxwell, Louise explained how she was influenced by May's detachment from the material world: "As often as I looked upon her, and contemplated her attitude to life and her disposition of it, I would distinctly feel that she was only visiting here."[13]

Above all, it was Lua Getsinger who first influenced the spiritual lives of May Maxwell and Louise Stapfer at a time when each was in search of the spiritually reviving and world-embracing vision of the teachings of Bahá'u'lláh. May's spiritual search began when she was spiritually despondent in Paris in 1899, and Louise's began when she was overcoming the death of her fiancé, William Moore, in 1906.[14]

After over a decade of such close friendship, how deplorable it must have been for May and Louise to hear the news of Lua Getsinger's untimely death in Cairo at the age of forty-five:

May 5, 1916, Western Union Night Letter
From Montreal, Quebec, Canada
To Mr. John Bosch, Geyserville
 Tell Louise our blessed beloved Lua ascended to the Supreme concourse at Cairo on May 1. Her death was the consummation of her glorious life she attained her supreme desire the sacrifice of her life in the paths of God the mystery of her sacrifice became revealed at Convention on May 1, in deepest love. May.[15]

Louise Stapfer met John Bosch as the result of encouragement from Lua Getsinger and her husband, Dr. Edward Getsinger, who knew John Bosch from the Temple Unity Convention in 1909. Two years later, in 1911, when Lua made her historic teaching trip to California, she became better acquainted with the spiritual nature of John Bosch's character. Furthermore, Dr. Getsinger had been in John Bosch's company in 1912 during the days of the Master's visit to New York, and it was Edward Getsinger who led John into the hotel room where the Master seemed to be awaiting his visit. These coincidences led Edward Getsinger to suggest to Louise Stapfer that she begin a correspondence with John Bosch, and he persuaded her that she would find comfort in writing to a fellow countryman from Switzerland who was also a devoted Bahá'í.[16]

John and Louise Bosch have extended family members who were Bahá'ís and living in the United States; they are the Somerhalders, and they are related to John on his sister's side. In the "In Memoriam" article about Louise Stapfer Bosch, Myrle and Irvin Somerhalder cited a Tablet from 'Abdu'l-Bahá written to Louise Stapfer. It was dated 1913, a year before Louise's marriage to John Bosch. When one pauses to consider the propitious nature of the Tablet, one cannot help but think that this Tablet from the Master is intuitive of Louise's spiritual development:

> Oh thou daughter of the Kingdom
> Thou art one of the old believers and belongest to the firm and steadfast maidservants of the Kingdom. Therefore in the estimation of 'Abdu'l-Bahá thou art favored. Thank God that thou art firm in the Covenant and hast turned thy face toward the Kingdom of Abhá. I hope from the bestowals of Bahá'u'lláh that He may so enkindle thee as to move that region, that thou mayest unloose thy tongue in guiding the people and attract the souls to His Holiness Bahá'u'lláh.[17]

When she received the above Tablet from 'Abdu'l-Bahá, it must have influenced her thoughts regarding her courtship with John Bosch. In a sense, 'Abdu'l-Bahá guided Louise to John by giving her the confidence that she could travel to other regions and serve the Cause. It is clear that John was also praying for such a partner with whom he could teach the Cause of God to others, having written that in "'1913 Louise came to my rescue.'"

At the end of John's life, Marzieh Gail interviewed him and asked him about how he and Louise met. Marzieh Gail asked, "'Where did you meet Louise?'" and John replied, "'I didn't meet her,'" as though he could not place a certain time when he had first met her because he had always known Louise.

Later in his interview with Marzieh Gail, John elaborated upon the subject in a tone that reveals a far more playful attitude than the respectful timidity of his younger days: "'I started to correspond with her through Lua Getsinger. I had met Lua in San Francisco in 1911. She spent a week at Geyserville, staying in the long front room of what is now the Collison house. Lua said there was a young Suissesse at Briarcliff Manor [in New York], servicing as health officer, who was a Bahá'í. So I dropped her a few lines.'" He said that he thought a Swiss girl from Zurich who had a position like that would be just right for him. (Louise had also worked four years in Eliot, Maine, with Sarah Farmer.)

Marzieh Gail asked, "'Did you propose to her before she came out West?'"

John Bosch replied, "'Just as much as I could by mail.'"[18]

Louise's own remembrance of how they met is told by her in this way, many years later, after the passing of John Bosch in 1946: "'I am remembering how I met John Bosch, after we had corresponded, and how I knew immediately he was the man who would share the deepest concerns of my heart.'"[19]

It was Louise who took the first step toward correspondence with John. Here is her first letter to him, dated September 20, 1912, written from her place of residence and work, Briarcliff Manor School in New York. Curiously, she writes the letter in English, even though Swiss German was a first language for each of them. Perhaps she chose English because it was less familiar than their shared native language; English would allow her to maintain a certain formality in her letter to someone she did not know. Only the first page of the letter survives:

Allaho'Abha!
My dear brother in El Baha,
Ever since the immemorial Feast that Abdul Baha gave to the believers at Englewood, New Jersey, June 29th, I intended to write to you, but I did not find time to do so until now. It was at that Feast that my dear friend, Dr. Getsinger, first told me of you and said: "Do you know that there is a Bahai countryman of yours living in California? He is a man of fine spirit and you might write to him; it would give him pleasure to hear from you since you are both from the same country."

I felt happy over this news and I intended to write you very soon. Afterward, Mrs. Getsinger (whom I know you love too) told me more of you while in New York, and afterward also Mrs.

Hoag whom I had the great pleasure to meet again after 10 years in Montreal. Always I thought of writing to you, but I could not. Finally a telegram was received from Lua Getsinger, which caused a little commotion as both your and my name were mentioned in it. I still could not write, yet I was pleased to think that someone wished to hear from me so much.

And that I am at last writing to you it seems as if it were not the first time that I am addressing you, that I had spoken to you before, and you to me.

Indeed we are not strangers in this age of oneness in which we find ourselves through the religion of Truth, such a thing is not possible. Rather it is . . .[20]

Sadly, what remains of the letter is lost. One month later, Louise wrote again to John, but this time she wrote in German. As the following letter suggests, Louise is beginning to make her decision about John, and she makes subtle hints in his favor by suggesting that his occupation as a vintner is a subject of minor importance that can be overcome, that his hard work all his life has pleased 'Abdu'l-Bahá "as it has others," and that even though she has never lived on a farm, she believes her heart belongs to the farm country. Most endearing is her query about his age—suggesting that his life experiences gave her the impression that he was "1,000 years old." She must have felt the spiritual capacity of his soul. Louise was forty-three years old when she wrote this letter, and John was fifty-eight.[21] The letter has the number nine centered at the top, which was a letterhead used frequently by the early believers in America. Here is the translation of the letter:*

---

* Mrs. Louise Semple has translated the letter from German to English and notes that the translation is a literal one in order to reflect Louise Stapfer's informal style of German.

- 9 -

October 22, 1913

Dear Friend,

I will try to also write a few words in German to you; yesterday I quickly responded to your last letter which contained the newspaper extract of Oct. 1899. Yes, that is a very interesting article. I read it through twice on the way home from New York to Briarcliff. Naturally the question occurred to me immediately what you were going to do, or what you will have done since the Revelation of Baha Ullah cast a new light on wine-making for you. I also thought of the conversation we had with Abdul Baha at table in Acca one day. Mr. and Mrs. Maxwell took me along to Acca five years ago, and we were there for six days. Abdul Baha told us how it had come about that Muhammad had forbidden the drinking of wine. He said that one day the disciples of Muhammad at table (or in any case while eating) had started quarreling over an argument, and finally one of them took the bone of a leg of mutton that they had just eaten and hit his opponent with it. In the end Muhammad had to be called to come and separate the quarrelling men and restore peace. As they had all drunk wine with their food, they had got rather heated. That day Muhammad forbade the drinking of wine in the future and made it into a law. And so it is customary among the Muslims to this day to drink no wine, although in these days of breaking away from all prophetic laws, that law has long since been broken. But Abdul Baha added that the law of Muhammad has been renewed by Baha Ullah, Who had explained or revealed that it is not good to drink (or eat) anything which has fermented outside the stomach: all food or drink should be fermented inside the stomach and by the stomach.

I have little doubt that you will have talked to Abdul Baha about your business of wine-making and that He will have given you an explanation. Also, Abdul Baha said to a friend in New

York that one should give up the habit of drinking only <u>gradually</u>, and this will at any rate apply also to the human race, and so it would take at least two or three generations to change the habits of one's ancestors.

I had previously thought that you were dealing only with unfermented wine, or grape juice. I had thought so because of what is printed on your letters or envelopes, but these are minor matters.

You must have worked very hard all your life to achieve all that you have achieved, and you must have genius. That pleases Abdul Baha, as it does others.

The newspaper extract talks about your travels and your studies abroad in Germany, France, and Spain, yet you wrote to me in your first letter that you had already come to Nebraska in 1876, and now I would like to know how old you are. I think that you must be 1000 years old! In the picture you look terribly young, but one cannot tell anything from this kind of picture. I would prefer a photograph, if you have had time to make an appointment with a photographer.

What you are telling me about a journey to the old homeland to explain the truth to the people there, yes, that would certainly be ideal. I cannot at all imagine my doing so, but as for you I can imagine it very well, you appear to have been called to do this and will probably do it. You may believe me when I say that I would like to be part of it, since it is also <u>my</u> people, yet there would have to be considerable changes in me to achieve this.

Do you still have relatives in Switzerland? I still have an old aunt there who has a noble soul, but until the present day it has been impossible for me to inspire her with belief in the truth of Baha Ullah. She is old (but spiritually young), and I know that God will not hold it against her that she cannot see or recognize the light of her Lord Jesus in the words of the Holy Spirit for this day. Perhaps we may meet once more in this life, then we may be able to discuss the matter, which would be better than letters. I shall now write to her that I have found a Bahai compatriot in you, and that will please and interest her very much: a compatriot from the Toggenburg—that really sounds quite romantic, do you not think so?

In your last letter, you did not tell me whether the Toggenburg is <u>in fact</u> real farm country; please do not fail to make that clear to me when next you write to me. Since I have never been in farm country, I have only vague conceptions of it, but it seems to me nevertheless that I must have been in real farm country once— perhaps as a child with my so greatly loved grandfather, which is entirely possible since he had a brother in the Toggenburg. Undoubtedly there must be such a place somewhere that I have in mind. Other than that, I feel as you do. It is very strange, but in fact I would not like to end my life anywhere but in <u>America</u>, in the United States. My aunt does not find that strange, since I, as she wrote, have spent the greater part of my life here and have gathered all my experiences here. That obviously ties one to the land, as you must also have felt. I also like the spirit of this country and the mainly newness that comprises it. My artistic friends, of whom I have a few, tell me that only those who have no feeling or genius for art or antiquities can prefer this country to Europe. Then I always tell them that I belong to the farm country.

I am ending this at last—the bell of the last class of the day is just sounding, and they will now come running in order to inform me of their various ailments!

With best wishes, hoping that our Lord may visit your apartment in Geyserville, I remain your devoted,
Louise Stapfer[22]

John David Bosch and Louise Sophie Stapfer were married in San Francisco on January 19, 1914. The marriage was a small ceremony performed by Joseph S. David, Minister of the Gospel, and witnessed by John's sister and her husband, Mr. and Mrs. Zuberbuhler, who had moved near Geyserville, in Knightsen, California. The wedding announcement simply said that they were married on "Monday, the nineteenth of January, nineteen hundred and fourteen, in San Francisco, California" and are now "at home in Geyserville, Sonoma County, California."[23]

The Master was pleased with the union, for He wrote a Tablet to them, signed His name in Persian and in English and addressed it to the newly married couple:

> To his honor Mr. John D. Bosch and the maid-servant of God,
> Louise Bosch,
> Geyserville, California.
> Upon them be Baha'u'llah el Abha!
> He is God!
> O ye two souls of pure spirit!
> Praise be to God that you have spread the feast of union and prepared the banquet of rejoicing. It is blessed. I beg of God that this union be eternal and the means of everlasting happiness, thus, in all the divine worlds ye may live together!
> Upon ye be Baha El Abha!
> [Signed in English alphabet]: abdul "Baha" abbas
> Mount Carmel, Haifa
> March 31, 1914[24]

5 / Awakened by the Tablets of the Divine Plan

Within the first year of their marriage, John and Louise succeeded in attracting many souls to the teachings of Bahá'u'lláh. In order to appreciate the scope of their teaching work, it is important to understand the community of Geyserville in which they lived.

Located about seventy-five miles north of San Francisco, Geyserville is a small agricultural town with a population that has remained at about one thousand for the past century. Its winters are mild but often rainy, and its summers are as warm and dry as a summer in central Italy. In winter, its hills and dales are lush and green; in the summer, they are dry and golden brown. Geyserville became known for its hot springs, which were mistakenly called geysers. In the 1850s, the "geysers" became an attraction for such notables as Ulysses Grant, Theodore Roosevelt, and even the Italian military hero Giuseppe Garibaldi—perhaps because the land is so reminiscent of Sicily. The stagecoach ride into the untracked region of Geyserville was rugged terrain, and the hotel attracted tourists by boasting of an "easy informality" as a euphemism for its rustic accommodations. In 1870, the San Francisco and North Pacific railroad was extended to Cloverdale, and its trains stopped in Geyserville.[1] Cattle roamed the land, and vineyards flourished in the rich soil and warm summer climate. In those days, the lucrative agricultural crops were pears and prunes. It was not until the

1970s that Geyserville's grape-growing became the dominant agricultural crop, so in 1914, John Bosch was one of the only professional viticulturists in the region and the "absolutely pure and non-alcoholic" grape juice that John made on his property was likely the only such grape juice in town. Except for the dozen or so wineries that circle the town today, Geyserville is a place that remains very much unchanged from the time when John and Louise lived there.

As John and Louise began their life together in Geyserville, a global war was about to engulf humanity and dramatically change the world as they knew it. The Universal House of Justice characterized the world of 1914 as one dominated by wayward leaders whose lust for personal power led them to "blindly [edge] their way towards the universal conflagration which pride and folly had prepared" and that the widespread rejection of religion was a result, in part, of the rise of communism and its doctrine that "faith in God was a neurotic weakness indulged in by the human race." This lust for power and the spread of godlessness combined to bring humanity to its knees in a war against itself so that "when the great conflagration did break out, therefore, the nightmare far surpassed the worst fears of thoughtful minds." There was no place on earth untouched by the catastrophic upheaval of the war, and although the consequences of the war were unparalleled in human history, a global consciousness emerged that had not existed before the war. People all over the planet began to think about the world as one, and although John and Louise lived inconspicuously in Geyserville, California, they felt this growing urgency for world unity no less than any soul on the planet longing for a spiritual unification of humanity.[2]

'Abdu'l-Bahá described this growing sense of world unity in one of His talks given in America in 1912:

Today I wish to speak to you upon the subject of the oneness of humanity, for in this great century the most important accomplishment is the unity of mankind. Although in former centuries and times this subject received some measure of mention and consideration, it has now become the paramount issue and question in the religious and political conditions of the world. History shows that throughout the past there has been continual warfare and strife among the various nations, peoples and sects; but now—praise be to God!—in this century of illumination, hearts are inclined toward agreement and fellowship, and minds are thoughtful upon the question of the unification of mankind. There is an emanation of the universal consciousness today which clearly indicates the dawn of a great unity.[3]

Writing after the Great War, Shoghi Effendi elaborates further on the source of this universal consciousness as a "God-born Force, irresistible in its sweeping power, incalculable in its potency, unpredictable in its course, mysterious in its workings, and awe-inspiring in its manifestations [. . .] acting even as a two-edged sword, [and] is, under our very eyes, sundering, on the one hand, the age-old ties which for centuries have held together the fabric of civilized society, and is unloosing, on the other, the bonds that still fetter the infant and as yet unemancipated Faith of Bahá'u'lláh."[4]

In this landscape of world travail, 'Abdu'l-Bahá began writing the Tablets of the Divine Plan, which are a series of letters giving instructions on how to spread the teachings of Bahá'u'lláh throughout the world. The aim of these Tablets is to awaken those ready souls willing to travel to various regions throughout the world to establish a foundation of universal peace—a peace founded on the principles of the oneness of God, the oneness of religion, and the oneness of humanity. Since the goals outlined in these Tablets are spiritual in nature, the Tablets are often referred to as a Bahá'í Charter for the spiritual conquest of the planet.[5]

Without such a charter, it would have been easy for someone like John Bosch to become so distracted and discouraged by world events as to render him unable to respond to the magnitude of discord spreading across the globe in 1914. The Tablets of the Divine Plan called upon the American believers to arise and emancipate the world from the fetters of religious tyranny, racial prejudice, and political corruption. Such a systematic approach required that the American believers sanctify their own souls from tyranny, prejudice, and corruption so that they may teach others and thereby prove the power of spiritual transformation—a power that attracted both John and Louise to the Cause of Bahá'u'lláh and awakened in them the desire to put into practice the very teachings they had espoused. The Tablets of the Divine Plan outlined for them a method by which they could participate in a unified global effort to affect a great spiritual transformation in the world.

Comprised of fourteen Tablets and written in 1916 and 1917 while the Master was confined in Haifa during the darkest days of the War, each Tablet was addressed directly to the believers in the United States and Canada, and each one called upon the followers of Bahá'u'lláh to arise and spread the teachings of God throughout North America and across the globe. The scope of the Divine Plan was at once broad and specific as the Master mentioned cities, regions, and countries by name and outlined the spiritual victories to be achieved there. The personal responsibility He entrusted in the American believers was awe-inspiring, as it was part of a Plan that called upon them to deliver a spiritual solution to the world's war-weary and wounded souls longing for something better than what they had. In one of the Tablets, 'Abdu'l-Bahá wrote:

> . . . this world-consuming war has set such a conflagration to the hearts that no word can describe it. In all the countries of the world the longing for universal peace is taking possession of the consciousness of men. There is not a soul who does not yearn for concord and peace. A most wonderful state of receptivity is being realized. This is through the consummate wisdom of God, so that capacity may be created, the standard of the oneness of the world

of humanity be upraised, and the fundamental of universal peace and the divine principles be promoted in the East and the West.[6]

Five of the Tablets were published in the United States in the autumn issues of *Star of the West* in 1916, and the Bahá'í community responded with a loyalty to the Center of the Covenant that had been inspired by 'Abdu'l-Bahá four years earlier when He visited the United States and Canada. The editors of *Star of West* introduced the Tablets as "a trumpet call to action," stating that 'Abdu'l-Bahá, "in his love and wisdom, is now giving each and all of the American Bahá'ís a special opportunity to awaken to their responsibilities and to arise in love and sacrifice for this 'superhuman service.'" The National Spiritual Assembly also made clear that funds would have to be raised in order to support the teaching work and that the American community had now been given the bounty of two great projects at hand: the building of the Mother Temple of the West and the execution of the goals of the Divine Plan.[7]

These two great projects would require a unity of thought among the believers. In a letter to the Bahá'í Temple Unity (which later evolved into National Spiritual Assembly), Ella Goodall Cooper wrote, "We cannot over-estimate the effect of this united service. The spiritual and practical results of our efforts will depend upon our joyous, enthusiastic and prompt obedience to the command of the Center of the Covenant." Furthermore, the enthusiasm of the editors of *Star of the West* was effective in encouraging broad participation in the Plan by calling to mind the cries of a despairing humanity and the opportunity to propagate the divine teachings by the end of the Great War: "What an inspiring thought that in responding to this call the Bahá'ís may be instrumental in helping to bring to pass the prophecy of 'Abdu'l-Bahá that the Cause will be known the world over by 1917!" In the issue of *Star of the West* that followed three weeks later, the headline announced "The New Work Now Before Us" and in the front-page article, Ella Goodall Cooper wrote:[8]

The great Tablets have come. Abdul-Baha himself gives us the plan, and it is as clear as daylight—that we should instantly drop every other consideration and concentrate all our energies and resources upon this great work. This is a call to the whole body of believers. The very first thing is to arouse all of the friends to the tremendous significance of this new work, this "superhuman service" as Abdul-Baha so justly calls it. Indeed it is so big that we should lose no time getting at it. The friends here in the West are alive to the supreme opportunity and we feel sure that their joyous enthusiasm is going to carry them through and make their work effective.[9]

It is interesting to note that five of the Tablets of the Divine Plan were mailed to Joseph Hannen but addressed by 'Abdu'l-Bahá to individual Bahá'ís in certain regions of the United States and Canada. For example, the Tablet to the Northern territory was mailed to Mrs. May Maxwell. The Tablet to the Southern territory was mailed to Mr. Joseph Hannen. The Tablet to the Eastern territory was mailed to Mr. Hooper Harris. The Tablet to the Central territory was mailed to Dr. Ziá Bagdádí. The Tablet to the Western territory was mailed to Mrs. Helen Goodall. Even though the Tablets were mailed to individuals, each Tablet was intended for the whole body of believers in the territory.[10]

In a spirit of individual and collective action, the Bahá'í Temple Unity decided to organize the teaching work around the persons to whom the Tablets of the Divine Plan were sent, and this plan of action was announced in the October 16, 1916 issue of *Star of the West*: "It has been suggested that we publish the names and addresses of the individuals through whom the five recent great Tablets were received, as well as the states mentioned in each territory, that all may turn to a center, as it were, in their respective territory as the first step in the Teaching Campaign. It has been suggested that each one communicate at once with their respective center in order to be informed of the plans of its

Teaching Committee, which, doubtless, is already chosen and at work." Through partnership and consultation with the Bahá'ís of a region, the teaching teams would teach by giving public lectures and meetings, by establishing personal contacts, and by visiting those contacts with follow-up teams, as suggested by Ella Goodall Cooper in a letter to the Bahá'í Temple Unity: "Regarding the teachers: It might be well if they could go two by two. Abdul-Baha approves of that. Our idea is that if two or three relays were to follow one another a few weeks apart perhaps, it might be a very good thing, because that always keeps up the interest in the subject among the people [. . .]. Any of the friends who have points of contact in any state should write to the sections where the Tablets have been received, so that all such information can be in hand as soon as possible." How providential that the point of contact for John and Louise was their closest Bahá'í friend, Helen Goodall in San Francisco—and John and Louise were an instant teaching team.[11]

In the first year of their marriage in 1914, they made frequent automobile trips to teach in Santa Rosa, a larger town nearby. By the end of their second year of marriage, they had made many new contacts with people interested in the teachings of Bahá'u'lláh—in fact, their teaching methods and efforts were at the forefront of the teaching work, for they were already enlisting traveling teachers to the region. For instance, in a letter dated December 30, 1915, Louise addressed an old friend, Alfred Lunt, a prominent Boston Bahá'í lawyer who became a Bahá'í shortly after hearing a lecture by Dr. Ali Kuli Khan in the winter of 1905. At the time, Alfred Lunt served as one of the editors of *Star of the West*, and he served as secretary of the executive board of the Bahá'í Temple Unity.

In the letter below, Louise wrote that Dr. Ali Kuli Khan and his wife Florence had come to give talks on the Bahá'í Faith. Dr. Khan and his wife Florence are best remembered in America for having hosted 'Abdu'l-Bahá for a reception dinner at their home in Washington, DC in April 1912. At that dinner, the Master insisted that Louis Gregory, an African American Bahá'í, be seated at His right at the dinner table. The Master thereby set an example to the other guests of the central principle of the teachings of Bahá'u'lláh: the oneness of mankind. Furthermore, Ali Kuli Khan's marriage to Florence Breed was the first Bahá'í Persian-American union. Their daughter Marzieh Gail is known for her erudite and eloquent translations of the holy writings of Bahá'u'lláh, most notably her translation in 1945 of both the Seven Valleys and the Four Valleys. As mentioned earlier, it was Marzieh Gail who was able to glean, through interviews, so much of John and Louise Bosch's life history. The intimate trust shared by John and Louise and Marzieh must have begun when Marzieh was a little girl, for they spoke to her in those interviews as though she were their own daughter.

Here is Louise's letter to Alfred Lunt where Louise was actively recruiting traveling teachers who could help expand and consolidate their teaching efforts in the Geyserville area.

Geyserville
December 30, 1915
Allaho' Abha!

Am so excited dear brother and cannot rest until I scratch off a word to you to say that [Ali Kuli] Khan was up here with Florence [. . .] and left again this morning.

He came in <u>your</u> place you see and we mentioned you during their presence here.

We had a meeting of 50 people here and about 100 in Santa Rosa. Now the great day of God has dawned upon humble Geyserville thru my dear husband and his efforts and his desire for the townspeople he loves so well.

Khan stayed 24 hours at Geyserville. Only in the eternal kingdom shall we see and know what has really happened during those extraordinary 24 hours.

Your Xmas card received. Your telegram of April 28 received and also later your very kind letter. Had never time to answer you. But in spirit I did.

Is it true that dear Mr. Randall is going out as a teacher to all parts? Will he come to Geyserville? We expect him. We hope he may follow up Khan's work at Geyserville.

In El Baha ever yours,
(signed) Louise Bosch[12]

Louise's spiritual intuition is evident in her clairvoyance about "the eternal kingdom," where the results of one's teaching work will finally be known. Also, Louise's reference to Harry Randall was providential and demonstrated Louise's discernment of effective Bahá'í teachers— for Harry Randall would later be remembered by the Guardian for his "unsparing efforts which he exerted for the promotion of the Faith, the passionate eloquence with which he diffused its teachings, the mature judgment and ripe experience which he contributed to its councils, the liberality with which in days of prosperity he supported its institutions, and above all his upright and generous character, . . . traits that will long live after him, and which bodily separation can never remove."[13]

Harry Randall was not the only one who gave liberally to the funds. John and Louise Bosch understood that giving to the Bahá'í Fund was central to the teaching work and vital to the success of the Plan. In the following letter, Alfred Lunt's response to Louise's letter seemed to be an instruction to himself more than John and Louise, as he was reflecting upon a spiritual attitude of sacrifice in giving and in teaching that was already integral to the life of John and Louise:

ALLAHO ABHA!
Boston, Mass., Jan. 20th, 1916.
Mrs. Louise Bosch
Geyserville, Calif.
My dear Sister:

I am glad that [Ali Kuli] Khan and the family went to Geyserville and gave such an inspired talk and attracted the hearts of the people. I heard also from Santa Rosa that that meeting was most helpful.

Please give my warm Bahai love to your dear husband and tell him that the service of the servants of God is not one of personality or of any identity save entire thraldom at His Threshold so that this meeting was surely a meeting of the believers of God in which all were serving, both speaker and listeners; so that I feel that Khan did not come in my place, as you say, but as a servant of the servants.

I have never lost my keen regret at not being able to meet the dear friends in your town, and if God pleases I shall do so whenever I have the opportunity. I am sure they would have served me more than I could possibly have served them.

My dear sister, I have much confidence in your spiritual intuitions and judgment. Have you any thought or suggestion at this time for bringing the aspirations and ideals of the believers into concerted expression by way of contributions to the Holy Edifice between now and the April Convention. Abdul Baha says [to Corinne True in a letter dated 10 April 1910], "Now you must collect contributions." We must not shrink from the task nor handle it gingerly but firmly. We must not be afraid of the name of money and its tremendous power when employed in obedience to the command of God. It is my constant prayer that between now and April matters may so develop that a really substantial sum may be accumulated which can be reported to the Convention—not $10,000 but $100,000 should be our smallest goal. We are thinking of putting into effect a sort of contingent pledge system, by having all state the utmost they will give voluntarily during the next twelve months provided others will give enough to make up a certain sum. I think that many of the believers have withheld their larger contributions hoping the fund would first become more substantial, but the rule should be that he who gives promptly gives most.

Can you give me some light on the situation? What are the convictions of your own heart on this most vital matter?

In His Love,
Faithfully your brother,
(signed) Alfred E. Lunt[14]

There are several letters among the Bosch papers that attest to John's good business sense, as the letters are rich with practical suggestions regarding the Fund. John and Louise responded to Mr. Lunt's inquiry by making a suggestion as applicable today as it was then: When the followers of Bahá'u'lláh are kindled with a love of God and His Religion, giving to the Fund of God's Cause is a natural expression of that love and needs no prompting from outside influence.

Five years after their marriage, Louise made a solo trip to Green Acre to visit old friends. This left John alone for the first time since his marriage, so naturally, he decided to write to the closest relative he had—the Master:

Geyserville, California
September 18th, 1919
Oh my Beloved Abdul Baha:
Thou willst remember me, who had the wonderful privilege to meet Thee in 1912 in New York and was permitted to travel with Thee from New York to Washington and from Washington to Chicago.
At the Ansonia in New York Thou hast given me the name "Nurani."
Oh how wonderful were those days and hours to have been in Thy presence and then again to have been in the midst with Thee in San Francisco.
Since Louise came here we have taught many souls and many of them have become firm believers in the Covenant.
We also have traveled in our automobile nearly fifteen thousand miles on this coast in California visiting believers and given many the Bahai message.

I thank Thee with all my heart for the blessing Thou hast given us and supplicate that thou willst help us in all the future times.

The town we are living in is small and we have meetings and feasts in our home and in the homes of the believers we have given the teachings.

Louise is a wonderful teacher and loved by all the people. She is not very strong for traveling on long trips, but she always makes the effort and has good results.

Louise made the trip to the meeting of believers at Green acre on August 1st and she informs me that she will now return to our own Western district and start giving the message in New Mexico and Arizona and return by way of southern California.

I am going to meet her in New Mexico about Oct. 1st and then travel together in the Cause.

I pray that we will be assisted by Thee.

I am longing to receive a tablet from Thee and again to meet Thee.

Wouldst Thou give us permission to visit Thee in Haifa and on our return home to give the message in Switzerland and Germany, wherever the German language is spoken.

Mr. and Mrs. Whitton of Geyserville expressed a desire to meet Thee. Both are on a trip to the eastern states at this time.

Of course I am not a teacher myself, but I am always ready to tell the people about the importance of the Bahai Cause and start them with books to read.

To all appearance this country will become prohibition and wine will not be used any more as a daily beverage.

My small vineyard here, which formerly has brought a fair income, will have to be uprooted and planted into fruit trees.

Wouldst Thou advise me to form a trust of this property so about 20 to 50 believers could share in it for the preparation of a Bahai School or College for teaching to prescribed Bahai courses of the pure teachings of Baha Ullah and Abdul Baha's interpretations?

With a very small help from a few believers that are firm, all this could be accomplished, the only consideration would be that Louise and myself would have the right to occupy a home or lot during our lifetime and that the income of the place could be used by us for Bahai purposes.

The place and situation is very attractive, only a few hundred feet from the Post Office and Railway Station and bordering on the town of Geyserville. Some believers could build small cottages and make their home here. Parents could bring their children here to be educated in [local public] high school, as we just have voted for a new up to date high school building to be completed this next season.

Oh my beloved Abdul Baha! I pray that thou willst attract more and more souls to this assembly we have started at our home here at Geyserville, and that all will become firm believers in the Covenant and hope that Geyserville in a few years will become wholly Bahai.

Bless us all, let the rain of Thy love shower over us.

I am longing to meet Thee again and pray to be guided by Thee in spirit and ever be occupied in Thy Service.

In Thy Covenant

(signed) John D. Bosch

P.S.: Enclosed herewith description of land, buildings and photographs.[15]

The establishment of the Bosch's property for use as a Bahá'í school would be realized in due time, but not before the consummation of two significant events in the lives of John and Louise: a pioneering teaching trip to the island of Tahiti and a pilgrimage to Haifa to see 'Abdu'l-Bahá one last time.

Before Louise departed for Green Acre, Maine, she had been re-reading all of the Tablets of the Divine Plan. In an interview with Marzieh Gail, Louise explains the spiritual awakening she had upon reading the Tablets: "I was reading that entire book from one end to the other and begging the Almighty to let me know when I had come to the place that was to be for me. When I reached the Polynesian Tablet, I perceived a stir, so I stopped and read it thoroughly many times. The next morning, or soon after, I awoke at the very earliest gray light of dawn, because something had wakened me. It was a voice that said, 'Loti, Loti.' I sat up and thought, 'Well, this is strange. What is this Loti?'"[16] She wakened John, and they looked up the word "Loti" in an encyclopedia and found that it was a book called *La Mariage de Loti* written in 1880 by French author Pierre Loti. Furthermore, they learned that the book was known by an alternate title: *Tahiti*. That same day Louise went to San Francisco to borrow the book from the library, but it was already checked out to someone else.

Louise returned from the San Francisco library empty-handed and continued on her journey to Green Acre where she and May Maxwell stayed as guests in the home of Sarah Farmer. Louise was praying for certitude in their choice of a pioneering post, and she found confirmation in the most unexpected way:

> Mrs. Maxwell asked me to wait a few moments in the big upstairs hall [of Sarah Farmer's house], while she got ready for luncheon. It was a warm day, but there was a draught through the hall from the open doorway. I started to shut the door when I saw a little book on a small table just inside. Thinking from the size that it was the *Book of Iqán* [*The Book of Certitude*], I picked it up and sat down on the top stair in the hall to read. I opened the book and instead of the beloved title, to my surprise it said *Le Mariage de Loti*. Imagine my feelings. That trip of three thousand miles I had to take to get it.[17]

John and Louise embarked for Tahiti in March of 1920. They were in their spiritual youth: John was sixty-five years old, and Louise was fifty. While on the ship, John encountered a fellow passenger who happened to be reading a book by Pierre Loti but of a different title than *La Mariage de Loti*. John asked to see the book, and its title read, *Vers Ispahan*, or "Toward Isfahán." Such a book might suggest to Louise that they should postpone fulfilling a goal of the Divine Plan and travel first to Isfahán, the very heart of Iran and the city to which the Báb traveled upon leaving His native Shiraz, and the city wherein the martyrdoms of the King of Martyrs and the Beloved of Martyrs took place. John promptly returned the book into the hands of its owner and said, "For heaven's sake, don't let my wife see that book!"[18]

6 / Tahiti

John and Louise sailed on the *RMS Moana* from San Francisco to Tahiti on March 20, 1920 and arrived three weeks later at the port of Papeete, Tahiti, on April 8 at sunset. Their decision to pioneer to Tahiti was of interest to many of their fellow Bahá'ís, including Howard MacNutt, who wrote to them saying, "Tell us something of Tahiti, its climate, fruits, inhabitants, and natural conditions. How we wish we could sail away from the Coast and lose our thoughts of New York for weeks upon the bosom of the mighty ocean, then cast anchor for a year or so in some quiet Papeete. We are driven and distracted by the din of cities; by the sordid money-mad metropolis whose minarets 'Abdu'l-Bahá said are the towering office buildings and where the Religion of God is defiled and trailed in the dust."[1]

Tahiti is part of a five-island group named the "Society Islands" by British explorer Thomas Cook due to the appearance of the five islands as an integrated community of islands huddled together and surrounded by the vast solitude of the southern Pacific Ocean. The islands that make up this group are Tahiti, Moorea, Raiatea, Bora Bora, and Huahine. In the early nineteenth century, the Society Islands became a French protectorate and a religious stronghold for French Catholic missionaries. The capital city of the island chain is Papeete, Tahiti, and even though the early Bahá'í teaching work took place there, the greatest expansion of the Bahá'í Faith today has taken place on the island of Huahine. Today, the population of French Polynesia is approximately three hundred thousand, while in 1920 it was a tenth that size, with approximately thirty thousand people living across all five islands. Of that population, eleven thousand resided in Tahiti at the time of John and Louise's arrival.[2]

A word about pioneering should be mentioned here. A "Bahá'í pioneer" is a term used to describe a person who leaves his or her home to settle in another locality, city, or country in the world with the purpose of establishing the Bahá'í Faith there. 'Abdu'l-Bahá described such pioneers as "wanderers in the Path of God" for whom "the blessing of homelessness shall endure forever." In effect, the ultimate goal of a Bahá'í pioneer is to advance the prosperity of humanity through the application of the teachings of Bahá'u'lláh. In order for a Bahá'í pioneer to be effective, he or she must become involved in the life of the society to which they have settled, learning to walk side by side with those whom they hope to teach. It is interesting to note how learning is acquired from the experiences of the early pioneers of the Faith—a learning that informs the teaching work carried out today. For instance, in its December 2015 message to the Conference of the Continental Boards of Counselors, the Universal House of Justice surveyed the learning in the teaching work world-wide and noted, "What is required from those involved, however, is long-term commitment and a yearning to become so familiar with the reality of a place that they integrate into local life and, eschewing any trace of prejudice or paternalism, form those bonds of true friendship that befit companions on a spiritual journey." John and Louise's experiences in Tahiti are part of an aggregate composite of learning from the last century that continues to reveal insights into how best to serve the Cause of Bahá'u'lláh in the pioneering field.[3]

Although John and Louise stayed only five months in Tahiti, they developed relationships that would last another twenty-five years and more, and they became closely linked to the fates and fortunes of three persons in Tahiti: Mr. Alexandre Drollet (a local Tahitian), Mr. René Gasse (a Frenchman living in Tahiti), and Mr. Georges Spitz (a Tahitian-born European). The story of how each of these men responded to the message of Bahá'u'lláh is complicated, yet highly instructive when learning about teaching the Cause in a tightly-knit island community such as the one in Papeete. The story of Mr. René Gasse and Mr. Georges Spitz begins with the story of Mr. Alexandre Drollet, the government interpreter for Tahiti and the first person to whom John and Louise delivered the message of Bahá'u'lláh upon their arrival at the port in Papeete.

After meeting Mr. Drollet on the wharf, the Bosches were invited to his home where they gave the Message of Bahá'u'lláh to Mr. Drollet's wife and their eight children. Of that experience, Louise wrote to Mrs. Edna True in July of 1920:

> He (Mr. Drollet) was the first who became a believer and the first who heard the Truth. We presented the Truth to him and his wife in French at their home, not long after our arrival here. He uses the Greatest Name every morning, and he prays that wonderful prayer on page 58 of the Divine Plan. Without our telling him, he has selected that prayer for himself. In every way his rapid spiritual growth has amazed us, and words are unable to express our thankfulness to God. How great is the mercy of Abdul-Baha to have permitted us to come here to find such a soul! Mr. Drollet told us that always he had wished and hoped to do something sometime for the Polynesians here and he said that he knew now that he would translate some of the teachings of Abdul-Baha into that language.[4]

It is possible that the prayer to which Louise refers is the prayer in the Tablets of the Divine Plan where 'Abdu'l-Bahá prays that God will relieve mankind of the darkness of the Great War. This prayer is especially topical given the expansion of that war into the far reaches of the globe, including the remote islands of French Polynesia. In the early stages of the war, two German warships bombarded Papeete. In terror, Tahitians took refuge in the hills of the island during and after the attack.[5] Therefore, the following prayer would have been deeply reassuring to Alexandre Drollet. Here is the prayer, in part:

> O God, my God! Thou seest how black darkness is enshrouding all regions, how all countries are burning with the flame of dissension, and the fire of war and carnage is blazing throughout the East and the West [. . .]
>
> O Lord! Draw up the people from the abyss of the ocean of hatred and enmity, and deliver them from this impenetrable darkness [. . .]
>
> O Lord! The ocean of rebellion is surging, and these tempests will not be stilled save through Thy boundless grace which hath embraced all regions.[6]

Alexandre Tahea Drollet was born in Tahiti in 1871 and would have been fifty years old when he met the Bosches on Pier 33 in Papeete. His wife, Anne Marie Anamu Naumi Drollet, was also born in Tahiti the same year as her husband. Together they had eight children, all of whom would have been present when the Bosches arrived as their guests to explain the Message of Bahá'u'lláh. Of the eight children, four of them would figure into a storied history of the Drollet family's relationship with John and Louise: Jane (Drollet) Gasse, Alfred Drollet, Roger Drollet, and Ariane (Drollet) Marchel.

Within two months of John and Louise's stay in Tahiti, Alexandre Drollet and his son Alfred (age 21) and his eldest daughter Jane (age 24) sailed to San Francisco. They were seeking medical advice for Jane, who suffered from elephantiasis, a disease that causes dramatic swelling in the lower legs. By way of introduction from the Bosches, Alexandre Drollet met Dr. Frederick D'Evelyn, a Bahá'í living in San Francisco. In the following letter, Alexandre Drollet sends news of his voyage to John and Louise, who were still at their pioneering post in Tahiti:

On board SS Tofua, June 11, 1920
Dear Madam Bosch,
Before my arrival at San Francisco I wish to write these few lines to let you know how sorry I was that evening we left to hear that Mr. Bosch was not feeling well and that you were kept from coming to the wharf. I hope Mr. Bosch is well again and enjoying a good health. Oh! how sorry I felt to leave my dear family, and especially my two babies Francis and Newton [grandchildren from eldest daughter Jane Drollet Gasse.]

This voyage has passed quite rapidly [. . .] I have not been able to do much for our Cause on board but had very interesting talks with one old passenger who had heard of the Bahai movement but knew nothing about it so I handed him a few booklets. After he read them, he said he absolutely agreed with this teaching and that he would look for the Bahai groups everywhere he would be in the States. So you may realize how happy I felt of my little success [. . .]

Kindly give my best regards to Mr. Bosch and believe me your most loving friend, Alex. Drollet.

PS: Written from San Francisco, June 15th:

My son Alfred and I have met yesterday Doctor D'Evelyn at his Office and he was delighted to see us. He invited us to join the Bahai meeting Friday evening, which we accepted with great pleasure [. . .]

I met here a great many Tahitians who do not wish to return to Papeete because they are so happy in California.

As I have much writing to do I am going to leave you and say good-bye for the time being.

Your loving,
Alex. Drollet[7]

When one considers that Alexandre Drollet became a Bahá'í sometime in April of 1920 and that by June of that same year he would be in San Francisco meeting Dr. Frederick D'Evelyn, Mrs. Helen Goodall, and Mrs. Ella Goodall Cooper—all three of whom had been in the presence of 'Abdu'l-Bahá during His visit to America—it is a miracle, indeed.

By August of 1920, John and Louise had left Tahiti and returned to Geyserville, California, having stayed in Tahiti for only five months. Louise makes it very clear that they left Tahiti for no other reason except that they felt they had exhausted their influence due to the Tahitian preconception that the Bosches were German. Only five years earlier, the Tahitians had endured the attack by German warships in the early stages of the war. Even though the Tahitian queen had no political power, she had sway over Tahitian attitudes toward both French and German people. Louise explained it in this way:

> Fain would we have given the Bahá'í Message to the ex-Queen, but an extraordinary circumstance prevented it. The fact was that our name was "Bosch." We were in a French colony. It was soon after the war, and when the war feeling against the Germans was apparently at its height. Although we are Swiss, not German, yet because of our name we were believed to be German, and it was rumored that we had come to Tahiti to instigate the natives against the French. As there was already existing a good deal of estrangement between the Tahitians and the French, it was easily possible to credit the rumor. At all events, a false motive was assigned to our coming there, and the Queen sent her regrets at her inability to meet us. This she did very kindly, through one of her sisters. This sister was, however, sufficiently interested in us to suggest that my husband change his name. My husband replied that this was a good suggestion, but that he feared he might not always be able to remember his new name. But we met a sufficient number of people whose interest we had gained and whose eyes we had directed toward the Bahá'í Cause. It seemed, therefore, best to leave that field then with the hope that we would return at some later time.[8]

Although John and Louise did not return to Tahiti, they kept in very close contact with their Tahitian friends. For instance, John and Louise learned that Alexandre Drollet had sailed from San Francisco to France, where he could obtain a medical operation through the French government services for Tahitians. From Paris, he wrote several letters to the Bosches in Geyserville about the personal transformation he was experiencing as a new Bahá'í. In the letter that follows, Alexandre Drollet explained to John and Louise that four months into his medical rehabilitation in France, he was feeling the confines of his cage and was struggling between selfish passion and surrender to the Will of God. He recognized that his tests were a healing medicine to the soul, but he had difficulty rising above his material concerns until slowly his material concerns began to affect his spiritual attitude. In many ways, reading about Alexandre Drollet's experience is a lesson in how one learns to apply the teachings of Bahá'u'lláh to the daily changes and chances of life. Furthermore, his deep understanding of the principles of the Cause is a credit to the unfailing guidance he received in so short a time through the efforts of John and Louise.

Despite these periods of doubt and despair, Alexandre Drollet's enthusiasm for the teachings inspired him to attempt to translate Bahá'í pamphlets into Tahitian, and he wrote to Roy Wilhelm about the project. Roy, who was the treasurer of the Bahá'í Temple Unity Fund at that time, took a personal interest in making sure that translations of Bahá'í literature were accurate. Roy wished to see the translations of Bahá'í pamphlets that Alexandre Drollet promised, but while in France, Mr. Drollet's problems seemed to multiply. He became entangled in a petition to receive unpaid wages for his work as a government translator, including payment for his return passage to Tahiti. His petition remained mired in obfuscation, and once again, Mr. Drollet began to lose hope. In one of his letters to the Bosches, he confessed his disappointment in human nature when he wrote, "I am learning a sad lesson about the justice of men."[9]

Mr. Drollet's letters are not solely limited to his internal struggles about human nature. He also wrote to the Bosches about some of the

Bahá'ís he met in Paris—some of whom were taught by Miss May Bolles during her Paris years before her marriage to Mr. Sutherland Maxwell. For Louise Bosch, reading about Mr. Drollet's experiences must have felt like watching a grand circle completing the arc that began with Louise and May Bolles and circled around to Tahiti, where it touched the life of Alexandre Drollet and carried him back to Paris where the arc had begun. This letter was written after John and Louise's return to Geyserville from Tahiti. As Alexandre Drollet was the first person John and Louise met upon their arrival in Tahiti, John and Louise must have read this letter with great interest because it was telling of Alexandre Drollet's spiritual path. Clearly his life had changed since becoming a Bahá'í, but with those changes had come challenges of how to adjust his material outlook on life to the spiritual transformation that was taking place:

Paris, December 10, 1920
Allaho'Abha
My dear Sister in El Abha,
Your very kind letter was received on the 7th of this month and first of all I must present you and my good friend Mr. Bosch my best thanks for your so kind invitation to [son] Roger to stay with you at Geyserville. Alfred had written to me already about all your kindness towards my children.

Concerning the clock-works Mr. Bosch wants me to bring back, I will surely do my best to give him satisfaction. I have already noted a junkshop where I might be able to get one at a reasonable cost. But you give no description whatever of the kind and size of the mechanism because as I have learned the clock-making trade, I could have selected just what Mr. B. wants. Anyhow, if I cannot get here what we need, I have in Papeete a good "Coucou clock" with brass works in good order that might fill the requirements. Kindly give me more information about the size and disposition of the wheels.

TAHITI

I have just received a good letter from Roy Wilhelm concerning the proofreading of the booklet in the Tahitian dialect. I am going to write to Mr. Roy Wilhelm that I will be only too glad to help the accomplishment of this work, and in order to save time, that he may send the proofs by first chance because I do not know yet exactly when I will be able to go back to America and to my beloved home island.

As you see, I am still here in the hospital where things are taken very slow. I have been many times at the "Ministére Des Colonies" with no satisfactory result and it is only last Monday that they decided to send a wireless message to the governor of Tahiti asking him to settle my case. But since I left the island, they have treated me in the meanest way, giving no answer to my written requests and not paying me one cent of my wages, so I had to borrow a little money for my personal needs.

Oh! my dear friends, nobody will ever know the heartbroken state I am feeling since I arrived in France. Many would have turned mad but as the Master says in the little leaflet enclosed in your letter: "The more difficulties one has in the world, the more perfect one becomes." Yes, indeed, I am learning a great lesson but I can't help telling you that my tears are running every day and if it was not for the benefit of my health, I would feel sorry all my life of having left behind my wife, my home and specially my dear little [grandchildren] Francis and Newton whom I am so anxious to see again. And when I think that I have no idea when that day will come, Oh! I feel awfully sad. That is one of the main reasons that kept me away from those I would have been so happy to meet in Paris.

Paris is a prison to me from which I am anxious to escape. I have visited very little of it and have no desire to go anywhere having only one idea in mind—like the wild bird in a cage that is to get out and never come back anymore. My moral sufferings are indescribable since the French government would not let me have at least the hope of being sent back to Tahiti. And it is so cold now that I can hardly go out of my room. Today I have seen my first sight of snowfall, it is really very strange, *mais ce spectacle me met la tristesse dans l'ame et je pense a la famille qui est si loin et que je pleure sans cesse. Non, nul ne saura jamais ce que je souffre en silence.* [Author's translation: But this show makes me sad in the soul, and I think of my family who are so far away, and I cry constantly. No, no one will ever know that I suffer in silence.]

Last Friday I went at last and met Mr. and Mrs. Scott [Bahá'ís in Paris]. They were really happy of my visit and the next day, Saturday evening, I was invited to the meeting and there I had the pleasure of being introduced to the Bahai friends among which was Miss Edith Sanderson and a couple of very nice Persian young men. On Tuesday evening I was invited at Mrs. [Loulie] Matthews' at Columbia Hotel, Avenue Kléber, where another Bahai meeting was held. They were all anxious to hear about the spreading of the cause in the South Sea Islands and also how myself and family came in contact with you and Mr. Bosch. Mr. Ali Akbar was there and through him I learned that Mr. and Madame Dreyfus had gone to Saïgon to bring the Bahai cause in those countries.

About a week ago I received a long letter from Mrs. Cooper of San Francisco, dated <u>August 15</u> and sent to the care of my cousin who kept it until the other day when I went to see him. I was very sorry of the accident and I am sending my excuses and my regrets to Mrs. Cooper who had been so kind to me while I was in San Francisco.

Yes, I received your good letter of July last and those written later and also some cards. The box address to reach me anytime, even after I leave Paris, is: "c/f L. Petillot, 42 rue de l'Echiquier, Paris X." Do not miss the "X" after Paris, it makes it much easier for the Post Office.

Now I am going to close, hoping to hear from you soon again. It encourages me in my great distress. I feel your loving spirit constantly around me, and perhaps also that of the good friends of San Francisco who sent me their love through Alfred.

Hoping this will find both of you and Roger in good health and happy feeling,

I am with best Abha's greetings,

Your most loving friend and spiritual brother,

Alex Drollet[10]

As the correspondence from Alexandre Drollet waned, John and Louise relied on Mr. Drollet's son-in-law, Mr. René Gasse, to keep them informed of the spiritual health of the Drollet family. When the Bosches arrived in Tahiti and first met René Gasse, he and Jane Drollet had been married for five years and had two children, Newton and Francis. John and Louise did everything in their power to ensure the Drollet family's firmness in the Covenant of Bahá'u'lláh, despite the personal tests and trials various members of the family faced in the years that followed. John and Louise seemed especially interested in receiving news of Ariane Tepoe Drollet, who would have been nineteen years old when the Bosches arrived in Tahiti in 1920. Although Ariane accepted the teachings of Bahá'u'lláh, she was not immune to the moral decline that was gaining pernicious strength in societies across the globe—including the society of islanders in Tahiti.

Nevertheless, they all endeavored to transform their lives according to the high standard of the teachings. John and Louise's encouragement of these new Bahá'ís was likely informed by their own understanding of Bahá'u'lláh's condition of suffering in the Path of God: "But for the tribulations which are sustained in Thy path, how could Thy true lovers be recognized; and were it not for the trials which are borne for love of Thee, how could the station of such as yearn for Thee be revealed? Thy might beareth me witness! The companions of all who adore Thee are the tears they shed, and the comforters of such as seek Thee are the groans they utter, and the food of them who haste to meet Thee is the fragments of their broken hearts."[11]

The society in Tahiti suffered under the pervasive influence of moral licentiousness to which no society is immune, yet it caused John and Louise a great deal of anguish. They worried about the Drollet children as though they were their own children. When Alexandre Drollet became a Bahá'í, he essentially declared his whole family to be Bahá'ís, which included children who were already grown, married, and settled into a certain morality that may have been at odds with the high standards of the Bahá'í teachings. Infidelity was not uncommon; therefore, their adaption to a new moral standard was gradual, to say the least. In this regard, René Gasse wrote to the Bosches for guidance on how to live a Bahá'í life. Similar to Alexandre Drollet's letters to the Bosches, René Gasse's letters are a window into his spiritual development, revealing once again John and Louise's spiritual influence on the souls they encountered in Tahiti.

Bearing in mind that English was not René Gasse's first language, the sincere and personal nature of the news he shared with John and Louise was, at times, awkwardly expressed. He wrote of his wife Jane, who was Alexandre and Marie Drollet's eldest daughter. Jane and René were having marital difficulties, and René was trying to figure out how the Bahá'í teachings could help to spiritualize his marriage. René's letter is a humbling reminder that when a Bahá'í enters the field of teaching the Cause to others, the results of one's Bahá'í teaching efforts are sometimes inscrutable to the teacher. Toward the conclusion of the following letter, René Gasse wondered about writing to Shoghi Effendi and worried that he would not be able to conceal his pride from the Guardian:

Allaho'Abha
Papeete Le 20 Juillet 1925
Dear Mr. and Mrs. Bosch
    I am sorry to have missed [mailing a letter to] you by the last steamer, but I was so busy and also so sorry that I feel so bad I did not write to you or anyone else a single word.

The children, Jane and I are well now. Jane was suffering lately of Elephantiasis and now it seems that the sore is going away little by little. So Jane is as well as possible. She, now, asked my little boys to say their prayers every night before sleeping and they do so very nicely. I have to think Jane is now much better than before, but she remains a little doubtful because she did not receive from her father the right education and she seems to be very anxious to learn much more about the truth. However she seems to have abandoned her wrong life and she tries to do everything to make me pleased as much as possible. Marie Drollet [Jane's mother] believes in God and in a better life after death . . .

I have to tell you something: One night I was very sorry and I asked to Jane if she was a very Bahai <u>she said yes</u> because I have always on my finger the little ring you gave to her. Her mother is a good mother for her and the children and also to me. She comes very often to my place and passes almost every Sunday with us [. . .]. Later on we will see what will happen

About Ariane [Jane's younger sister] she is still with Bataille and she seems happy now. He gives her all she likes to have and I have heard that Bataille has already bought the drug store from Mr. Lebrazidec.

I have received your letters sent by the last mail and I have been seeking about those mats "Peue." I found only some of too small sizes so I will send them to you as soon some will arrive from the islands.

Please give me the address of Shoghi Effendi if you think there is no inconvenience from my part. I have never write to such a personality and He could find me too proud. Send me also please a small Bahai stone for I lost mine before I spare the money to make it mounted. [. . .]

The business is very quiet here at the present time and I hope without certainty to succeed in the settlement of my affairs.

Never mind, all will be well if God permit that become so.

I remain in El Baha ever,
Yours,
René Gasse[12]

Jane and René eventually divorced, resulting in divided loyalties between the families, but René remained a firm believer. He became a wireless (telegraph) operator on steamships that ran routes from Tahiti to San Francisco, and sometime after 1930, René Gasse married Jeanne Moua, a Tahitian who was living in San Francisco. He died in 1965, and Jeanne died in 1967. Both are buried in the Italian Cemetery in Colma City, San Mateo County, near San Francisco.

René remained devoted to the Cause of Bahá'u'lláh, as the following letter affirms. It was written in 1945 when René would have been fifty-four years old and still working as a wireless operator "somewhere in the Southwest Pacific" aboard the *S.S. Abigail Adams*—one year before the passing of John Bosch in 1946. On the front of the original letter, Louise wrote a note in her own handwriting that reads "From René Gasse, of wonderful mind and soul."

May 6, 1945
Somewhere in the Southwest Pacific
My Very Dear Friends,

My thoughts are very often with you. I will miss you both very much. I certainly hope John is well and happy. Jeanne and I are hoping to pay you a visit if Jeanne has some time off on my return. I read and re-read Bahai literature that I brought along and feel more and more deeply about it. Jeanne is 100% Bahai and wishes her health was better as she cannot do any work at all. Wonder how you are and when [Geyserville Bahá'í] summer school will start, although I cannot make any definite plans as yet.

I do not know if I will make another trip after this one. Jeanne worries herself sick. However this was a good means to achieve our goal of repaying our debts.

I am somewhat at a loss to understand how we could manage financially should we decide to live over there [at Geyserville] as much as we desire it to be so, so that we (or rather I) could work for you and the Cause at the same time. It should be borne in mind that Jeanne is not fit to do any manual work, and I do not know what the work would consist of, and how to get an income sufficient to pay all debts besides current normal expenses.

I think I will be back in San Francisco in about two months if everything goes well.

Hope this letter finds you both in the best of health and I am looking forward to seeing you.

Always yours affectionately,

In El Baha,

René Gasse[13]

In addition to Alexandre Drollet and René Gasse, a third figure stands out as one of the most curious and fascinating of the people John and Louise met in Tahiti. His name was Georges William Henri Loulou Spitz, and he was born in Tahiti in 1885 and died there in 1949. He was the son of photographer Charles Spitz, resident of Papeete and owner of "Spitz's Curio Store." It is interesting to note that when the post-impressionist painter Paul Gauguin arrived in Papeete, he found inspiration in the photographs in Spitz's curio shop. Although Gauguin's famous paintings of Tahitians appear to be painted from real life, actually most of his paintings were inspired from Charles Spitz's photographs.[14]

After Charles Spitz's death in 1894, his widow, Elisa Jane Hills, continued running the curio shop until her son Georges was old enough to assume responsibilities of the store. It just so happened that in 1920, when young Georges Spitz was thirty-five years old and proud proprietor of "Spitz's Curio Store," John Bosch strolled in with a more precious treasure to offer Georges Spitz than all his curios combined.

Not only did Georges Spitz become a Bahá'í, but his Tahitian wife, Martha Tetuara, declared her Faith as well. They had four children who did not declare themselves as believers, but their two daughters, Fifi and Irma, kept in close contact with Bahá'ís. Because the Bosches stayed only five months, they relied on deepening these new Bahá'ís through frequent correspondence between Geyserville and Tahiti. In this way, even though John and Louise were thousands of miles away from their Tahitian friends, they remained so spiritually connected with the friends in Tahiti that it was as though no distance separated them.

In the personal papers of John and Louise Bosch, there are forty-six letters from Georges Spitz to them. In almost every letter, he remembers to thank the Bosches for bringing the message of Bahá'u'lláh to him and to his wife. Georges Spitz did not accept the Truth right away, but when he finally did, he bemoaned his initial reluctance in a letter to John and Louise, whom he called "Tihoni" and "Ruita": "How sorry I am and will always be for not accepting Tihoni when he first proposed the great Light in my shop."[15]

In time, Georges Spitz read earnestly the various Bahá'í books sent to him by the Bosches. One such book was John Esslemont's *Bahá'u'lláh and the New Era*, a book that Rúhíyyih Khánum later referred to as the "textbook" of the Bahá'í Faith.[16] In the following letter, Georges "Ruru" Spitz wrote to John and Louise in Geyserville from a hospital in San Francisco (where he had gone for gallbladder surgery) and told the Bosches of the profound impact the "New Era" had on him:

Alláh-u-Abhá!
San Francisco
St. Francis Hospital
January 6, 1926
Dear Ruita and Tihoni,
    Your dear letter, dated yesterday, made us both as happy as ours did you. Like in everything in which I was confident since we came to Geyserville, I am fully confident also in the Star of

Guidance because I am more and more lightened by it daily. I want its light more and more. I feel that I need same much more and I am searching for more. Yes, more and more all the time.

I am at page 75 in the *New Era*. Oh! how sweet and how beautiful every line of it is. And how more happy I am to possess and to hold a book of such value. In this World how many cannot imagine how such dear teachings renew one's life; if they only knew it or if they could only have the lucky chance to come across it like dear Tihoni had and us all.

One must read and understand before they can realize the meaning of the word Baha'i, which both you and Tihoni tried to explain the night before we left peaceful Geyserville.

I came across it in Chapter V [of *Bahá'u'lláh and the New Era*] and I saw what really one has to do before being able to call himself or herself a Baha'i.

I know I have lots to do yet but I have the feeling and the will of many years already, with these it will ease my climbing to the cliff where I can see the Light of Love which Baha-u-llah brought us poor sinners etc.

We are so glad that we are not forgotten in your meetings.

Sweet Martha had a good laugh over what you mention about Mr. Feldmeyer whom she does not remember and she wishes to know! It's the same everywhere, my beloved wife is liked; Ruru is proud of it. Like your good selves, we hope you are coming to see me. Sure, we would be glad to go with you to a meeting here in San Francisco.

The way everything looks, the Doctor says I will be able to leave the hospital on or about the fifteenth [. . .] we will leave [for Tahiti] by the mail steamer; leaving here on February 24th. This will give me plenty of time to heal up everything and to have a last good look at San Francisco and especially to see you again.

We noticed the real way of spelling the "Greatest Name," thank you. I like the idea of it being left in Persian.

What I meant by 5 stones is that the removed gall-bladder had in it 5 stones and same I will see with the appendix at the Doctor's office after I leave here. If I ask for them or a report the Doctor will let me have same.

I am sure I will be a well man from now on.

I also hope, like you are wishing, that spiritually I will also be a new man. Like the little vessel out in the ocean and in bad weather drawing nearer to the lighthouse; that's the way I feel and hope to be drawn too.

Before very long I can see myself surrounded by my family, friends, their friends which will become mine; reading the glorious teachings of our most perfect Baha-u-llah and Abdul-Baha. By last mail I wrote to René Gasse saying that him and I are going to have long evenings together.

To Marchal's mother [Georges Spitz's aunt] I wrote saying that Ernest [Spitz's cousin] must hold tight to what he obtained from Mr. and Mrs. Bosch of Geyserville. My aunt's reply will show me the road I have to take.

What you say about them will surely take place.

We are expecting you both on Friday; how nice it will be, how happy we will be to see our most kind and sincere friends, the good ones that we also care a lot for.

We hope you are having good weather in splendid Geyserville [. . .] Here [in San Francisco] we have plenty of fog in the morning but the Sun we brought from Tahiti seems to find itself thru it.

Love and best wishes to every one we knew in dear Geyserville, and like yourselves we wish to be ever yours in El Baha,

Martha and Ruru[17]

In the time of 'Abdu'l-Bahá, new believers would write directly to Him and declare their belief in the teachings of Bahá'u'lláh. Likewise, in the Guardian's time, new believers would write directly to the Guardian to declare themselves believers, especially if those new believers were in areas such as Tahiti, where a Bahá'í administration was not in place. John and Louise guided these new believers in Tahiti toward an understanding of the fundamental verities of the Faith and the significance of the Greater Covenant (a covenant between God and His creation) and the Lesser Covenant (a covenant between God's Manifestation and His followers). Because Georges Spitz lived in a region where there was not a Bahá'í Local Spiritual Assembly, writing to the Guardian was an added assurance that a believer in a remote region would come under the shadow of the protection of the Administrative Order directly through Shoghi Effendi.

A survey of the correspondence of Alexandre Drollet, René Gasse, and Georges Spitz suggests that all three had intended to write to the Guardian. According to the archival records available at this time, only Georges Spitz followed through with this intention, and he received a letter in return from the Guardian. Spitz's joy of having what he regarded as a "sacred" letter in the Guardian's own handwriting caused him to recognize the "splendid light" that was now running through his veins. The feeling caused him to recognize the sharp contrast between the Bahá'í way of life and the society in which he was living: Georges Spitz's neighbor had recently converted his home into a saloon, and Georges had become distressed over the drunken licentiousness and moral decline that was beginning to spread in the neighborhood. It seems clear that Georges' enlightened spiritual state had brought about a greater awareness of the needs of the society in which he lived, and, as the following letter demonstrates, the sacred and the profane became parallel realities in his life:

"Allah-u-Abha"
Papeete March 7, 1927
Dear brother and sister,
   What joy to receive your letters and the two from Haifa. I can hardly believe that I have Shoghi's handwriting in my possession.

What a blessing. Ethel Rosenberg* wrote a splendid one, but when I read the following words by our great Shoghi, I don't feel my old self no more.

Something ran through my veins while Martha and myself were reading same. How thankful we are to have come across you both and to have had the chance of finding the splendid light which we are trying to reach. In my mind it seems like I see in a distance a proud standing light to which we are aiming for.

And now we are rid of our horrible neighbor who was shot dead by a young woman he tried to rape. This took place during the night of the 24th of January. One bullet went thru his heart and a second thru his face. The shameful house is closed until everything is settled. Let us pray that some one else won't reopen it. What an end the fellow had, nearly everybody says he deserved it all. I am glad that I am not the only one that thought it. How happy we are without all that terrible noise etc.

If you must not write dear Ruita [Louise], don't do it, we will understand. How happy we feel when we see all your good words about our daughter Fifi, who is getting on beautifully. And also to know that the Mullanes [cousins in San Francisco] love her like their own child.

If everything continues the same I pray that my two daughters never return here to live; for a visit now and then.

When Martha feels that she is ready I will write what she will dictate to Shoghi. I won't write for her, neither did I get anyone to do mine when I wrote to him.

Sure dear Ruita that letter from Shoghi will be kept, it's sacred. René is soon leaving by a motor schooner the "Bretagne" about the 19th [. . .].

I spoke to him about waiting until later, or after the Cause is established. He said it was impossible for him to remain on

---

* Details about Ethel Rosenberg are given in Chapter 7.

account of the separation. I think he is wise to get out of it for the time being. I told Mrs. Wilder about Miss Agnes Alexander visiting you, how she spoke good of same person. Mrs. Wilder phoned this afternoon telling me that the Guilds had met you. How nice.

I will see them on Sunday to thank them for being so kind to Fifi. When I see it's time, I will talk to them about the Cause [. . .].

We are glad that dear Tihoni [John Bosch] had a delightful time in Canada. Atta boy.

I won't have the time to answer Miss Rosenberg and our Great Shoghi letters by this mail; I am sorry. If you should write them, please mention it to them.

How much happier I feel since all this new light, how thankful I am to you both dear sister Ruita [Louise] and dear Brother [John Bosch] in the Bahai Cause.

Until next time I will say tata and God Bless you both, Always yours in El Abha,
Martha and Lulu[18]

Nearly all of Georges Spitz's letters to John and Louise are addressed to them with the endearing term of "Ruita" for Louise and "Tihoni" for John. Georges was European by descent but Tahitian by culture. English was his third language, after Tahitian and French, and he had an endearing manner of addressing himself in the third person and then switching between his three Tahitian names of "Loulou," "Lulu," and "Ruru." For instance, in one letter Georges writes to John and Louise about feeling alone in the Cause: "There I sit [. . .] and get all sorts of ideas that could make one lose their mind. But nothing of that can get hold of your Lulu who has hold of a bit of His robe on which I hold as tight as possible [. . .] I pray that He knows I am sincere."[19]

In 1927, Georges Spitz was homesick for his wife, Martha, and two daughters, who had all gone to San Francisco so that Martha could receive medical attention and so that the girls could receive an education and, of course, be near John and Louise in Geyserville. Again, Georges Spitz does not neglect to express his gratitude to John and Louise for teaching him the "great Name" of Bahá'u'lláh:

"ALLAH-U-ABHA"
Papeete, October 16, 1927
Dear Ruita and Tihoni,
 Like another "Ray of Light" your letter dated the third reached me. Thank you, our beloved sister and brother in "El Abha" for all you always write me.
 Sincerely I never will forget you both for being the only cause of your Ruru finding what he was so long searching for.
 Again and again thank you, and may my daily prayer be heard; because every time you are included.
 With the little I know I am full of joy, full of courage, full of life since the great "Name" was known to me [. . .][20]

Georges and Martha Spitz's good intentions to teach the Cause were perpetually delayed. At times, Georges felt that the spread of moral licentiousness and the corrosive effects of alcoholism were destroying the social fabric of his community. John and Louise continued to urge Georges Spitz to focus on spreading the spiritual principles of the Cause regardless of the social ills of his community. Georges felt that he had to eradicate those problems first before he could teach the Cause to his friends and family. In this excerpt from a letter dated June 28, 1926 he wrote about his efforts to convince the government to condemn the saloon that had resumed operation next door to his home and curio shop:

> I had a fearful row with the deputy mayor at the Town hall the other day over the saloon or horrible place next to us. The proprietor is the deputy mayor's biggest friend and as I am fighting

to have same place closed, he thought he would master me. Dear Ruita and Tihoni, you both cannot imagine what we are standing with that same place. Ever since we landed the fight began and still I am at it. This morning I called to the Courthouse for evidence on things I could never tell you [. . .] Terrible—Terrible—Terrible it is. The worst and lowest women and men get in there drinking, singing and speaking horrible words. Acting fearfully, etc, etc. The good public is shocked. We cannot read, nor write, no sleep before ½ nine and very often until eleven. Sundays it impossible to do a thing the whole day. It is so bad that sometimes I cry with anger. And all this is the result of Politic, trouble, and favoritism.

No doubt it takes time to attract people to anything new like the Beautiful Bahai Cause, but where there is a will there is a way, and if there is no way we make one. But as long as our government tolerates places like the one near our home, we will have a hard battle. But do not be afraid, Lulu and Martha will find the way, as we always promised and believe. Time is what we need and the rest will come itself.[21]

Although his teaching efforts withered, Georges coveted the hope that he could be instrumental in raising the first Tahitian-born Bahá'í. John and Louise suggested this to him in a letter and explained that if a child were born a Bahá'í on that island, that child could become a cornerstone of a future Bahá'í community. Georges became inspired by this idea:

"Allah-u-Abha"
Papeete, April 29, 1928
Dear Ruita and Tihoni
Your nice long letter found us as usual; well and happy. How we enjoyed reading its contents, how we felt proud over all you

say about us and to know that Tihoni will say a few words to the believers in Chicago [at the United States Bahá'í National Convention] about us here in far away Tahiti.

But above all how pleasing it is to hear and to know all what you've told us about the great number of followers in the Great Cause. Oh how we would be happy to have started the work down here to be able to tell you and everyone else that the first Bahai stone has been layed.

Since our return here we have told you all and the reason of the delay; but never mind how long it will take, the stone will be layed one of these days. Do not worry our dear Sister and Brother in "El Abha."

And to prove my or our "Faith" we want to make a "Bahai" out of our grandson Oscar Alcide Georges Tamahere Spitz, here our eldest son's first child.

Kindly let us know what to do about it. Has the Bahai any baptism? or not. That would be a splendid first stone for the foundation of "Bahaism" here.

Thank you, our dear ones, for your wishes which fill us with joy.

Yes, Lulu wishes he was going to that Chicago convention with dear Tihoni and to enjoy that <u>TEA</u> from Haifa, the City of our Beloved Lord.

How great the work of "Father and Mother Dunn" in Australia; how happy they must feel over it.

We will love to meet them when they do call to see Tahiti.

I, Lulu, will try to think to write them [. . .].

Martha my dear wife and myself are fine and always busy.

Sincere love from both of us to you dear Ruita and Tihoni.

(Signed) Martha and Ruru[22]

Ironically, after struggling against what he described as the "dirty politics" of Papeete, Spitz decided to join the political arena, a decision that took him further away from the protection and guidance of Bahá'í principles. Louise recognized this danger and, at the top of the original letter received from Georges Spitz, she wrote a note to herself that reads "Write to Paris for a translation of Shoghi's *Dispensation.*"

The Dispensation of Bahá'u'lláh is an epistle regarded as Shoghi Effendi's own will and testament, and it outlines the stations of the Báb, Bahá'u'lláh, and 'Abdu'l-Bahá and describes the safeguards of the Administrative Order. Furthermore, *The Dispensation of Bahá'u'lláh* outlines "certain truths which lie at the basis of our Faith" that the Guardian said will "powerfully reinforce the vigor of our spiritual life."[23] *The Dispensation of Bahá'u'lláh* may have fallen on deaf ears by the time it reached Georges Spitz, who was now forty-nine years old, had abandoned a spiritual solution to his community's problems, and had replaced it with highly unpromising political efforts. This letter from Georges Spitz is the only letter of all of the forty-six letters he sent to the Bosches where he omits the accustomed salutation "Alláh'u'Abhá," which means "God is Most Great," and it is the last letter the Bosches received from him:

Papeete, January 29th, 1934
Dear Ruita and Tihoni,

Please excuse my, or our, very late reply to your many and kind letters and printed matter. I have been so very busy in mind and everything else that I have even neglected my own work. And my health, of course, has not been good during and since the great fight I had to lead and win with my good and clean friends.

Some of our officials wanted to deport me; I was dragged in court but I came out on top. The battle is not altogether over as some of the bad eggs are still holding their position. The worse one, the acting Governor of the time, has been called home; the second bad egg is leaving soon. Three or four more and our dear little Tahiti will be cleared of its filth.

Never in our history has anyone else stood or fought like we did during the latter part of 1933. Our new Delegate at Paris paid us a visit and his report is well-known by now [. . .]. Lack of education prevented me accepting the Mayor's job after Cassiau's death. Georges Bambridge is the new Mayor. He is a Tahiti born.

The $9.00 reached me; you should not have done so. I am more and more ashamed of myself when I think of all my promises to do such a lot for the cause.

The older I get, the more I estrange from everything called religion, etc. I have undergone and have seen so much injustices that I have become a free thinker. I am almost disgusted with everything called government. I have suffered so much for doing good to my people that I am surprised to feel myself alive or out of the asylum where the many crooks of Tahiti wanted me to go.

I don't think my health will ever get back to where it should be. That's my recompense for fighting the dirty politics of our far-away little group of islands.

Our friend Alexandre Drollet is as bitter against everything. He was one of US during the great fight. Mr. Drollet now lives at Mataiea; I will send word to him [. . .].

Everyone at home outside of Lulu is well.

All wish you both "BONNE SANTE."

Ever yours,

Ruru[24]

Georges Spitz remained in John and Louise's thoughts. Georges' lack of correspondence was a clear sign of his apathy toward the Cause, but John and Louise did not allow his apathy to estrange them. The following letter from Louise to Georges is an example of the transparency of her affection for him, and it is difficult to imagine that Georges Spitz was not influenced, even slightly, by Louise's broad and encouraging vision of the future:

Geyserville, California, U.S.A.
September 16, 1939

Our dear Ruru,

Lacking new letters from you, we have been reading over your dear old ones again.

Now that the world is going through such difficulties, we think of all our friends in Tahiti, and especially of you. We are happy to tell you that the Cause is now stronger than ever before. It has spread even to parts of the African continent, and there is also a National Spiritual Assembly of the Bahá'ís of Australia and New Zealand.

Under the Guardianship of Shoghi Effendi, and the strong Administrative Order which he has established in accord with the Will and Testament of Abdu'l-Baha, the Faith is already a realization of the world unity which Baha'u'llah has promised.

We know that even more troubled times are ahead, but the Guardian assures us of lasting victory and a new world civilization, to follow the present world chaos.

Dear Ruru, will you please write us soon [. . .] John and I are very well, and always thinking of you. With loving Baha'i greetings to you, Martha and the children,

Ever yours,

Ruita[25]

Georges Spitz died in Tahiti in 1949. He is featured in the "*Histoire de L'Assemblee de la Polynésie Française*" in an article called "*Personnages remarquables*" ("Remarkable Persons") wherein he is recognized for his twenty-five years as deputy mayor of Papeete. It is clear that Spitz's intentions toward the betterment of society were sincere. His numerous letters to the Bosches suggest that he understood how lasting societal change begins when the members of that society avoid the pitfall of finding fault with one another. Bahá'u'lláh warns, "Speak no evil, that thou mayest not hear it spoken unto thee, and magnify not the faults of others that thine own faults may not appear great; and wish not the abasement of anyone, that thine own abasement be not exposed."[26]

Louise understood the value of these Hidden Words from Bahá'u'lláh, and she presented Bahá'u'lláh's wisdom to Georges Spitz in the most gentle way:

Thursday night, May 14, 1929
Dearest Ruru,
When the great confirmation will have descended upon you, the confirmation of the fire of the love of God, and a confirmation of which you are capable of, then you will find excuses upon excuses for even the greatest sinners among men. Your heart will overflow with compassion and mercy.

Ah my dearest Ruru, you will be so changed that you yourself will be unable to recognize yourself.

These are the wonders of God and His miracles. It is unbelievable what transformations can take place in a true believer.

God is doing it unbeknown to ourselves, when sufficient sacrifice on our part has been rendered and when our hearts have become severed from the things of this world. This may take ten, twenty, thirty, or fifty years, time is nothing with God, but evolution is a quality of the human soul and it will finally reach perfection.

For this perfection is in store for you, it is in reserve for you and one day you will possess it. At that time, you will understand the reason of things, you will understand why this one or that one is bad or demoralized, and with that knowledge comes love for that defective one. This is one of the laws of God.[27]

Although Georges Spitz's desire was that his newborn grandson would become the "splendid first stone for the foundation of 'Baha-ism'" in Tahiti, it would not be so. Genealogy records show that Georges Spitz's first grandson, Oscar, was born in 1928, died in 1970 at the age of forty-two, and had no children. It is actually the family of Alexandre Drollet that may well be that "splendid first stone" of the establishment of the Cause of Bahá'u'lláh in Tahiti because several of his descendants are Bahá'ís. What a wonderful blessing for the Drollet family—a blessing given to them by 'Abdu'l-Bahá in the following Tablet addressed to the Bosches:[28]

To his honor Mr. Bosch and Mrs. Bosch
Upon them be Baha'u'llah El Abha!
He is the El Abha!
O ye two blessed souls:
Truly I say you have arisen in the service of the Kingdom of God, you hastened to the Island of Tahiti, summoned the people to the Daybreak of the Sun of Reality and become the cause of the guidance of souls.
Convey to Mr. Alexandre Drollet on my behalf the utmost respect and happiness. It is my hope that that honorable family may become the means of the enkindlement of the glowing Fire of the Love of God in that Island;—so that the splendors of the Sun of Truth may shine forth and the verses of Guidance be chanted. Rest ye assured in the Confirmations of His Highness Baha'u'llah which are descending uninterruptedly.[. . .]
Upon ye be Baha El Abha,
[Signed] 'Abdu'l-Baha Abbas.
May 1, 1921
Acca, Bahji
Translated by M.A. Sohrab[29]

John and Louise returned to San Francisco from Tahiti on September 9, 1920, exactly five months from their arrival in Tahiti. To a casual observer, their teaching efforts in Tahiti may seem to have yielded little fruit. Decades later, in 1953, the Guardian launched an ambitious teaching campaign called the Ten Year Crusade, which had four main goals to be carried out over a ten-year period: the further development of Bahá'í institutions at its World Center in Haifa, Israel;

the consolidation of the twelve countries in the world where the Bahá'í Faith was already well-established; the consolidation of territories of the world already opened to the Bahá'í Faith; and the opening of the "chief remaining virgin territories" around the globe that had, as yet, not been established as having permanent Bahá'í communities.[30]

When the Guardian launched the Ten Year Crusade and named those "virgin territories," two women from Australia arose to fill the post in Tahiti. They were Miss Gladys Irene Parker and Miss Gretta Stevens Lamprill, both in their sixties. Gladys was hostess at the Haziratu'l-Quds in Sidney. (*Haziratu'l-Quds* means *sacred fold* in Arabic, and the name is used to refer to a Bahá'í national administrative center). Gretta was secretary of the National Spiritual Assembly of Australia. When the Guardian called for pioneers, Gretta Lamprill and Gladys Parke sent a cable to the Guardian: SHALL LAMPRILL PARKE VOLUNTEER TEACH TAHITI. The cabled reply from the Guardian read: HEARTILY APPROVE. LOVE, SHOGHI. The "twin G's," as they were called, arrived at their pioneering post in December of 1953 and, in time, established the first Spiritual Assembly of Tahiti. In recognition of their service in the Ten Year Crusade, they were both named Knights of Bahá'u'lláh by Shoghi Effendi. Surely the spiritual success of these two women rests, in part, on the spiritual foundations established in Tahiti by John and Louise Bosch.[31]

Louise is often noted for saying that we may never know of the fruits of our teaching efforts until we reach the next world. Nevertheless, there are promises of spiritual rewards for the soul who travels away from his or her homeland to teach the Cause of God. In the section of the Tablets of the Divine Plan wherein the Master lists Polynesia as a goal territory, He explains what will happen when a believer pioneers to spread the Message of Bahá'u'lláh to these territories: "The moment this divine Message is carried forward by the American believers from the shores of America and is propagated through the continents of Europe, of Asia, of Africa and of Australasia, and as far as the islands of the Pacific, this community will find itself securely established upon the throne of an everlasting dominion. Then will all the peoples of the world witness that this community is spiritually illumined and divinely guided. Then will the whole earth resound with the praises of its majesty and greatness.[32]

Although their pioneering adventure to Tahiti lasted only five months, John and Louise achieved their purpose of planting the seeds ahead of a future time when those seeds would yield fruit. 'Abdu'l-Bahá described this process in this way:

> These are the days of seed sowing. These are the days of tree planting. The bountiful bestowals of God are successive. He who sows a seed in this day will behold his reward in the fruits and harvest of the heavenly Kingdom. This timely seed, when planted in the hearts of the beloved of God, will be watered by showers of divine mercy and warmed by the sunshine of divine love. Its fruitage and flower shall be the solidarity of mankind, the perfection of justice and the praiseworthy attributes of heaven manifest in humanity. All who sow such a seed and plant such a tree according to the teachings of Bahá'u'lláh shall surely witness this divine outcome in the degrees of its perfection and will attain unto the good pleasure of the Merciful One.[33]

A year after John and Louise returned from Tahiti, they journeyed to Haifa to see the Master. Louise wrote the following:

> We did not stay long at home after our return to America, but set out again as soon as we had sufficiently recovered from the effect of our sojourn in a tropical climate. It was just about a year after the above occurrences that we found ourselves in Haifa, Palestine, in the presence of 'Abdu'l-Bahá.
>
> We were, of course, most anxious to tell Him of our stay in Tahiti. During our first day in Haifa we made several attempts to draw His attention to our experiences there. On the following

day some Persian pilgrims, who had arrived in Haifa a few days before us, came to the Pilgrim House in the early morning from the Tomb of Bahá'u'lláh, bringing with them from the Tomb a handkerchief full of blossoms. These they emptied into a dish which they set upon the dining table. How great was my surprise when I noticed among these blossoms the national flower of Tahiti, there called the "Diadem." I had not known that this most fragrant flower grew elsewhere, as here in Akka. In Tahiti wreaths are made of these flowers. Loti says that both men and women wear them, and we have witnessed this.

I could not refrain from telling 'Abdu'l-Bahá, when He came to lunch with us at the Pilgrim House, of this coincidence. He looked weary and spoke but little. Could I have foreseen that within a very few days 'Abdu'l-Bahá would be taken from us I should hardly have ventured to trouble Him. In my ignorance, however, I asked for permission to speak, which was granted. I then told of some Tahitians who had made wreaths of these flowers for our heads. I had not mentioned any of the humble circumstances leading to the making of these wreaths when 'Abdu'l-Bahá said: "You must try to attain to the diadem of the flowers of Christ... These flowers here wither quickly, whereas those others remain forever fresh." I looked at Him. I had not understood. He then said, "The flowers of Christ are the disciples of Christ."

Another day I laid the photograph of an old full-blooded Tahitian lady of several generations back at 'Abdu'l-Bahá's place at the table. He took it up and looked at it, asking whose it was. I told Him it was the picture of the wife of a native chief whose present-day descendants had listened to the Message we had taken to them. His reply: "She was a good tree, she has borne good fruit!"[34]

7 / 'Abdu'l-Bahá is in the Utmost Longing to See You

Seven months after their return from Tahiti, John and Louise wrote to 'Abdu'l-Bahá requesting permission to visit Him. On April 8, 1921, they received a telegram from the Master that read: "Bosches permitted. Abbas."[1] By the end of April, they set out on a journey to Haifa, which was preceded by a modest teaching trip through Europe, where they visited the regions of their childhood. They traveled through France, Switzerland, Germany, and Italy, and they reached Haifa on November 14, 1921. For Louise, it was her second pilgrimage. For John, it was his first. They would be among the last pilgrims to be in the physical presence of the Master.

There were six Western pilgrims in Haifa in the two weeks leading up to the ascension of 'Abdu'l-Bahá on November 28th: Dr. Florian and Grace Krug from New York, John and Louise Bosch from California, Ethel Rosenberg from London, and Fraulein Johanna Hauff from Stuttgart. The only other Western believer present in Haifa at the time was Curtis Kelsey from the United States, who was in Haifa to install electrical lighting in the Shrine of the Báb.[2] Because of the profound significance of the events that unfolded before, during, and after the passing of 'Abdu'l-Bahá, it is important to understand something about the lives of these seven Western believers who were present at the time of His ascension.

Dr. Florian Krug, a successful surgeon in New York, became a Bahá'í directly through 'Abdu'l-Bahá when the Master visited his home in 1912. Grace Krug was Florian's second wife, and she became the stepmother of young Charles and Louise Krug. The following account of Dr. Krug's acceptance of 'Abdu'l-Bahá is recorded by Marzieh Gail in her book *Arches of the Years:*

There were historic family quarrels after Grace, their determined stepmother, became a Bahá'í. The siblings cowered, watched and trembled on their perch at the head of the stairs, as their father below them would scream at his wife and hurl down Bahá'í books.

In spite of everything, Grace Krug invited the Master to speak at their home, and the young people heard their father shouting, "If that old man comes into this house I'll have the doorman throw him out!" Both Charles and Louise Krug described the fateful day of the visit. Charles said his father's attitude was: "Now I can get my hands on the ringleader of this bunch!"

Louise Krug said, "We were terrified. Charlie and I were standing there by the door as 'Abdu'l-Bahá came in. He put His arms out with that wonderful gesture—you could feel the love pouring out. He walked right up to my father and looked him straight in the face. And He said: "'Dr Krug, are you happy?'"

"I don't know," Louise [Krug] went on, "my father just wilted. He was like a bird letting its wings down, to enjoy the sun. From that time on, never a word against the Master."[3]

While in Haifa, the Krugs were given the room of 'Abdu'l-Bahá during their stay, and 'Abdu'l-Bahá took another room across the garden in the main house. Grace Krug remembers the moment of hearing of the Master's ascension:

We retired as usual, but Dr. Krug had a premonition that he would be called to the Master's bedside before morning. About one fifteen o'clock we were awakened by screams from the Master's house, "Come Dr. Krug, the Master, the Master!" Like a flash, the Doctor was up, dressed, out of the room and across the garden into the house. You see, friends, had we not occupied 'Abdu'l-Bahá's room over the garage, Dr. Krug could not have reached the Master so quickly. I stood absolutely petrified with fear. Finally I was able to slip a one-piece dress over my night robe and rushed after the Doctor. Friends, how can I describe that scene in the Master's bedroom! Dr. Krug stood in the center, his hand raised, saying: "Silence, our Beloved Master has ascended."[4]

Another Western believer on pilgrimage in November 1921 was Ethel Rosenberg. In 1899, she was the first English-born woman to become a Bahá'í through the teaching efforts of May Bolles (Maxwell). She was forty years old when she became a Bahá'í, and over the next thirty-two years of her life, Ethel visited the Master in Haifa on three separate occasions, stayed for long periods, and received instruction from the Master Himself. Perhaps the most notable instruction she received from 'Abdu'l-Bahá was the answer to her question about Bahá'u'lláh's "Tablet of Wisdom," wherein Bahá'u'lláh explained that the philosophers of the ancient world "acquired Wisdom from the treasury of prophethood" and that the "essence and the fundamentals of philosophy have emanated from the Prophets." Ethel Rosenberg's biographer wrote that her "curiosity to know more of, and understand better, the teachings of Bahá'u'lláh led to her questioning 'Abdu'l-Bahá about the fact that Bahá'u'lláh's account of the Greek philosophers differed from other historical documents. In reply to Ethel Rosenberg, 'Abdu'l-Bahá wrote a Tablet known as the 'Rosenberg Tablet' wherein He explained that 'Holy Writ is authoritative, and with it no history of the world can compare.'"[5]

Ethel Rosenberg was beloved of 'Abdu'l-Bahá's family, and after the passing of the Master, the Guardian relied on her impeccable usage of the English and French languages to assist him with translations of the sacred texts. On this point of her mastery of the art of the English language, Ethel Rosenberg's biographer further notes "at the very end of her life, Ethel worked with [George] Townshend in the final major achievement of her distinguished life of service to the Bahá'í Cause— assisting Shoghi Effendi in the translation of the *Hidden Words* of Bahá'u'lláh into matchless and majestic English." Upon Ethel Rosenberg's first visit to Haifa in 1901 she met the young Shoghi Effendi who would have been a child of only four years of age at that time and she knew him twenty years later when he was at Oxford. When Shoghi Effendi became the Guardian of the Cause, Ethel Rosenberg served as one of his first corresponding secretaries. She is named in the document *Century of Light* as one of those great heroes who are among "a galaxy of unforgettable women who became the principal exponents of the Bahá'í message on both sides of the Atlantic." Upon her passing on November 17, 1930 at the age of seventy-two, the Guardian sent this cable to the Bahá'ís of the world:[6]

DEEPLY GRIEVED PASSING ROSENBERG ENGLAND'S OUTSTANDING BAHÁ'Í PIONEER WORKER. MEMORY HER GLORIOUS SERVICE WILL NEVER DIE ABDU'L-BAHÁ'S FAMILY JOIN ME IN EXPRESSING HEARTFELT CONDOLENCES HER BROTHER RELATIVES URGE FRIENDS HOLD BEFITTING MEMORIAL SERVICE. SHOGHI[7]

Along with the Krugs and Ethel Rosenberg, there was Johanna Hauff, the daughter of a Bahá'í family from Stuttgart, Germany. When 'Abdu'l-Bahá made His journey to the West, He visited Stuttgart and made several public addresses there. John and Louise stopped in Stuttgart on their way to Haifa, so it is likely that Johanna joined their party from there. Johanna Hauff's age in 1921 is not known, but in his memoirs, Ali Yazdi writes of having visited the Hauff family in 1919 when 'Abdu'l-Bahá sent him to Germany to contact the Stuttgart believers after the war. Johanna Hauff was the oldest of the three Hauff children, so she may not have been beyond her teen years.[8] Her youthfulness is particularly tender in her letters written to her parents in Germany after the passing of 'Abdu'l-Bahá—and how wonderful to have a youthful point of view of such a spiritual experience. She wrote two letters to her parents describing events that had taken place. The following are excerpts from each letter:

> Haifa, Palestine, November 28, 1921
> What terrible hours were these tonight at the deathbed of the beloved Master! At one o'clock at night (Monday morning) we were called and told the Master was very low. Quickly we went down into the sorrowing house, to His bedside; for a long time I did not know whether He was still with His body or had ascended into His Kingdom. He is no longer among us! Oh, no, we must not say this; His spirit is perhaps a thousand times nearer to us; but it is incredible, unbelievable, because this great loss came so swift—so unexpected. We are all stunned. I cannot say anything; I do not know what will happen![9]

> Haifa, Palestine, December 3, 1921
> As in a dream these last days have passed. Since I wrote to you on Monday, after the incredible had happened—incredible because it happened so unexpectedly—much has come to pass. Before I tell you something about it, I wish to thank you from the bottom of my heart, that you let me come here, that I was allowed to be here during these wonderful, hard and indescribably beautiful times [. . .] I am not worth it, that those radiant, luminous, penetrating blue eyes should have rested on me, that that kind mouth should have spoken loving, beautiful words to me—and how useless my life would appear to me if the power of the experience does not give me strength to really remold my life and to lead it to a high purpose.[10]

Aside from the Bosches, the Krugs, Miss Rosenberg and Miss Hauff, the only other Western believer present in Haifa at the time of the passing of 'Abdu'l-Bahá was Mr. Curtis Kelsey from the United States.

Curtis Kelsey lived in New York, and through Dr. Krug he learned of the Faith of Bahá'u'lláh, became a Bahá'í in 1917 at the age of twenty-three, and was subsequently elected to the Spiritual Assembly of New York that same year. Around that time, 'Abdu'l-Bahá was making plans to install the first electrical lighting to illumine the mausoleum of the Báb. (The dome and superstructure were not completed until 1953.) One of Curtis Kelsey's fellow Spiritual Assembly members, Roy Wilhelm, had been corresponding with the Master about this endeavor. In the "In Memoriam" article written about Curtis Kelsey, Florence Mayberry wrote:

Roy one day asked Curtis, "How would you like to go to Haifa?" Roy had sent three lighting plants to the Holy Land and had written to 'Abdu'l-Bahá asking that Curtis, whose hobby was electricity, be permitted to install them. The Master replied by cable: CURTIS KELSEY PERMITTED. Curtis felt very strongly that he must go at once, sold his possessions and with some financial help from his father and Roy Wilhelm left almost immediately.

He arrived in the Holy Land in September, 1921, and stayed until April of the next year, during which time he illumined the Shrine of the Báb, the Mansion at Bahjí and the home of 'Abdu'l-Bahá, No. 7 Haparsim Street, Haifa. The Master passed away on November 28, 1921, before the completion of the work, but His wish, that the lights be turned on, the first time, simultaneously, was fulfilled. Curtis often said he did not fully appreciate at the time the priceless privilege bestowed upon him, but as the years passed and his awareness deepened, the full realization impressed itself upon him. He was able to repair the car that had been a gift to 'Abdu'l-Bahá and in which he took the Master for rides; he walked with Him by moonlight along the shore of the Mediterranean; he stood behind Him in the Shrine of Bahá'u'lláh while the Master chanted the Tablet of Visitation; he ate his meals with 'Abdu'l-Bahá; even his diet was selected for him by the Master.

On one occasion 'Abdu'l-Bahá summoned Curtis into His room, had him sit opposite Him, and just looked into his eyes for several minutes, not saying anything.[11]

Curtis Kelsey was twenty-seven years old when he made the first installation of lights for the resting place of the Báb. Having been a Bahá'í for only four years, his Spiritual Assembly in New York must have been filled with joy and awe upon hearing of Mr. Kelsey's role in assisting 'Abdu'l-Bahá in fulfilling one of His lifelong determinations to bathe the Shrine of the Báb in light. Dr. Ziá Bagdádí, an Eastern believer living in Chicago, wrote to the members of the Spiritual Assembly of the Bahá'ís of New York City. It is important to note that this letter was written on June 9, 1922, after the ascension of 'Abdu'l-Bahá:

I beg to inform you of the joyful report this servant received from Haifa in regards to the illumined and sincere youth, Mr. Curtis Kelsey, who has been wonderfully blessed and confirmed in rendering one of the great services to the Cause of God. He has successfully illumined the Holy Shrines of Bahá'u'lláh, 'Abdu'l-Bahá and the Báb, and above all the blessed Master was very pleased with him. This is, I am sure, because of the purity of his heart, sincerity of his aim and obedience to the blessed Commands. Verily, God confirms whomsoever He wishes in whatsoever He wishes.

I will never forget how the Master acted and what He said regarding the illumination of the Blessed Shrine (of the Báb). It was on the anniversary of the martyrdom of His Holiness the Báb, while all pilgrims were at the Sacred Shrine. The beloved Master remained silent for (a) few minutes standing at the Holy Threshold. His silence broke with gushing tears and (He) cried loudly, saying: In all the years of imprisonment (in Máh-kú), *the Báb spent all the nights in utter darkness. Yea, not even a candle was allowed* (Him) . . . Therefore, God willing, I shall illumine His Sublime Shrine with one hundred electric lamps. . . . Now the news has come that on the last day of the Feast of Ridván (April 1922) the three Blessed Shrines were illumined with electricity and the light is flooding the Bay of 'Akká. Indeed, Mr. Kelsey deserves a thousand praises and commendations.[12]

In thinking about these seven Western believers, one cannot help but wonder at this propitious assemblage of souls present at such a calamity as the ascension of 'Abdu'l-Bahá—souls that could arise to the requisite needs that such a spiritual and historically significant event would demand. It is known that the Master made necessary plans to ensure that the integrity of the Cause would be preserved even at the very moment of His passing. In *The Priceless Pearl*, Rúhíyyih Khánum confirms that "a few weeks before 'Abdu'l-Bahá died, suddenly He came into the room where Shoghi Effendi's father was and said, 'Cable Shoghi Effendi to return (from Oxford) at once.' His mother told us that on hearing this she consulted with her mother and it was decided that to cable risked shocking Shoghi Effendi unnecessarily and so they would write to him the Master's instruction; the letter arrived after He had ascended."[13]

Munavvar Khánum, one of the daughters of 'Abdu'l-Bahá, also affirms that the Master anticipated His ascension. In a letter to Mrs. Ruth Randall in Boston, dated December 22, 1921, Munavvar Khánum wrote the following: "The beloved Master knew exactly beforehand when he would leave us. The reason I know this so certainly is on account of a dream which he had about two weeks before the end (the dream was that Bahá'u'lláh appeared to him and said: 'Destroy this room in which you are' (the 'room' being his blessed body), and also because he requested us to send for Shoghi Effendi to come back from Oxford, England, 'for a very great and important reason,' as he said."[14]

Some of these Western pilgrims who were present at 'Abdu'l-Bahá's passing seemed to fulfill a specific purpose that arose out of the events that unfolded: Curtis Kelsey served to fulfill the final wish of 'Abdu'l-

Bahá, Dr. Krug served as physician, Ethel Rosenberg served as a trusted assistant to Shoghi Effendi, Johanna Hauff served as a youthful observer, and Louise served as correspondent to the Western believers. Even the dynamics between these pilgrims gave the Master an opportunity to give final instructions about how the friends should regard their fellow man. For instance, in her book *Arches of the Years*, Marzieh Gail relates a story told by Dr. Krug's son, Charles Krug, who explained to Marzieh Gail that his father was not a naturally congenial man:

"Father had crotchets, and he might for no reason take a dislike to someone. Among those whom he took a dislike to was the famed early Bahá'í, Ethel Rosenberg.

One day in the Holy Land, 'Abdu'l-Bahá was giving a talk on love and unity. The Master said that we must learn to love everybody.

Dr. Krug said, 'Everybody, 'Abdu'l-Bahá?'

'Yes, Dr. Krug, everybody.' Then pointing His finger, 'Abdu'l-Bahá said: 'But you stay away from Miss Rosenberg!'"[15]

A week after the passing of 'Abdu'l-Bahá, Louise wrote to Ella Cooper about the Master's design in having them there: "The holy mother [Monireh Khánum, the wife of 'Abdu'l-Bahá] said that we could never in this life appreciate the privilege of having been here [in Haifa] at just this time. She said that in our presence here all of the American friends were also present, and in Johanna Hauff's presence here, all the German friends were present."[16]

In addition to these seven Western believers present at the time of the Master's ascension, there were many Eastern pilgrims present, as well as the members of the holy family. Despite the intimation made by the Master Himself, His passing was unexpected by the members of His household. In a letter to the friends in England, Ethel Rosenberg recounts two occasions when the Master indicated that He knew His ascension was near. Here is that letter, in part:

Haifa, Palestine, December 8, 1921
Beloved friends in England,
I know so well how heartbroken you have all been at this (for *us*) sad, sad news and how you must all be longing for a word directly from this sacred spot—made doubly sacred for all of us now as it is the resting-place of our Beloved Abdul-Baha [. . .].

During the previous week he had given his family many hints of His approaching end, if they had but understood them.

To Rouhi Effendi he said, "I have decided to go far away, where no one can reach me." Rouhi Effendi and another young man who was present thought he was joking and Rouhi Effendi said, "You know, Master, that is impossible; they will always find you."

About ten days before the end, he left his little bedroom in the garden and came into the house. He told his family that he had dreamed in the night that BAHA 'ULLAH had come to him, and had said, "Destroy this room immediately," and therefore he did not like to sleep outside any more, but would come into the house. The family were thankful, as they felt he would be nearer to them if he needed any service during the night. They now understand the spiritual symbolism of the saying—the "room" being the Beloved One's body.[17]

Before the passing of 'Abdu'l-Bahá, one of the members of the holy family took his own life when he suspected that the Master's death was imminent. The day after the ascension of 'Abdu'l-Bahá, one of the Persian teachers in Haifa, Ahmad Tabrizi, wrote to Dr. Ziá Bagdádí, a member of the editorial staff of *Star of the West*, appealing to him to educate the friends about the Master's teachings forbidding suicide. Here is the letter, in part:

Haifa, Palestine, November 29, 1921
My dear brother:

I am grieved to announce to you in brief that the Master, Abdul-Baha, has ascended to the Kingdom by his own will. In some of his writings and Tablets which are not yet made public, he clearly stated in regard to his departure. [. . .] Mirza Abul Hassan Afnan (a noble gentleman from the family of the Bab, for many years living near Abdul-Baha), realizing the approach of the most great calamity—the Master's ascension—could not wait to see it, and therefore he drowned himself here, in the sea.

The Master, in advising us and all the friends, said: "You must not injure yourselves or commit suicide. . . . It is not permissible to do to yourselves what Mirza Hassan Afnan did to himself. Should anyone at any time encounter hard and perplexing times, he must say to himself, 'This will soon pass.' Then he will be calm and quiet. In all my calamity and difficulties I used to say to myself, 'This will pass away.' Then I became patient. If anyone cannot be patient and cannot endure, and if he wishes to become a martyr, then let him arise in service to the Cause of God. It will be better for him if he attains to martyrdom in His path. Arise ye in service to the Cause of God as the Apostles arose after the departure of Christ."

The Master has left a will, which is His Covenant, written with his own blessed hand. As soon as it is read, I shall write to you what it contains. It is the hour of firmness and the moment of steadfastness. Blessed are those who are faithful to the Cause and loyal to the Covenant.

Your brother,
Ahmad[18]

The concern about protecting the friends from resorting to suicide was repeated by Louise Bosch in a letter to Ella Cooper about what Ahmad Tabrizi had written. Louise's explanation shows the clarity of her mind, the understanding of her heart, and the consecration of her soul: "Yesterday one of the Persian teachers said that if it were not for the closing of the doors of suicide and the opening of the doors of martyrdom, many Persian believers would now find it unendurable. As the expenditure of life through martyrdom is accepted before God, so we may soon hear of many Persian Bahais killed; they will throw themselves recklessly into the stream of the consequences of fearless open teaching."[19]

The news of the ascension of 'Abdu'l-Bahá spread rapidly through the city, the region, and indeed throughout the whole world. Thousands of people of various faiths, race, and rank gathered for His funeral; any differences of religion, race, and rank receded behind the unifying forces released by the Master's ministry. Shoghi Effendi wrote that the passing of 'Abdu'l-Bahá "brought to a close the ministry of One Who was the incarnation, by virtue of the rank bestowed upon Him by His Father, of an institution that has no parallel in the entire field of religious history, a ministry that marks the final stage in the Apostolic, the Heroic and most glorious Age of the Dispensation of Bahá'u'lláh."[20]

At such a pivotal moment in Bahá'í history, a special honor awaited John Bosch—one that he could never have imagined: the sacred privilege of helping to place the precious body of the Master into His coffin and to assist in bearing the coffin upon his shoulder as it was carried from the room where the Master had ascended. John Bosch's account of the preparation of the Master's precious body is held at the United States Bahá'í Archives and printed here in part:

> The hour for the funeral had been set for nine-o'clock the next morning, Tuesday, November 29th [. . .]. By eight o'clock the house, yards and garden were filled with mourners. They came in great numbers to attend the funeral. At half past eight a picture was taken of the room and the bed wherein Abdul Baha had passed away. In this picture the ladies of the family appeared.

Then another photograph was taken, with the sons-in-law and some others of the household surrounding the bed.

At a quarter to nine a sudden command was given to the hundred or more people who were standing in the large center hall. Instantly they all moved toward the front door, but my wife, Johanna and myself, not understanding what had been said, remained standing by the wall. In a moment Mirza Jalal, known to the believers as the son of the King of the Martyrs, appeared, and walking toward me, motioned for me to accompany him. I did not know what he wanted, but I followed as he led the way to one of the north rooms. As we entered the room I saw, to my surprise, a casket. It was very plain, of white wood, unpainted. We carried it across the hall to the room in which lay the body of Abdul Baha. We placed it upon two chairs, and when it was uncovered I observed that it was zinc lined. Two of the persons present placed in it a most exquisite silken comforter, leaving the sides hanging over. Turning to the bed, I noticed that the body of Abdul Baha was wrapped in three white silken sheets which were folded over him from both sides. Rouhi Effendi and others then prepared to place the body in the casket. They were at the head, Mirza Jalal at the center, I at the feet. We gently laid it [His body] in the casket and someone put a silken pillow under the head. The best attar of rose was sprinkled over Abdul Baha, then both sides of the comforter were drawn up and laid over him. The cover was then placed upon the casket and at once, as from an invisible command, six of us raised it to our shoulder, I being at the head. We carried it to the large room outside and lowered it to the floor. A beautiful ivory silk cover was laid over it, also one of the many wreaths that had been sent. A call was given, the doors were opened, and many people entered the room [. . .]. Sharply at nine o'clock the casket was lifted from the floor by the appointed pallbearers, who carried it out the front door, down the steps and through the gate, along the short street about the length of two of our city blocks, to the road which led up Mount Carmel.*

About 40 carriages were waiting at the gate to join in the funeral cortege, but only about five were occupied, as all who possibly could wished to honor the Master they had loved by humbly walking after his remains. Even the British High Commissioner, who had come specially from Jerusalem, walked with the others. Beside him, in full uniform, was the Chief of Police of Haifa, who had left his horse standing in the street near the house of Abdul Baha. The Governor of Phoenicia also walked. There were men of all nations, of all creeds, of all walks in life, high and low, rich and poor. It seemed that never had there been such a funeral procession before. So great was the desire to help carry the casket up the mountain that some of the men were wrangling for the privilege of only touching it with their finger tips. For an hour and a half that great mass of people slowly moved along the winding road up the steep incline of Mount Carmel.

It was a perfect day, one of the most beautiful one could imagine. As I turned and looked back now and then many were the thoughts that came to me as I watched all those people wending their way up the mountain. Ahead was the Tomb of the Bab. Behind were the blue Mediterranean and the bay of Haifa, and nine miles away was the old city of Akka, and in the far distance the Lebanon Mountains. Never can I forget that scene.[21]

Of the many thoughts that came to John in that scene, one must have been the memory of the Master asleep on his shoulder while riding in an automobile through the city of New York in 1912. Louise wrote to

---

* In 2019, the Universal House of Justice announced that 'Abdu'l-Bahá's permanent resting place and shrine would be built near the Ridván Garden, between 'Akká and Haifa.

Ella Cooper of this glorious privilege bestowed upon John: "Tomorrow it will be one week since we carried our blessed Lord's earthly temple to Mount Carmel. John had the great privilege that day to assist in carrying the coffin into the room which our Lord lay, and John also assisted in placing the holy body into the coffin. This is John's everlasting bounty for his services rendered to the Cause, and because of the privilege he had of lifting the holy body of his Lord, John can never be the same being any more. And he is and looks different, too."[22]

Although we cannot know for certain what was in the mind of 'Abdu'l-Bahá in the days preceding His passing, one cannot help wondering that John Bosch's arrival in the Holy Land at that time was providential. Marzieh Gail wrote that "John Bosch was one of those whom 'Abdu'l-Bahá chose as a companion for the time when He should leave the world. Afterward, the friends saw that the Master knew the moment of His passing and had prepared for it. Some who had asked permission to visit Him at that time, He had gently turned away, but to John He had written 'I am longing to see you.'"[23]

John and Louise received this assurance that the Master was "in the utmost longing" to see them, but they did not receive the Tablet until their return to America nearly a year later. As it happened, the Master wrote the Tablet to John and Louise six months before His ascension, but the Tablet was not translated until a year after the passing of 'Abdu'l-Bahá. What a touching confirmation it must have been for John and Louise to receive this Tablet after their return from the Holy Land. Surely it was an assurance that their presence during the Master's ascension was His wish. Here is the Tablet, in part:

To his honor Mr. Bosch and Mrs. Bosch
Upon them be Bahá'u'lláh El Abha!
He is the El Abha!
O ye two blessed souls,
You have permission to come into the presence in the coming winter or spring. 'Abdu'l-Baha is in the utmost longing to see you.

Upon ye be Baha El Abha,
(Signed) 'Abdu'l-Baha Abbas.
May 1, 1921
Acca, Bahji
Translated by M.A. Sohrab
December 14, 1922
Los Angeles, California[24]

In the following account of his last visit with the Master, John Bosch expressed how unworthy he felt of such attention:

The last time Abdul Baha spoke to me was in the morning of November 25, 1921, when I longed to have a glimpse of him. I entered the garden near his house where he gave instructions to the gardener and then he walked up and down the lane on the north side of the house taking exercise like most any morning, then picking a few oranges and mandarins from the trees with his own hands, giving them to the visitors there—several Persians, Hindus and Arabs were standing there—and then when he approached me he gave me one mandarin and said in English with his usual smile, "Eat! Good!" I always remember his words in the magnetic tone he spoke them to me. He seemed to be very happy at that time and smiled at me. I wondered then if I was worthy of that smile of our Master, not knowing then that I would be called to help laying his earthly body in the casket in the morning of the fourth day after this occurrence. He then walked into his house and at the same day at noon he came to lunch at the Pilgrim House where he spoke to several of us, and when serving rice when we only took a small portion he always said in English, "Again, again" meaning that we should again take rice and eat plenty. How wonderful it was to be a guest of the host of the world during his last days on earth. Never shall I forget the farewell of the Master. When he rose from the chair and after his usual ablution as is the custom there after meals, he proceeded towards the door, then turned to us and standing in a majestic position outstretching his hands toward us and then raising them to his forehead, his face illumined, said in a smiling way to all of us, three times, "Good afternoon. Good afternoon. Good afternoon." And with each time stretching his hands forward, palms upward, and raised them to his forehead. How happy we were to see him happy and how little we knew then that those were his last words to us.[25]

In the same account, John describes the night he and Louise were called to the house of the Master just moments after His soul ascended:

After midnight, we were awakened in the Pilgrim House by a few loud knocks given in rapid succession and we wondered what had happened. My watch pointed to 1:20 o'clock. My wife said, "Something must have happened to Abdul Baha. Let us hurry and find out what this unusual call is." In a few minutes we were running to the house of Abdul Baha where we found that it was only too true that our Master had just passed away. Doctors were leaving the house and we entered the room finding all of the family of Abdul Baha there, Abdul Baha resting in bed as though he were still alive. Approaching the bed I could not resist to take his hand, not trusting he was dead. It was warm and lifelike. Then I touched his forehead and hoped that he still might utter a word, but it was only too true that our Master had passed away, his spirit had departed. The Greatest Holy Leaf then kindly reached her hand to me and motioned me to sit beside her, which I did. The room became filled with friends and people from the town and the antechamber and the hall too became filled. It is indescribable to describe the sorrow and weeping uttered by the people in that hour. To me it seemed that thousands of thoughts went through my mind in those moments. Sometimes there comes to all of us feelings that sigh for expression when only our silence really registers the depth of our emotion, and our moist eyes suggest what words could never reveal, so I cannot express the deep stirrings within me when all in deep silence I arose again and touched the hand and forehead of Abdul Baha still warm. I said, "Oh Abdul Baha!" And Rizwanieh said later how they loved it that in the deep silence someone called the name of the Master. Again I was seated alongside the Greatest Holy Leaf who through her calmness was an example to us all. Through her poise and calmness a change came over me, a relief, the thought that our Master was at last released and relieved from all the persecutions and the answering to questions of all the friends and inquirers and curiosity seekers. I felt that his precious body now was at rest, his spirit alive, that we were all equal now regardless of position, that each and every one of us could find him and serve him only in spirit and in his teachings, the greatest of privileges and also the greatest of obligations![26]

John then explains that he was permitted to see the Master's body one last time before His burial: "Just before dark [on Monday, November 28th] Rouhi Effendi called us to say that we were permitted to have a last look at Abdul Baha." In a letter to her parents, Johanna Hauff describes this sacred moment: "Mr. and Mrs. Bosch, Dr and Mrs. Krug and I were almost constantly in the most intimate family circle. On Monday night we were permitted to see the face of the Master once more—the only ones besides the family. How beautiful it was! Such Peace! Such rest! I do not believe that I shall ever in my life see again such an unspeakably beautiful face as that of Abdul Baha in life and in death."[27]

Louise adds further spiritual insight to the sanctity and significance of that night. Metaphorically, the Master is often characterized as the "moon" and His Father the "Sun." The moon has no inherent light of its own; rather, it achieves all of its brilliance by becoming a perfect reflection of the light of the Sun. Louise writes of this analogy, in a letter to Ella Cooper dated December 5, 1921: "We [. . .] were in the room together with the holy family, and the Holy Mother [Moníreh Khánum, the wife of 'Abdu'l-Bahá] held my husband's hand and the Greatest Holy Leaf held mine. After a time we went back to the Pilgrim House, leaving the holy family alone. It was still night—no moon at all. Not long afterward the dawn broke, and at last the sun rose with great effulgence over the scene of this memorable night."[28]

The imagery of the sun and the moon allude to the Covenant of Bahá'u'lláh. Poetically, the imagery suggests that despite the darkness caused by the setting of the Sun (the ascension of the Bahá'u'lláh) and the passing of the Moon (the ascension of 'Abdu'l-Bahá), the Leaves of the tree of the Holy family, Moníreh Khánum and Bahíyyih Khánum, served as channels of that Light, much as a leaf photosynthesizes the light of the Sun and gives life to the tree. Bahíyyih Khánum, the sister of 'Abdu'l-Bahá, known as the Greatest Holy Leaf, arose to a capacity unrivaled by any woman in the history of religion: When Shoghi Effendi learned that he was named Guardian of the Cause of Bahá'u'lláh, he was devastated by the news and retreated to the mountains of Switzerland to conquer himself so that he would be fit to lead the Cause of Bahá'u'lláh.[30] While the Guardian was away for nine months, the Greatest Holy Leaf stood at the helm of the Cause at its darkest hour, and she maintained written correspondence with the Bahá'í world in the Guardian's absence. In one of her letters, the Greatest Holy Leaf explained Shoghi Effendi's temporary travel away from the Holy Land: "Since the ascension of our Beloved 'Abdu'l-Bahá, Shoghi Effendi has been moved so deeply [. . .] that he has sought the necessary quiet in which to meditate upon the vast task ahead of him, and it is to accomplish this that he has temporarily left these regions. During his absence he has appointed me as his representative, and while he is occupied in this great endeavour, the family of 'Abdu'l-Bahá is assured that you will all strive to advance triumphantly the Cause of Bahá'u'lláh."[29]

In *The Priceless Pearl*, Rúhíyyih Khánum explains that after the passing of 'Abdu'l-Bahá the members of the holy family looked for burial instructions for Him and "discovered His Will—which consists of three Wills written at different times and forming one document—addressed to Shoghi Effendi. It now became the painful duty of Shoghi Effendi to hear what was in it; a few days after his arrival they read it to him."[30] Shoghi Effendi was at Oxford when he received news of his Grandfather's passing and he did not arrive in the Holy Land until December 29, 1921, one month and a day after the passing of his beloved Grandfather.

Adib Taherzadeh, in his book *The Child of the Covenant*, explains the details of the reading of the Master's Will:

> Although the Will and Testament of 'Abdu'l-Bahá was read out to Shoghi Effendi soon after his arrival in Haifa, it had to be formally presented to the members of the family and others in the Holy Land. On 3 January 1922, in the presence of nine persons, mainly senior members of 'Abdu'l-Bahá's family, and in Shoghi Effendi's absence, the Will and Testament was read aloud and its seal, signature and handwriting were shown to those present. Later, the Greatest Holy Leaf sent cables to Persia and America—the two major communities at that time—informing them that according to the Will and Testament of 'Abdu'l-Bahá, Shoghi Effendi had been appointed "Guardian of the Cause of God."[31]

A few days after the formal reading of the Will, another reading was held at which John Bosch was present. He described the occasion in detail:

> On January 7th, just 40 days after the passing of Abdul Baha, at nine in the morning, we were invited to assemble in the large hall of the residence of Abdul Baha to listen to the reading of the will

'ABDU'L-BAHÁ IS IN THE UTMOST LONGING TO SEE YOU

and testament of Abdul Baha. It was in Arabic.* Jusuf Khan of Tihran, Persia, began to chant the first part of the testament. He began at 9:55 and finished at 10:50. That part of the testament (which had been affected by many years of dampness) had been written by Abdul Baha when Shoghi Effendi was about six years old, and therein Abdul Baha referred to him as "the young and tender branch." The second part was chanted by Muhammad Taki of Cairo. That part was finished at 11:20. Then followed the chanting of the third part by Jusuf Khan, which he finished at a quarter to twelve o'clock.

At this reading of the testament there were 120 persons present. Many had come specially from Cairo, Alexandria, Port Said, Jerusalem, Damascus, Beirut, Persia, India and England. Six Americans were present: Dr. and Mrs. Krug, Mrs. Hoagg.,** Curtis Kelsey of New York, John D. and Louise Bosch of California.[32]

Bahíyyih Khánum was very much aware of the Master's affection for John and Louise, and she invited the Bosches to stay with the Holy family during a forty-day period of mourning. The privilege of such intimate association with the members of the family of 'Abdu'l-Bahá at such a calamitous time is telling of their love for these two American believers. 'Abdu'l-Bahá demonstrated this love for John Bosch at a meeting held at His home nine days before He passed away. It was 'Abdu'l-Bahá's custom to host a regular six o'clock evening meeting

---

* Each of the three parts of the Will and Testament of 'Abdu'l-Bahá contains sections revealed in Arabic and sections revealed in Persian, according to Omid Ghaemmaghami, Assistant Professor of Arabic at Binghamton University (State University of New York). He holds a PhD in Middle Eastern and Islamic Studies from the University of Toronto and an MA in Islamic and Near Eastern Studies from Washington University in St. Louis.

** For further information on Imogene Hoagg, please see http://bahaiblog.net/2016/12/emogene-hoagg-spiritual-giant/.

called "The Persian Meeting," where He would discuss various aspects of Bahá'u'lláh's teachings and laws to as many as sixty friends at one time. It was at that meeting, held on November 19, 1921, that the Master invited John Bosch to attend. He was the only Western believer present. Dr. Lutfu'lláh Hakím took notes during the meeting, while Mírzá Mohammad Ali Afnan translated. Here is a portion of what 'Abdu'l-Bahá said at that gathering, which was His last public meeting at His home before His passing. 'Abdu'l-Bahá opened the meeting by speaking directly to Mr. Bosch:

> Although you are here with these assembled friends and cannot speak with them nor they with you, yet you can speak with one another through the heart. The language of the heart is even more expressive than the language of the tongue and is more truthful and has a wider reach and a more potent effect. When lovers meet it may be that they cannot exchange a single word, yet with their hearts they speak to one another. Thus do the clouds speak to the earth and the rain comes down; the breeze whispers to the trees; this is the way in which the hearts of the friends talk together. It is the harmony between two persons and this harmony is of the hearts. For instance, you were in America and I was in the Holy Land. Although our lips were still, yet with our hearts we were conversing together. The friends here love you very much. They have a real attachment for you, although with the tongue they cannot express it.[33]

Nearly two months had passed since John and Louise's arrival in Haifa. Their unique pilgrimage and extended stay with the Master's family had come to its end. The time had come for John and Louise to prepare for their reluctant departure from the Holy Land. John kept an hourly record of the events that followed: At 5:00 am on January 17, 1922, John Bosch visited the tomb of the Báb and 'Abdu'l-Bahá. At 8:30 am, John and Louise bid their farewell to the holy family and then to Shoghi Effendi, who took them to view the picture of Bahá'u'lláh. Then the Guardian made an extraordinary request of the Bosches: he entrusted a copy of portions of the Will and Testament of 'Abdu'l-Bahá to the worthy care of John and Louise Bosch, asking that they deliver this document to the Bahá'í National Convention in Chicago to be held in April of that year.[34]

It is important to note that it was the Greatest Holy Leaf, and not John and Louise, who would first communicate to America the contents of the Master's Will. The Greatest Holy Leaf cabled the United States on January 16, 1922: "In Will Shoghi Effendi is appointed Guardian of the Cause and Head of the House of Justice. Inform American friends."[35] Furthermore, John and Louise were not the only individuals to whom the Guardian gave early copies of the Will and Testament. Rúhíyyih Khánum wrote that immediately after the events following the Master's ascension,

> Shoghi Effendi selected eight passages from the Will and circulated them among the Bahá'ís; only one of these referred to himself, was very brief and was quoted as follows: "O ye the faithful ones of 'Abdu'l-Bahá! It is incumbent upon you to take the greatest care of Shoghi Effendi [. . .] For he is, after 'Abdu'l-Bahá, the guardian of the Cause of God, the Afnán, the Hand (pillars) of the Cause and the beloved of the Lord must obey him and turn unto him." Of all the thundering and tremendous passages in the Will referring to himself, Shoghi Effendi chose the least astounding and provocative to first circulate among the Bahá'ís. Guided and guiding he was from the very beginning.[36]

One can only imagine what it must have felt like to John and Louise when the Guardian entrusted portions of the Will and Testament to them. So astonishing is this honor, so sacred the privilege, so astounding the significance of bearing the Master's Will and Testament to America, that it is important to pause this narrative of John's life and consider the singular importance of the Will and Testament of 'Abdu'l-Bahá—a document the Guardian described as the Master's "greatest legacy to posterity, the brightest emanation of His mind and the mightiest instrument forged to insure the continuity" of Bahá'u'lláh's Dispensation.[37]

The Will and Testament of 'Abdu'l-Bahá, together with Bahá'u'lláh's Most Holy Book (the Kitáb-i-Aqdas), form the Charter for a new world civilization. Shoghi Effendi explains that the Will and Testament of 'Abdu'l-Bahá is unique in the history of religion, describing it as "the Document establishing that Order, the Charter of a future world civilization, which may be regarded in some of its features as supplementary to no less weighty a Book than the Kitáb-i-Aqdas; signed and sealed by 'Abdu'l-Bahá; entirely written with His own hand."[38]

In one of his letters to America, written seventeen years after the passing of 'Abdu'l-Bahá, the Guardian explains that the Will and Testament of 'Abdu'l-Bahá is the distinguishing feature of the Bahá'í Dispensation and the believers are urged "to grasp the fundamental difference existing between this world-embracing, divinely-appointed Order and the chief ecclesiastical organizations of the world."[39] Further in that letter, the Guardian elaborates on the schisms that divided the Dispensations of the past, and then asserts:

> Not so with the Revelation of Bahá'u'lláh. Unlike the Dispensation of Christ, unlike the Dispensation of Muḥammad, unlike all the Dispensations of the past, the apostles of Bahá'u'lláh in every land, wherever they labor and toil, have before them in clear, in unequivocal and emphatic language, all the laws, the regulations, the principles, the institutions, the guidance, they require for the prosecution and consummation of their task. Both in the administrative provisions of the Bahá'í Dispensation, and in the matter of succession, as embodied in the twin institutions of the House of Justice and of the Guardianship, the followers of Bahá'u'lláh can summon to their aid such irrefutable evidences of Divine

Guidance that none can resist, that none can belittle or ignore. Therein lies the distinguishing feature of the Bahá'í Revelation. Therein lies the strength of the unity of the Faith, of the validity of a Revelation that claims not to destroy or belittle previous Revelations, but to connect, unify, and fulfill them. This is the reason why Bahá'u'lláh and 'Abdu'l-Bahá have both revealed and even insisted upon certain details in connection with the Divine Economy which they have bequeathed to us, their followers. This is why such an emphasis has been placed in their Will and Testament upon the powers and prerogatives of the ministers of their Faith.[40]

The Will and Testament of 'Abdu'l-Bahá is so unrivaled in the history of religion that it takes one's breath away to imagine the unique bounty and singular blessing bestowed upon John and Louise Bosch by the Guardian when he asked them to be the bearers of this document, which was the blueprint for the future world civilization and an invaluable guide for the American Bahá'í community—a community that the Guardian would later describe as the "cradle of the Administrative Order."[41]

The Guardian's commendation of this weighty and precious document into the hands of John and Louise is a demonstration of the deep trust he had in them—a trust that had its beginnings during the Master's visit to the United States when the Master told John Bosch that he is "one of the family now." It is a trust that also had its beginnings when May Maxwell gave birth to her daughter Mary Maxwell (Rúhíyyih Khánum), as it was Louise (Stapfer) Bosch who was like an auntie to little Mary. When Shoghi Effendi and Mary Maxwell were married on March 24, 1937, uniting forever the believers of the East with those of the West, John and Louise Bosch sent a cable to Haifa that read "Illustrious nuptial thrilled the universe" to which the Guardian cabled a reply on March 31, 1937 that read "Inexpressibly appreciative thrilling message. Deepest Love, Shoghi." Two months after her marriage to Shoghi Effendi, Rúhíyyih Khánum wrote a most precious, handwritten letter to John and Louise:[42]

Haifa, Palestine
26 May, 1937
My Dear Ones:
Your lovely letter made me very happy. Indeed I love you both so much and have always felt so close to you and during these weeks when the infinite Bounty of Baha'u'llah has been so unexpectedly and abundantly showered upon me, I who have never deserved it in any conceivable way! My thoughts have often gone out to you both.

This union of East and West is so far above personality. I feel myself only an instrument caught up in the power and majesty of the Plan of God; I can only pray, and ask others to pray with me, that I may become worthy and render our beloved Cause great services. It seems to me I stand at the bottom of a mountain—my privilege and responsibility to climb ever higher, and I hope you will pray for me.

My love I send you both, always.
Rúhíyyih[43]

With a copy of portions of the Will and Testament of 'Abdu'l-Bahá in their protective care, John and Louise, along with their young traveling companion, Johanna Hauff, departed Haifa at 10:00am on Tuesday, January 17, 1922. The party of three journeyed first to Jerusalem, where they stayed the night. The next day, they traveled to Bethlehem to the Church of the Nativity. The day after that, they traveled in an "overland automobile" to the Dead Sea, Jericho, and the Lamentation Mountains where Christ fasted and prayed for forty days. They concluded the day with a trip to the Mount of Olives. On Friday, January 20, Johanna returned to Haifa while John and Louise carried on toward Jerusalem and arrived in Cairo on Saturday, January 21 at 11:00pm.

They stayed in Cairo for one week as the guests of Muḥammed Taqíy-i-Iṣfahání, whom they had met in Haifa. (Taqíy-i-Iṣfahání was the one who chanted in Arabic the second part of the initial reading of the Will and Testament of 'Abdu'l-Bahá in the Master's residence in Haifa. After his death in 1946, the Guardian named him a Hand of the Cause of God.)[44] They had several meetings with the friends there, and they visited the gravesites of Lua Getsinger and Mírzá Abu'l-Faḍl. The reader may recall that Lua Getsinger considered Louise Bosch one of her "special five" souls she nurtured in the Cause; while travel-teaching for the Cause, Lua died unexpectedly in Cairo on May 1, 1916 and is buried there.

Mírzá Abu'l-Faḍl was the beloved servant of 'Abdu'l-Bahá who, at the Master's request, traveled to Paris and to the United States with Laura Clifford Barney (who compiled a collection of 'Abdu'l-Bahá's responses to questions on religious topics in the book *Some Answered Questions*) in order to ensure that the new believers had a clear understanding of the teachings and laws of Bahá'u'lláh's revelation. Mírzá Abu'l-Faḍl died in Cairo while visiting at the home of Mírza Muḥammad Taqí. Of Mírzá Abu'l-Faḍl's book *The Brilliant Proof*, the Master said that the Bahá'ís should "memorize and reflect upon" this book so that "when accusations and criticisms are advanced by those unfavorable to the Cause, you will be well armed."[45]

From Cairo, John and Louise traveled to Alexandria and Ramleh, where they spent two days meeting with the Bahá'í friends there. On Saturday, January 28, the friends came to the Windsor Hotel to bid them farewell, and John and Louise departed on the *SS Adriatic* to sail through the Mediterranean Sea toward Europe. Their travel teaching efforts continued to be inspired by the direction given to them in 'Abdu'l-Bahá's Tablets of the Divine Plan, where He calls upon the believers to travel to Europe after the Great War and spread the teachings to those longing souls:

This world-consuming war has set such a conflagration to the hearts that no word can describe it. In all the countries of the world the longing for universal peace is taking possession of the consciousness of men. There is not a soul who does not yearn for concord and peace. A most wonderful state of receptivity is being realized [. . .] Therefore, O ye believers of God! Show ye an effort and after this war spread ye the synopsis of the divine teachings in the British Isles, France, Germany, Austria-Hungary, Russia, Italy, Spain, Belgium, Switzerland, Norway, Sweden, Denmark, Holland, Portugal, Rumania, Serbia, Montenegro, Bulgaria, Greece, Andorra, Liechtenstein, Luxembourg, Monaco, San Marino, Balearic Isles, Corsica, Sardinia, Sicily, Crete, Malta, Iceland, Faroe Islands, Shetland Islands, Hebrides and Orkney Islands.[46]

In Italy, John and Louise organized public meetings on the Bahá'í Faith in Naples, Rome, Florence, and Como. From there they passed into Locarno, Switzerland and made their way toward Zurich, Louise's birthplace, and then to St. Gallen, the place of John's birth, where they stopped for one week.

From Switzerland they traveled to Germany, where they stayed for nearly a month and focused their teaching efforts on the cities of Stuttgart, Esslingen, and Bad-Mergentheim because these were cities that had been visited by 'Abdu'l-Bahá in 1913. Germany was beloved of the Master, as His assurances to the German people testify. For instance, in the Tablets of the Divine Plan, the Master associated Germany with His wish that He Himself could travel to these countries:

Miss Knobloch traveled alone to Germany. To what a great extent she became confirmed! Therefore, know ye of a certainty that whosoever arises in this day to diffuse the divine fragrances, the cohorts of the Kingdom of God shall confirm him and the bestowals and the favors of the Blessed Perfection shall encircle him.

O that I could travel, even though on foot and in the utmost poverty, to these regions, and, raising the call of "Ya Baha'u'l-Abha" in cities, villages, mountains, deserts and oceans, promote the divine teachings! This, alas, I cannot do. How intensely I deplore it! Please God, ye may achieve it.⁴⁷

When John and Louise visited Germany, they spent a great deal of time with Wilhelm Herrigel (with whom John had corresponded regarding the translation of Thornton Chase's book *The Bahá'í Revelation*). Herrigel was beginning to question the Administrative Order outlined in the Will and Testament of 'Abdu'l-Bahá, but his dissent had little effect on dividing the Bahá'í community in Germany—a community that remained firm in its acceptance of Shoghi Effendi as Guardian of the Cause. In a letter written two years after the ascension of 'Abdu'l-Bahá, the Guardian reassured the friends in Germany, instructing them to remain steadfast and to set their sights on the greatness promised them by 'Abdu'l-Bahá:

4 December 1923
To the dearly-beloved friends throughout Germany.
Care of the National Spiritual Assembly
My well-beloved friends:
What a joy to correspond with you again, and express, after a long and unbroken silence, my warm sentiments of love and affection for those tried, and yet steadfast, lovers of 'Abdu'l-Bahá! Your trials and sufferings have been a constant source of anxiety and painful sorrow, not to me alone, but to the Ladies of the Household as well as to the friends at large.
True, humanity is to-day widely afflicted with unprecedented ills and calamities, but you, the chosen and favoured children of 'Abdu'l-Bahá, have, by some wisdom inscrutable to us all, received the fullest measure of this distress, and are carrying the burden of your cares with heroic fortitude, unflinching faith, and

undaunted courage worthy of the admiration of even the most severely tried of your fellow-sufferers in far-away Persia.

Your only consolation lies in the ever-living words of our departed Master, who confidently declared that the days are not far distant when Germany will shake off her present humiliation, and will emerge, mighty, united and glorious, not only to take her destined place in the councils of nations, but to raise high the triumphant banner of the Cause in the very heart of Europe.

Your ceaseless activities since His departure from our midst have been steadily extended as your tribulations and anxieties have multiplied, and I feel hopeful that ere long the true Faith of God will blaze forth in that land, and will herald publicly the Message of Salvation to that distracted continent.

I am so desirous to receive from the National Spiritual Assembly, frequent, comprehensive and up-to-date reports on the present position of the Cause throughout Germany, with an account of the activities of the various Bahá'í centers recently established throughout the land.

Your Bahá'í Magazine, I have regularly received and read with deep interest. I strongly urge you to devote a section of it, written both in German and English, to an account of the current activities of the Movement throughout the length and breadth of Germany, a step which I am sure will rejoice the hearts of our spiritual brethren and sisters the world over.

The members of the holy family and myself have joined lately the resident friends in the Holy Land in contributing towards the relief of the present distress in Germany, and we trust our modest efforts will mitigate to some extent the rigours of this coming winter in that afflicted country.

Hoping to hear from you, individually and collectively, and remembering you always in my prayers.

I am your brother and co-worker[48]

Toward the end of their month-long stay in Germany, John and Louise focused their attention on Berlin. They succeeded in organizing the first Bahá'í meeting there, which was held on April 5, 1922. Wilhelm Herrigel was the speaker. Among the papers of John and Louise Bosch, there is evidence that John wrote a full account of that first Bahá'í meeting in Berlin. Decades later, Miss Bijou Straun made efforts to obtain that account from Louise, and here is Louise's response to Miss Straun in 1948, two years after John's passing:

> Do not do anything until you have corresponded with Mrs. Nellie French who wrote to John years ago that his story of Berlin was to appear in the *Bahá'í World* and for him to send her the whole account of it. [. . .]. Much care was bestowed upon that story. John afterward received letters with questions in it in relation to the account (from Mrs. French), and she seemed very pleased with the work. I do not know whether or not it appeared in the subsequent issue of that *Bahá'í World* Book. That Mr. Perron was the one person who brought the knowledge of the name of Baha'u'llah to Berlin my husband and I heard from Mr. Herrigel. That was, of course, many years ago. Mr. Herrigel told us that Mr. Perron gave $100 at that time, at that earliest time, for the purpose of a start in Berlin. The lecture gotten up by Mr. Herrigel and John D. Bosch in Berlin was successful, even as the story of it shows. I was not present but ill in bed with measles in a hotel in Hamburg, Germany. My husband took that long and cold trip across Germany from Hamburg to Berlin, alone by himself, but both of us were booked to sail from Hamburg to New York soon after the lecture in Berlin.[49]

There is no record of this account in the U.S. National Bahá'í Archives, and it is possible that the manuscript to which Louise refers was lost. In a letter to Louise dated March 2, 1944, Nellie wrote, "By the way, several packages of the manuscript for Vol. IX of the *Bahá'í World* were lost at sea. I was heartbroken as I do not know what is gone. Horace [Holley] did not keep an accurate list and I had no duplicates of many of the articles."⁵⁰

To this writer, it is heartbreaking indeed, but perhaps better for posterity that Herrigel's talk in Berlin remained simply a footnote and, instead, the work of the German believers who remained steadfast was lauded. After all, the most significant German Bahá'í at the time of the passing of 'Abdu'l-Bahá was the youth Johanna Hauff; due to her presence at the ascension of 'Abdu'l-Bahá, all German Bahá'ís had the bounty of learning what transpired at His ascension. Furthermore, after the passing of 'Abdu'l-Bahá, the German Bahá'ís sent the following cable to the holy family: "All believers deeply moved by irrevocable loss of our Master's precious life. We pray for heavenly protection of Holy Cause and promise faithfulness and obedience to Center of Covenant."⁵¹

The special destiny of the German Bahá'í community is expressed in this letter from the Guardian to Dr. Adlebert Muhlschlegel (who would later be named a Hand of the Cause of God and have the unparalleled honor of washing and preparing for burial the precious body of Shoghi Effendi when he so unexpectedly passed away in London in 1957):

16 May 1933
Dear Dr. Muhlschlegel:
Dear and precious co-worker:
 I was so pleased to receive your letter. I long to hear more fully and more frequently from you. You are a tower of . . . and a pillar of His Faith in that land. Germany has a glorious future under the banner of the Faith of Bahá'u'lláh. Its mission is to champion the cause of God in Europe and establish it firmly in the heart of that continent. The tests and trials which have beset the Faith in that land were necessary and providential. It is for the German believers, who have weathered the storm, to arise and promote

the Cause, to proclaim the non-political character of their Faith, to establish its nascent institutions and prove by their words and acts their freedom from every taint of particularism and prejudice. May the Almighty guide their steps, sustain them in their efforts and bless their activities.

Shoghi[52]

Perhaps the most touching example of the steadfastness of the German Bahá'í community was seen at the onset of World War II when the Bahá'í Faith was officially banned in June, 1937. Two years before the ban, Miss Mary Maxwell (later Rúhíyyih Khánum, wife of the Guardian) pioneered to Germany in 1935; she was twenty-five years old. Of her early experiences there, she wrote to the American Bahá'í community the following:

The first contact that I made with the Bahá'ís of Germany was on the occasion of the Esslingen Summer School in August of 1935. Of all the many and varied impressions that flowed into my mind the deepest and most sacred was that of hearing the meeting opened by a reading of a Bahá'í prayer in German. Though I could scarcely understand it, the power and beauty of the creative Word was distinct and a consciousness of the innate and glorious oneness of the followers of Bahá'u'lláh the world over streamed into me with a sense of joy and gratitude.[53]

Having had a successful month-long teaching campaign in Germany, John and Louise departed for the United States on April 11, 1922, sailing on the *SS Resolute*. In his papers, John Bosch makes a special note about their ship being "the first large Steamer departing Germany since the War, under the American Flag." They were at sea for twelve days, arrived in New York on April 23, and were met by Miss Nelly Lloyd at the pier. Together they made their way to the train depot where Mrs. Kinney and Mrs. Kelsey were waiting to join them on the train to Chicago. There, they would, as requested by the Guardian, deliver a portion of the Will and Testament of 'Abdu'l-Bahá to the Convention in Chicago. In his journal, John Bosch wrote, "On April 24 we arrived Chicago at 2pm Monday and at Convention about 3pm, just in time when my name as a delegate of Geyserville was called. How happy we were to meet all the friends from so many states of the United States of America."[54]

After the Convention, they traveled to Portland and visited their good friends, the Latimers. From there, they took the train to San Francisco and arrived at their home in Geyserville on May 8, 1922 at 8:30pm, where there was a letter waiting for them from Soheil Afnan, a member of the family of 'Abdu'l-Bahá. (The Guardian would not have been in the Holy Land at this time, as he had already left on his sojourn to Switzerland on April 8, 1922).[55] Here is the letter, in part:

Haifa, Palestine
June 20, 1922
My Dear Mr. and Mrs. Bosch,
I was very glad to see some time ago the photo of Mr. Bosch among a group of whole-hearted German friends and I could not but realize what faithful servants Divine Love has wrought. One can hardly believe that a group of conflicting Westerners could unite under no common bond of friendship save devotion to our Eastern Lord and conviction in His sublime Cause.[56]

Such a letter must have reassured them of the success of their journey—especially to the country of Germany and for its people for whom the Master had promised so many glorious spiritual victories. Furthermore, the letter must have also brought back to their minds the fragrance of the Holy Land and the bounty of being in the presence of the Master one last time on this earth. It must have reminded John of how he felt meeting the Master for the first time, when he entered the Master's hotel rooms in New York in 1912—with a pocket-full of questions to ask Him:

The power of my speech failed. I was overshadowed by His Spirit. In His radiation I only could feel His universal Love. I was empty. In my heart I became aware of His greatness and of my littleness, of my unworthiness, of my nothingness. I spoke: "I regret very much that I have not the capacity as a teacher, that my work so far has only been by circulating books like Mr. Chase's *Revelation* and a few others."

'Abdu'l-Bahá replied: "You are doing well, you are doing better than talking. With you it is not words, or movements of or with the lips. With you it is the heart that talks. In your presence silence talks and radiates."[57]

In 1935, the National Spiritual Assembly of the Bahá'ís of the United States and Canada began formalizing its membership records by asking the Bahá'ís to fill out a card that was called the "Bahá'í Historical Record." The decision to issue the cards was recommended by the delegates at the United Stated Bahá'í National Convention that year in an attempt to get a "thorough and complete Bahá'í census" of the Bahá'í community—particularly its survey of racial, cultural and religious backgrounds.[58] The result was that about 1,813 believers—representing about 60% of the body of believers in America at that time—filled out the card. The added value is that the information collected has become valuable archival information for future Bahá'ís to look back at the remarkable circumstances under which these early Bahá'ís accepted Bahá'u'lláh as the Manifestation of God for this Day. In *Century of Light,* a document prepared under the supervision of the Universal House of Justice, the spiritual resolve of the Bahá'ís of both East and West in the first decades of the twentieth century is surveyed:

Their response arose from a level of consciousness that recognized, even if sometimes only dimly, the desperate need of the human race for spiritual enlightenment. To remain steadfast in the commitment to this insight required of these early believers [. . .] that they resist not only family and social pressures, but also the easy rationalizations of the world-view in which they had been raised and to which everything around them insistently exposed them. There was a heroism about the steadfastness of these early Western Bahá'ís that is, in its own way, as affecting as that of their Persian co-religionists, who in these same years, were facing persecution and death for the Faith they had embraced.[59]

John Bosch filled out his "Bahá'í Historical Record" card as follows:

1. Name: John D. Bosch
2. Reported through Spiritual Assembly: Geyserville
3. Address, city, state: Geyserville, California
4. Birthplace and birth-date: Switzerland, August 1st, 1855
5. Naturalization (if foreign born): Los Angeles, California, August 26th, 1887
6. National origin: Swiss
7. Race: Caucasian
8. Color: White
9. Sex: Male
10. Married?: Yes, January 19, 1914
11. Children or dependents: No children
12. Religious origin (religion before becoming a Bahá'í): Christian, reformed Protestant
13. Date of acceptance of the Bahá'í Faith: 1903
14. Place of acceptance of Bahá'í Faith: Oakland, California, at Mrs Goodall's
15. Date of enrollment in present Bahá'í community: April 21, 1923

16. General information you would like to have preserved in this historical record (about Bahá'í services, connection with the Cause in early days, special talents, etc.):
Was privileged to be sent to that early Chicago Temple Convention of 1909 as delegate of the Californian and Hawaiian believers. Was first Californian believer who went to New York to meet 'Abdu'l-Baha in 1912. Was travelling in 'Abdu'l-Baha's party from New York to Washington D.C. and was in the same party again 6 days afterward from Washington to Chicago. Was in Wilmette at the Laying of the Cornerstone of the Mashriqu'l-Adhkar. Was present in Haifa at the Passing Away of 'Abdu'l-Baha. On Day of His Funeral was called to assist with the Laying of the Body of 'Abdu'l-Baha into the Coffin.[60]

It is interesting to note the things that John Bosch does not list on the card. For instance, not only was he the travelling companion of 'Abdu'l-Bahá during His visit to America in 1912, but he was told by 'Abdu'l-Bahá that he was to be considered as a member of the family of 'Abdu'l-Bahá, and that 'Abdu'l-Bahá Himself gave John the name "Nurani," which means luminous, and wrote it on a piece of paper for John in His own pen.* John does not write that he and Louise were invited to stay with the holy family for two months after the ascension of 'Abdu'l-Bahá, and that upon their departure from the Holy Land in January, 1922 the Guardian would entrust portions of the Will and Testament of 'Abdu'l-Bahá into their care so that John would deliver it to the United States Bahá'í National Convention in 1922. John Bosch participated in some of the most pivotal and sacred events of the first centenary of Bahá'í history, yet how unvarnished is his account of the Bahá'í services listed on his historical record; his genuine humility is an example of his selfless devotion to the Cause of Bahá'u'lláh.

In the introductory pages of *God Passes By*, Shoghi Effendi described the first century of Bahá'í history, 1844–1944, by comprising it into

---

* Please see Chapter 3.

four periods: "These four periods are to be regarded not only as the component, the inseparable parts of one stupendous whole, but as progressive stages in a single evolutionary process, vast, steady and irresistible."[61] The fourth period in that evolutionary process spans from 1921–1944; its commencement is marked by the conclusion of the Apostolic Age with the passing of 'Abdu'l-Bahá in 1921, and punctuated by the execution of His Will in the years that followed—and it would be the United States that would become the cradle of that Administrative Order described in the Will and Testament of 'Abdu'l-Bahá. How fitting that the Guardian entrusted to John Bosch the delivery of a portion of the Master's Will to America, for it is through him that all American believers had the bounty of learning of the Master's ascension and learning of the contents of His Will as it was presented to the elected representatives of the American believers at their National Convention.

Yet the services of John Bosch were not at an end. During the "fourth period" of the first century of the Bahá'í Dispensation, from 1921–1944, John would offer his most lasting service to the community of the Greatest Name: he and Louise would begin a Bahá'í school that would provide what the Guardian later described as one "of those initial schools which, as time goes by, will, on the one hand, evolve into powerful centers of Bahá'í learning, and, on the other, provide a fertile recruiting ground for the enrichment and consolidation of its teaching force."[62]

8 / An Indefatigable Trio

In 1938, the Guardian wrote a seminal letter to the Bahá'ís of the United States and Canada. The letter is called *The Advent of Divine Justice,* and in it the Guardian outlined the spiritual requisites necessary for the United States and Canada to lead all nations spiritually. The first requisite is rectitude of conduct and is "specially, though not exclusively, directed to their elected representatives"; the second is a chaste and holy life and "is mainly and directly concerned with the Bahá'í youth"; and the third is racial fellowship and "should be the immediate, the universal, and the chief concern of all and sundry members of the Bahá'í community, of whatever age, rank, experience, class, or color, as all, with no exception, must face its challenging implications, and none can claim, however much he may have progressed along this line, to have completely discharged the stern responsibilities which it inculcates."[1] These spiritual requisites delineate the sharp distinction that must be made between the disintegrating forces of the material society in which the Bahá'ís live and the integrating forces of the spiritual civilization that the Bahá'ís are striving to build. To achieve such a spiritual victory over the corrosive material influences of American society, the individual believer must prepare himself to teach the Cause of God, and the Bahá'í summer school is one path to this preparation. The Guardian wrote, "If he attends his summer school—and everyone without exception is urged to take advantage of attending it—let him consider such an occasion as a welcome and precious opportunity so to enrich, through lectures, study, and discussion, his knowledge of the fundamentals of his Faith as to be able to transmit, with greater confidence and effectiveness, the Message that has been entrusted to his care."2

At the time that the Guardian wrote this message to the American believers, the existing permanent summer schools in America were Green Acre Bahá'í School in Maine, Louhelen Bahá'í School in Michigan, and Geyserville Bahá'í School in California. To appreciate the significance of the Geyserville Bahá'í School and its beginnings in 1926, it is necessary to understand the direction of the teaching work in the five years preceding its establishment and the paramount importance of completing the construction of the Bahá'í House of Worship in Wilmette, Illinois.

Rúhíyyih Khánum explained that when he became Guardian, Shoghi Effendi made clear that the completion of the Mother Temple of the West was an undertaking integral to the teaching work:

> The Guardian called the American Temple the "symbolic Edifice" of the Administration, "its mighty bulwark, the symbol of its strength and the sign of its future glory," the "harbinger of an as yet unborn civilization," the "symbol and harbinger of the World Order." Such "Mother" Temples, he said, were the great silent teachers of the Faith and occupied such a key position in its progress that he stated the American House of Worship incarnated the soul of the American Bahá'í Community in the Western Hemisphere. Although the first Temple was built according to 'Abdu'l-Bahá's own instructions in 'Ishqabad during His lifetime, the Guardian assured us that the first Temple erected in the New World was the holiest for all time because the Master Himself had laid its foundation stone during His visit to North America and it had been one of the undertakings dearest to His heart. By 1921, when Shoghi Effendi became Guardian, its foundations

had been laid but the building 'Abdu'l-Bahá had so longed to see erected before His passing was only a hideous black waterproofed cylinder, resembling a gas tank, sticking up above the ground.[3]

The Temple resembling "a gas tank sticking up above the ground" can be analogous to the progress of the teaching work in the years between 1921 and 1926. That is not to say that there was a lack of earnest endeavor on behalf of the friends; on the contrary, there were many Bahá'ís who had the capacity to deliver the message effectively and with eloquence and confidence, but they were relatively few in number. The teaching work in America would require thousands of capable teachers if the goals outlined in the Tablets of the Divine Plan were to be fully realized.

Developing capacity in the individual was a central concern to both the individual and institutions of the Cause. Furthermore, individuals and institutions sought ways in which to communicate the goals of the Bahá'í Faith to a broader audience of seekers. For instance, the Local Spiritual Assembly of San Francisco even used its letterhead as an avenue to communicate to that broader audience. The letterhead read, "The Bahai Movement: A Universal Movement Having For Its Purpose the Bestowal of Social Economic and Spiritual Unity Upon the World of Humanity." Although the institutions of the Cause are central to the teaching work, ultimately the obligation to teach the Cause of God rests with the individual. 'Abdu'l-Bahá stated in His Will and Testament, "Of all the gifts of God, the greatest is the gift of Teaching. It draweth unto us the Grace of God and is our first obligation. Of such a gift, how can we deprive ourselves? Nay, our lives, our good, our comforts, our rest, we offer them all as a sacrifice for the Abhá Beauty and teach the Cause of God."[4]

Therefore, it rests upon the individual believer to learn how to explain to others the practical application of the teachings, as well as learn to balance thoughtful prudence with bold confidence. In the early 1920s, there were many Bahá'ís in the region of Geyserville who were practiced in giving public talks; they were often called upon to speak at Bahá'í events so that the Bahá'ís themselves could learn how to present the teachings in a manner relevant to seekers at the time.

In 1922, at the unit convention for the Pacific Coast region, Leroy Ioas helped organize the convention speakers and program as outlined in this letter from him to John Bosch:

1415 Palm Drive
Burlingame, California
October 28, 1922
Dear Mr. Bosch,

It occurred to me you may not have seen the enclosed paper, published in Chicago a long time ago, how long, I don't know. It was interesting, when I found it in some old data my father had, to see your shining face among those early pioneers. If you wish to keep this among your valuable data on the early days of the Cause, you may do so.

We are looking forward to a wonderful congress and Convention. There should be about 20 coming up from Los Angeles, Pasadena, and Glendale. Just received word there will be three from Seattle. We have not heard definitely from Portland, but undoubtedly some will come from there. San Diego will not be officially represented, but I understand, one or two from near at hand will be present. The program is working out nicely.

Of course you and Mrs. Bosch will be here. We have not had the pleasure of seeing or hearing from Mrs. Bosch since the Convention in Chicago, and we must at this, the First convention of its kind on the Pacific Coast. She must come, that's all!

The outline for the Convention will be: of course, the business session Friday and Saturday, the 24th and 25th, in the morning and afternoons, each day. In the evening of each day will the public meetings for Teaching. The 26th, Abdul Baha's day, will be devoted to Memorial Meetings in the Morning, and Feast of Commemoration in the evening.* The program for the first Evening is Mrs. French of Pasadena, *The New East, Its Problems and Solution*; Ahmad of Los Angeles, *The Bahai Movement, Its Universal Appeal*; Mrs. Waite, Los Angeles, *Spiritual Success*. The second evening will be Mrs. Luther, Seattle, *The Oneness of the World of Humanity*; George Latimer, Portland, *Economic Right and Justice*; Dr. D'Evelyn, *The Mysterious Forces of Civilization*. The Memorial Service will be given to Mrs. Bosch principally, to tell of your wonderful trip, and the experiences in Haifa and Acca. You know the friends here have not heard of it, and you promised to devote a meeting to it. Then there will be the Friends here from the other cities, and it will be a most wonderful occasion, all the hearts receptive, and a beautiful spirit present. The Feast in the Evening will be a general Feast of Love and good cheer. Mrs. Frankland will be Chairman, and probably follow no set program, but just have different ones talk of experiences in the Cause, of the love of Abdul Baha, and the present heavenly Guardianship of Shoghi Effendi.

With the utmost love to you and Mrs. Bosch, in which Sylvia joins me, as ever,
Sincerely,
Leroy Ioas[5]

Topics such as the universal application of the Bahá'í teachings, the need for spiritual fulfillment, the application of the principle of the oneness of humanity, and the progress of civilization are topics that are as relevant today as they were to seekers in 1922. The United States had emerged from the First World War with damaging prejudices and

---

* Novermber 26, known as the Day of the Covenant, is a day on which Bahá'ís commemorate the recognition of 'Abdu'l-Bahá as the Center of Bahá'u'lláh's Covenant.

growing discontent with world affairs; it was imperative that the Bahá'í teacher be able to explain how the teachings of Bahá'u'lláh were distinctive in the application of spiritual principles for solutions to the world's problems. Shoghi Effendi, in his first year as Guardian of the Cause in 1922, made clear the distinctions between the aims of a material civilization and the aims of the divine civilization of Bahá'u'lláh, as described here by Rúhíyyih Khánum:

> Every time one goes into the details of any particular period in the Guardian's life one is tempted to say, "this was the worst period," so fraught with strain, problems, unbearable pressures was his entire ministry. But there is a pattern, there are themes, higher and lower points were reached. The pattern of 1922, 1923 and 1924 reveals itself, insofar as his personal life is concerned, as an heroic attempt to come to grips with this leviathan—the Cause of God—he had been commanded to bestride.
>
> With the passing of 1923 one could almost say that the winged Guardian emerged from the chrysalis of youth, a new being; the wings may not yet be fully stretched, but their beat gains steadily in sweep and assurance as the years go by until, in the end, they truly cast a shadow over all mankind. In his early writings one sees this mastery unfolding, in style, in thought, in power. [. . .] His questions are challenging, his thoughts incisive: "Are we to be carried away by the flood of hollow and conflicting ideas, or are we to stand, unsubdued and unblemished, upon the everlasting rock of God's Divine Instructions?"; ". . . are we to believe that whatever befalls us is divinely ordained, and in no wise the result of our faint-heartedness and negligence? Already in 1923 he sees the world and the Cause as two distinct things, not to be mixed up in our minds into one sentimental and haphazard lump. The Will of God he asserts is "at variance with the shadowy views, the impotent doctrines, the crude theories, the idle imaginings, the fashionable conceptions of a transient and troublous age."[6]

Rúhíyyih K͟hánum suggests the need to eschew sentimentality as a necessary precaution for the teaching work ahead of the American Bahá'í community. Furthermore, developing capacity in the individual teacher required a specific kind of training that the Bahá'ís in America had not yet experienced. Although Green Acre Bahá'í School was successful in attracting attendees to its summer session, the program at Green Acre was not specifically aimed at systematic training of teachers of the Cause. The twofold urgency of increasing the number of capable teachers of the Cause concomitant with the completion of the Mother Temple of the West required a unity of thought among the believers in the United States. Rúhíyyih K͟hánum explained the plan in this way:

> The Guardian conceived it as one of his major duties to complete this sacred edifice as soon as possible. It took him thirty-two years to accomplish this task which he called the greatest enterprise ever launched by the western followers of the Faith and the most signal victory won during the Formative Period of the Bahá'í Dispensation [. . .]. To the Convention held [in 1923] he sent a strongly worded message pleading with the American believers to resume the construction of their great Temple and this influenced them to initiate what became known as the "Plan of Unified Action," designed to raise money for the extremely costly work of the superstructure.[7]

The National Spiritual Assembly appealed to Local Spiritual Assemblies to enlist Bahá'ís across the United States to support the Plan of Unified Action, and, of course, John and Louise were included in the recruitment:

November 4, 1922
Dear Mr. and Mrs. Bosch:
    Presumably you two wonderful people have by this time received a copy of the attached letter direct from Mr. Lunt, relative to the Mashreq'ul Azkar work.

At the last meeting of the Spiritual Assembly, held Wednesday Evening, everyone was unanimous in their hope and desire that you two accept for the San Francisco and surrounding assemblies the duties of representing us, on this campaign, and cooperate with the National Assembly, as they request. The attributes which the National Assembly desire the representative to have, are all found in their full richness in your sweet lives, and we all hope you will find it possible to undertake this responsibility.

May I ask if you will let me know as quickly as possible, without hurrying you in any way, so I may advise Mr. Lunt.
With Bahai Love and Greetings,
In His Service,
Sincerely yours,
San Francisco Spiritual Assembly
Secretary, (signed) Leroy Ioas[8]

In the years between 1921 and 1925, John and Louise traveled to communities along the Pacific Coast range to promote the teaching campaigns that were launched as a response to the Tablets of the Divine Plan as well as the "Plan of Unified Action" for the completion of the House of Worship. Their teaching efforts naturally gave way to the necessary and arduous consolidation of new believers in order that they could begin to develop a Bahá'í way of life. John and Louise were effective teachers in every way: with ease they spread the seeds of interest in the teachings of Bahá'u'lláh, and with equal effectiveness they had the necessary patience and deep commitment to consolidating long-lasting relationships with new believers.

The numbers of people influenced by the spirit of love and fellowship so characteristic of John and Louise's appeal are too many to number in this biography. Perhaps looking at the life of one of those persons will give insight into how John and Louise became true brethren to so many.

Grace Bruckman Holley from Visalia, California, was one such believer, and she figured intimately into the story of the Geyserville

Summer School. She became a Bahá'í during the teaching campaign that was launched with the Tablets of the Divine Plan sometime around 1917. Prior to becoming a Bahá'í, she was one of the first women to graduate from Stanford University with a bachelor's degree in physics in 1904, followed by a teaching assistantship in physics at Stanford in 1905—all the while maintaining her chair as violinist in the university orchestra. She married fellow Stanford student Harry Holley in 1906; his geology degree led him to a civil and hydraulics engineering job in Visalia, California.

Grace Holley's first introduction to the Bahá'í Faith was by an invitation from Mary Burland of San Francisco. They attended a Bahá'í meeting that had been organized by Isabella Brittingham, who was one of the traveling teachers sent to the Pacific and Southwest States as a response to the Tablets of the Divine Plan. Grace Holley's granddaughter, May Hofman, wrote that when her grandmother was on her way home from that first Bahá'í meeting, she stopped in the middle of the street and said aloud, "It's true—Christ has come again!"[9]

Grace and Harry Holley built a home in Visalia, and it soon became a center of teaching activity for the many Bahá'í teachers who came through Visalia, as it was a natural stopover for traveling teachers en route from San Francisco to Los Angeles. Visalia is at the center of the great San Joaquin Valley of California and is the gateway to Sequoia National Park. The analogy of it as a fertile field where giant trees grow was not lost on the Bahá'ís of Visalia. In a letter dated January 14, 1925 to the Guardian, Grace Holley wrote, in part:

> We are praying, and solicit your prayers also, that from this little nucleus may stream forth such a radiance of love that others may be attracted to our center, and from here go forth to the rest of this great Garden of the Sun (San Joaquin Valley), in the center of which we live.
>
> Mr. Hyde Dunn patiently sowed seed here for several years, but for a long time saw no results. Yet, through Mary Burland, in whose heart his seed took root, Mrs. Brittingham was sent to us,

and here raised the Call of the Kingdom. That dear Maid-Servant said while here over ten years ago "I feel that you will sound the trumpet which will arouse this great Valley." This is our constant prayer.

Progress has been slow, partly because we are so lacking in vision, and do not grasp the privilege of our opportunity, but partly because all of us have limited means and all are parents of children, and so cannot travel as we would. But at last we can see, descending in torrents, the confirmations.[10]

Here is the reply to Mrs. Holley's letter, written on behalf of the Guardian by John Esslemont:

We hope that Mrs. Brittingham's prophetic intuition will be fulfilled and that your assembly will "sound the trumpet which will arouse the great San Joaquin Valley." Limited financial means and the care of children will not prove insuperable obstacles. Christ and his disciples had but little of this world's goods, and Bahá'u'lláh and the Master were prisoners for many years and unable to travel, but that did not prevent them from raising the Call of the Kingdom very effectually. As for the children, they will, it is to be hoped, soon become Heralds of the Cause themselves, and carry the Glad Tidings wherever they go.[11]

The generation of children to which this letter alludes is the generation that would be young adults by the time the Faith reached its first centenary in 1944. Therefore, the teaching work required a vision into the future—a vision toward the teaching force that would assume the lion's share of the teaching work in the decades ahead.

By 1925, John and Louise were seventy and fifty-five years old, respectively. They had been Bahá'ís for over twenty years, but their experiences directly with the Master, as well as their pioneering and teaching efforts, gave them the learning of a century. Their souls mirrored divine attributes that became an attraction to others who sought their fellowship—young and old alike. For instance, Grace Holley's daughter, Marion Holley (Hofman) was thirty-four years old in 1944 and full of eager excitement to serve the Cause, in part due to the spiritual ties she had with John and Louise, who watched her grow up. Like her parents, Marion was a student at Stanford (class of 1930) and an athlete in the 1928 Olympics in track and field. Marion later married David Hofman, who served on the Universal House Justice from 1963 to 1988. Grace Holley became like a sister to John and Louise, and Marion would grow up regarding the Bosches as one would regard a beloved aunt and uncle. Marion's development as a capable teacher of the Cause was largely due to her own natural ability and intuition but also due to her training at Geyserville. For instance, in this letter to John and Louise, Marion, at the age of thirty-three, demonstrates her insight into the precious act of teaching another soul about the message of Bahá'u'lláh. She remembers that there are two audiences when one teaches another—one is the physical reality of the person, and the other is the intangible reality of that person's soul. Marion Holley refers to these two audiences as "one we see, and another one":

2031 Ninth Avenue
San Francisco, California
December 16, 1943
Dearest Louise and John,
Your dear letters have come, two of them, and it makes me wish I were right back there with you. I know how you fret, sometimes, at being unable to do more—but if you only preserve a place where people can experience the real love of God, even for a few hours, then you have done the greatest service of all. I can't tell you how different it is in the City—even coming down on the bus is a different world—and the spirit seems to wither until you wonder if any of it survives at all. And then comes a letter

from you, and inhaling it I know that I still do survive, and long for these real and precious moments again. Somehow, I am never able to keep this wonderful feeling, except when I am with believers like you. This is where I envy Milly [Collins], who is always attached to the Guardian and inseparable from him and Haifa—and so of course she is always full of joy and exhilaration.*

I don't know why you liked the lecture so much, but I'm pleased that you did—for this means that the trip was not in vain. I never worry at all about numbers, for we deal with something more intangible. I have a feeling that the happiness which John's relative had that evening would make the effort worthwhile. And then we always have two audiences—one we see and another one.

Since returning I have put in twelve hours writing my radio talk for Sunday, and last night the Committee approved it, thank heaven. This is the hardest kind of work—much more difficult than a lecture, because one can leave nothing for the inspiration of the moment, but must drive through and get it all on paper in advance, and in addition try to say a lot in fifteen minutes. I hope you will be able to hear that station—which is KYA, 1260 on the dial, at 7:30 P.M. Sunday. You will see it advertised (one inch) on the radio page of the S.F. Chronicle, under the title of "Humanity's Coming of Age" [. . .].

Enclosed is the Fire Tablet, which I promised to send. Do let me hear how you like it. To me it is a like a great symphony, and is really a tremendous conversation between the Manifestation and God—and almost too intimate for us to listen in on.

---

* See chapter 10 for a summary of Milly Collins.

[. . .] And now my deepest love to you both—whom I miss already so much!

Marion[12]

John and Louise did not travel to the National Convention in 1944; John was in his eighty-ninth year, and the journey to Chicago a long one, so they relied on Marion Holley to report to them the historic events that took place at the House of Worship in Wilmette where the friends gathered and held a special commemoration of the First Bahá'í Century. Marion kept John and Louise as close to the experience as possible and focused on the aspects of the Convention that she knew would be most important to both of them:

May 12, 1944

Dearest Louise and John,

This is written from the train—somewhere in Wyoming—as we approach Chicago and the wonderful Convention. Mildred and I are going to Detroit for a few days first, to see her family. It seems like a dream that May 23, 1944 has come at last—for it has been the pivot of our hopes since I can remember.

I was up at four this morning to watch the sunrise—from pure excitement unable to sleep. I keep thinking of the Guardian—and I feel he must be very close to us at this time. What thrilling message will he send, and what will be the new phase of our work?

How we wish that you and John could be here—but of course you really will be, and we shall be thinking of you when the picture of the Báb is unveiled—and shall try to remember everything to tell you.

We have had a wonderful year in San Francisco, so full of activity—and I think thousands have now heard of the Cause who had never noticed its name before. Our symposiums have all been fine, with at least 500 present. The last one, two nights ago, was perhaps best of all—for all the speakers talked of the Faith, and Professor Rogers of Montezuma [School for Boys] made everyone very happy with his memories of 'Abdu'l-Bahá.* One remarkable thing he told us that the Master said to him on education: That he must always remember that he was teaching not only the mind of the youth, but his very atoms—so that in reality he was helping to educate all the kingdoms.

I was thrilled with the news of Mrs. Jeanne Gasse [wife of René Gasse from Tahiti.]. We too are taking in four new believers tonight in San Francisco, and two weeks ago, a lovely girl, daughter of Helen Wilson who used to live in Visalia, was confirmed [. . .].

Many thanks for your lovely letter—so like old times. My heart is often with you both, even though the gasoline and the lack of time have kept us separated. I shall think of you in prayers at the Temple—and when the beloved Guardian's message comes.

With deepest love always to you both,

Marion[13]

In all of their relationships with people, whether they were casual encounters or long-term friendships, John and Louise were remembered for their gentle kindness and unconditional love. Fellowship with others fosters spiritual perfections, as 'Abdu'l-Bahá wrote in His Will and Testament: "So intense must be the spirit of love and loving

---

* Dr. Ernest Rogers was founder of the Montezuma School for Boys in Los Gatos, California. He became a Bahá'í in the early 1900s, and when the Master spoke at Stanford University in October of 1912, Professor Rogers brought thirty of his students to hear Him. See Anita Chapman, *Leroy Ioas, Hand of the Cause of God*, 53.

kindness, that the stranger may find himself a friend, the enemy a true brother, no difference whatsoever existing between them. For universality is of God and all limitations earthly. Thus man must strive that his reality may manifest virtues and perfections, the light whereof may shine upon everyone."[14]

John and Louise must have been inspired by these words of 'Abdu'l-Bahá because on the first of August, 1925, nearly 150 friends gathered around the "Big Tree" that stood in the center of their Geyserville property to celebrate the Bahá'í Feast of Kamál/Perfection and to celebrate John's seventieth birthday. The next day, the San Francisco Bahá'í Assembly sent the following letter to John, and it included 132 signatures of the friends who were present at that Feast. The letter begins with a reference to "one and twenty years"—presumably the number of years since John first learned of the Message of Bahá'u'lláh:

August 2nd, 1925
Esteemed friend,

One and twenty years are not long as Time goes, but days eternal, when they register pilgrim steps on that highway whose finger-posts are fundamental realities, and whose goal is The Kingdom of Abha Destiny.

The rhythm of life, with the subtle meanings; the flow and the ebb; the surge and the calm; in its pulsings has not been unheeded or unknown by you; nor indeed by those who in varying measure share its purpose with you: whether as honoured and cherished <u>helpmeet</u>, long time <u>brother</u>; or spiritual <u>nursling</u>, whose trusting footsteps follow in guidance, though the vision be unseen and the story unread.

It is in this unity of kinship, this singleness of love; we whose signatures are attached, and further for those physically absent, but in soul and spirit present, be they of hearth and home, or of lands far distant; co-partners with us; tender you our <u>affection</u> and <u>high</u> <u>esteem</u> and beseech for you and yours the jewels of beat-

itude and to thine eyes an ever increasing radiance, made bright by beholding the signs of *Abha guidance.*
Fraternally yours,
San Francisco Baha'i Assembly
Dr. Frederick D'Evelyn[15]

The style of the letter may be grandiloquent, but the sentiment is sincere: the Bahá'ís held both John and Louise in the highest regard, and toward John there was a special feeling due to his association with 'Abdu'l-Bahá at His ascension. It gave one the sense that to be near John was to be near the Master, and as a result of John and Louise having been present at His ascension, the American believers felt a special relationship with them. One seeker, after receiving a Bahá'í book from John, described that nearness in this way: "I feel gratified to think that you should bestow such an honor on me, you, who have seen and know so much of the one, who I am trying to learn more about."[16]

The goals of the Tablets of the Divine Plan would require the training of Bahá'í teachers in ways that had not yet been systematized. Due to the increasing call for Bahá'í teachers in the Western States in 1926, and because of the great distance separating these states from Green Acre, the National Spiritual Assembly appointed a committee consisting of John Bosch (age 71), George Latimer (age 36), and Leroy Ioas (age 30); their mandate was to work out plans for a Bahá'í summer school on the Pacific Coast. A more capable trio could not have been formed. To appreciate the deep camaraderie of these three men, a brief survey of the record of service of George Latimer and Leroy Ioas is necessary.

George Latimer was from Portland, Oregon. He and his parents, James and Harriet (Rúhaniyyih) Latimer did much of the teaching work in the Pacific Northwest in preparation for 'Abdu'l-Bahá's visit in 1912. Although 'Abdu'l-Bahá did not reach Portland, the publicity and public meetings held in anticipation of a potential visit from the Master resulted in an even greater interest in the Master's visit as people wanted to know what it was they had missed. In her book *Memories of 'Abdu'l-Bahá*, Ramona Allen Brown explains that since the Master could not travel to Portland, the Portland Bahá'ís traveled to San Francisco to see Him:

> Harriett and James Latimer, my aunt and uncle, and their son, George, came from Portland, Oregon, and remained in San Francisco during the Master's stay there. He gave my aunt the name Ruhaniyyih and called her the "Mother of the Portland Assembly" (Community), as the Latimer family had established the Faith in that city. George traveled around the world teaching and fulfilling the wishes of the Master. He made two pilgrimages to Haifa to meet 'Abdu'l-Bahá and several pilgrimages to meet Shoghi Effendi. George served on the National Spiritual Assembly of the United States for many years until his death in June 1948. Soon after George's passing, my aunt received this letter from the National Spiritual Assembly:

> November 16, 1948
> Dear Ruhaniyyih:
> Now we can see and recognize the extraordinary spiritual unity of the great Bahá'í services rendered by you, your husband and your son. Such work could never have been done by any three individuals striving alone. It could only be a family accomplishment, a unity—one inspiration flowing through three harmonious instruments [. . .].
> With loving greetings from each member,
> Affectionately yours,
> Horace Holley
> Secretary[17]

The story of George Latimer is worthy of its own biography. He is an unsung hero and perhaps would prefer it that way, as he did not seek prominence or renown. He was confident but not overbearing, intelligent without an air of superiority, and he was fair-minded without being paternal. When 'Abdu'l-Bahá was in New Hampshire, George traveled to meet Him there. It was to George Latimer that 'Abdu'l-Bahá said these words about how to prepare teachers of the Cause:

> The Bahá'í must first be informed of the principles and Teachings of Bahá'u'lláh, then go forth and spread the Message. It is like unto a soldier, who must arm himself with the buckler and armor, and then he enters the battlefield to fight against the foe. But if he goes to fight without arming himself, he will be defeated. The Bahá'ís are the Army of God. Their defensive armors or weapons are: First, Faith; second, Assurance; third, Severance; fourth, Complete Attraction to the Kingdom of Abhá. If they are armed with these weapons, they will gain the victory in whatever field they may enter. As long as he is not equipped with these weapons, he will not be successful. He must cut himself entirely from all imitations.[18]

George Latimer had been on pilgrimage to meet 'Abdu'l-Bahá in 1919 and chronicled his experiences in a book called *The Light of the World*. He wrote eruditely yet colloquially on Bahá'í subjects, most notably a paper titled *The Call of God*, where he reviewed the progressive nature of God's revelation to mankind. He was elected to the National Spiritual Assembly in 1943 and served as chairman throughout the Centenary Year of the Bahá'í Faith in 1944, and he delivered one of the keynote addresses at the Centenary commemoration at the House of Worship.[19]

In a Tablet to Lutfu'lláh Hakím, 'Abdu'l-Bahá refers to George Latimer as an "illumined, God-like youth" and he was loved by both the Master and by the Guardian.[20] George Latimer traveled extensively for the Faith and died prematurely in 1948 at the age of fifty-eight. A proper and extensive review of his life will show a man free from self-interest in his service to the Cause—even succeeding in concealing his profession as a lawyer to the keenest of observers, as demonstrated in this letter to John and Louise where George mentions being under the watchful scrutiny of Barbara Yazdi Markert, who would have been a child at the time:

Dear John and Louise,
I had a nice thank-you letter from Marion and Ali Yazdi for the talk at their delightful tea in Berkeley the day following the big meeting at the Palace Hotel. I quote from their letter what dear little Barbara said to her mother the night of the big meeting in whispers: "Doesn't George look important. He would make a very good lawyer. See him looking so proud and restful"—I was quaking in my boots—"How can anyone who looks so important be so humorous?" Well I wrote down that I would like to have Barbara as my press agent.[21]

Perhaps the most revealing letter about George Latimer is the one written by the Master to George's parents, as it foreshadows the far-reaching record of service of George's all-too-brief life. Here is the Tablet, in part:

To their honours, Mr. James and Rúhaniyyih Latimer
Portland, Oregon—Upon them be Bahá'u'l-Abhá!
HE IS GOD!
O ye two faithful and assured souls! Praise be to God, your son, George Latimer, is enkindled with the fire of the love of God, and is with all his power engaged in service. This youth shall be confirmed and shall plant for you a tree that shall eternally yield fresh fruits [. . .].
At present the principle of the Oneness of Mankind resembles a seed which is sown and which at first commands no importance, but when the springtime of Universal Peace draws near, then it

shall grow and its importance be made known.
Upon ye be Bahá'u'l-Abhá!
(Signed) 'Abdu'l-Bahá
Translated by Shoghi Rabbání, Bahjí, 'Akká, Palestine, July 20, 1919[22]

One cannot help but wonder at the symbolic meaning of George Latimer growing up to plant a tree "that shall eternally yield fresh fruits" given his efforts to establish a "tree" of Bahá'í learning in the form of a permanent Bahá'í school.

The third member of the Pacific Coast Bahá'í Summer School committee was the incomparable Leroy Ioas. A brilliant biography of Leroy Ioas has been written by his daughter, Anita Chapman; however, a brief review of Ioas' life would provide a useful perspective on his work as a member of the Pacific Coast Summer School committee. Leroy Ioas was sixteen years old when he and his parents met 'Abdu'l-Bahá in 1912. In 1919, at age 23, he married Sylvia Kuhlman, and they moved to San Francisco, where Leroy began a career with the Southern Pacific Railroad—a career that would last forty years until he was called to the Holy Land to serve as secretary to the Guardian in 1951. Leroy would then remain in the Holy Land until his death in 1965.

His daughter Anita wrote that "his first act on reaching San Francisco [in 1919] was to address a letter to 'Abdu'l-Bahá, begging confirmation for all his family and his children unborn, and for his own severance, knowledge, and steadfastness 'that this faltering one may be quickened through that Divine Power, and thereby render some service which may be conducive to the happiness of the heart of 'Abdu'l-Bahá.' He had heard the Master's Divine Plan Tablets read at the American Convention in New York that spring, and his desire to serve had been fully awakened."[23]

David Starr Jordan, president of Stanford University, with whom Leroy had developed an association, recognized Leroy's aptitude and offered Leroy a scholarship to study at Stanford University, but Leroy turned it down, as he found that the needs of the Cause posed a greater demand than the needs of furthering his own material education. Anita wrote that her father "had a creative vision matched by practical sense and determination, and his hopes for the expansion of the Faith were boundless." Named a Hand of the Cause in 1951, he was herculean in his service to the Cause and was noted by the Guardian for his "vigorous spirit of determination and of noble enthusiasm," his "energy, judgment, zeal and fidelity," his "incessant activities and prodigious labours," and his "tireless vigilance, self-sacrifice, and devotion to the Cause in all its multiple fields of activity."[24]

Leroy Ioas wasted no time in convening the members of the summer school committee. In this letter, he mentioned Mr. Horace Holley, who was secretary of the National Spiritual Assembly at the time:

March 10, 1927
40-46th Avenue
San Francisco, California
 Mr. John D. Bosch, Geyserville, California
 Mr. George O. Latimer, Portland, Oregon
Dear Bahai Brothers,
 What a great privilege it is to be appointed on a committee with you two for the purpose of investigating the possibilities of organizing a Bahai Summer School, along the lines of that at Green Acre, for the friends of the Pacific Coast, who are mainly unable to attend the school in Green Acre.
 In order that we may all understand fully the preliminary steps, so far as my activity in this matter is concerned, I am quoting the following from a letter which I wrote to Mr. Holley on February 13th:
 Have you any record of the number of people from the Pacific Coast, or Western Region who attend the Green Acre Conferences or summer school? What I have in mind is this: we have one or two beautiful spots in the territory which are available for

gatherings such as are held in Green Acre, where the Bahais of the West might spend their vacations, and hold summer schools of instruction for children, as well as lay plans for speaking the Message. I have particularly in mind Mr. John Bosch's place in Geyserville. If there are few who attend the summer sessions in Green Acre from the Pacific Coast, we would not be cutting in, in any way on the development of Green Acre, but would be creating something ideal for the Bahais of the West. My idea would be simply to suggest to the Friends in the West, that as many as possible plan to spend their vacations at or near these places at the same time, so we might have these meetings and schools of instruction. As a result of the letter which was sent out to the Teachers in the West, a conference will no doubt be held in Visalia early next month and this subject may come up; so if you can favor me with your views by that time, it will be appreciated.

The teaching conference mentioned in the preceding paragraph was called for Visalia March 6th, but none but myself were able to attend. Mrs. Grace Holley and myself discussed the suggestion, and peculiarly enough, were able to synchronize the plans that some of the Visalia younger Bahais were planning, if possible, to go to Green Acre this summer, but thought it much better, if we could work out some concrete plan, for them to stay here, and devote the time and energy to building up a lasting instrument of service for the Cause in establishing a summer school.

The teaching conference will no doubt be held later in Visalia and I am wondering if you two could not come down there also to assist in the formation of plans for consecutive teaching in the new centers in California; as well as see if we cannot work out something constructive for this summer school idea for the Pacific Coast. We could meet before the teaching conferences and then submit the plan to those assembled as a definite program of action.

There are also steps being taken to arrange for a World Unity Conference in Fresno, California, April 22nd, 23rd, and 24th.

Wouldn't it be wonderful if we could have the Teaching Meeting at the same time in Visalia and then the Unity Conference Sessions in the evenings in Fresno. We might devote the 22nd to the discussion of the summer school and the 23rd and 24th to the Teaching Work.

Can we have any kind of preliminary conference soon. I will endeavor to make my plans to coordinate with anything that either of you suggest.

With deep Bahai Love, and the hope that our humble efforts may be the source of some service and advancement to the Cause, as well as be confirmed by Abdul Baha,

I am, in His Service,

(signed) Leroy Ioas[25]

Leroy's vision of the summer school becoming "a lasting instrument of service to the Cause" suggests that he felt the summer school should be used as a tool for the training of teachers, generation after generation. An instrument may also be thought of as a musical instrument that plays in harmony with other instruments; in that same way, all aspects of the teaching work operate in concert with one another. John Bosch, Leroy Ioas, and George Latimer recognized that the summer school could develop into a training ground for a teaching force and that the "increasing possibilities" of the summer school would require a larger committee than the three of them. In the meantime, Leroy made clear that he and John and George must not wait for reinforcements before getting the first summer school session underway:

640 46th Avenue
San Francisco, California
May 1, 1927
Dear George,

Both John D. and myself have been waiting for some word from you as to your views on the summer school idea for the Coast. We have been together a couple of times, and from our discussion and the study made, it appears that so far as this section is concerned, the ideal location for the school, bearing in mind the increasing possibilities of such an idea, and the consequent need of a suitable and permanent location, that the Bosch property at Geyserville is the best that can be made available. Of course, we have not been able to consider any location up north, feeling that you would do that, and then from the consultation, we would arrive at the proper solution.

Won't you write your views as to the advisability of going into such a plan. If we are to accomplish anything this summer at all, we will have to do some active work now. My thought is, that for the first year, all we can hope to accomplish, is just to have a few Bahais, who are definitely interested in becoming teachers, spend a month at Geyserville, say August, and have daily lessons in the various principles and phases of the Cause, as well as the history and development of the Cause. If we can definitely inspire a few as Teachers, and know they are properly qualified to teach, the work on the Coast will go forward by leaps and bounds this fall and winter. There is no doubt that the spirit of Abdul Baha has so impressed itself upon the world since His Ascent, that if we would only go forward with the proper teachers, and with appropriate follow up work, that the Cause would become established in various centers, very quickly. The need for some place and opportunity to train these teachers, I feel most strongly, and further am impressed that this is the most important thing to do. In the Bay region, we could use five or six capable teachers, but there are none, which for a Cause established in this territory for 20 years or more, is a deplorable condition. Those of us who are anxious to see the Beloved Cause spread, and at the same, see it prepared for its future growth, which we know is shortly coming, must put forth our efforts on every means that will lay a foundation for the future. The Cause is [not sufficiently propagated] today because there are not sufficient teachers fully qualified to present the Cause in its universal and dynamic force.

I don't suppose there is any opportunity for you to come down this way. If not, and anything can be accomplished, I will be glad at the first opportunity to go to Portland to discuss the subject with you. On the 15th of May, we are hoping that some of those who are actively engaged in the teaching work in the California territory will be able to come together in Santa Barbara, where Dr. Khan* will be exhibiting his articles of rare beauty, etc; and it would be wonderful if we could give some consideration to the summer school idea. Therefore, if you could give your suggestions before that time and we could jointly come to some conclusion before then, it would be helpful.

Mr. Bosch and myself feel we should change the recommendations made in the draft of memorandum to be sent to the National Assembly, to include nine in the Executive Committee, as follows: Mrs. Louise R. Waite, Mrs. Grace B. Holley, Mrs. Amelia Collins, Louise Bosch, Dr. Khan, May Maxwell and the three already appointed. Furthermore we should not in generalities speak of the Bosch property, but if that is selected, then give a definite idea of the expenses, etc. that would be incurred in making it a proper site, with accommodations for the Friends.

Of course that is one of the things for the future, but just now, if we could arrive at something concrete, then we could go ahead and for this year, just gather together those who are definitely

---

* Dr. Khan likely refers to Dr. Alí Kulí Khán.

interested in becoming teachers in future development of the Cause, and lay definite plans of teaching in the Fall and Winter.
With deep Bahai love,
(Signed) Leroy Ioas[26]

Leroy suggested that the committee should include May Maxwell, Louise Bosch, Louise Waite, Amelia Collins, Alí Kulí Khán, and Grace Holley—all of whom were experienced teachers of the Cause. Their appointment was not official until 1931, but in response to the suggestion, George Latimer replied, "I am extremely happy over their appointment. I feel it is a GREAT Committee."[27] In the meantime, John Bosch, Leroy Ioas, and George Latimer forged ahead with their plans to establish a training institute for teachers of the Cause—the first of its kind in America:

June 20, 1927
Dear Mr. and Mrs. Bosch:
Didn't we have a most wonderful day yesterday, and how happily all our plans came to such a constructive situation; so that only the future can tell how great will become this Bahai Village for service of the Cause. I am sure we now all feel more enthusiastic and re-assured. With such glowing testimony from Dr. Khan, who was for two years Chairman of the Green Acre Committee, we may be sure that we ourselves have not been carried away with the possibilities. Now we will see what the friends work out in our meetings and consultation, and I believe you will see that all will be surprised at the Confirmations, because it will become the incentive for renewed individual activity and responsibility, which is the great hope of the Cause. Each Bahai must become self-sufficient unto himself in carrying out the Will of the Master, so that if the entire world should be against the Cause, each Bahai himself could withstand any attack. This is

the spirit of service which I understand Shoghi Effendi is creating in the heart of everyone, and when each individual arises as an individual expression of the Cause, with these institutions of Spiritual Assemblies the coordinating influences for this great service, then will the Cause grow and develop.

If I may offer a suggestion, it occurs to me, it might be advisable to change the location of the proposed shower baths and toilet facilities, from the left hand side of the barn behind your new house, to the right hand side, and the reason is this: If we are having meetings under the 'Bahai Tree' of Life, and anyone wishes to use the shower baths, etc., it might create a disturbance which would detract from the attention of the Friends. If on the other side of the barn, then those entering and leaving the shower bath house, would not have to come near the gathering at all.

Another thing, Mrs. Bosch was to find out how much the room would cost in the farm houses nearby, and if you will do this, we will incorporate it in our circular which Dr. Khan and I will compose Tuesday night, leaving space for that data, which we will fill in Wednesday, if you can secure it and mail it Tuesday, so as to reach me Wednesday.

I am writing different ones about taking up one or two special subjects, at the different sessions; for instance, we must have Doctor D'Evelyn go into detail in his explanation of the Word of God, which is the most wonderful anyone ever gives; then Mr. Hurlbut should spend a session in giving the Bible Prophesies from the Old and New Testament, as well as from the other Bibles of the other Religions. Then Dr. Khan must explain in detail, the great station of the House of Justice, in Shoghi Effendi's ministration, as he explained it to us yesterday, because all the Bahais must know and understand these very vital matters, especially those who are to become the Teachers. Also the general subjects, which will be dealt with by Mrs. Waite and George Latimer, and your-

selves; Mrs. French, Mrs. Cooper, etc. I am looking forward to a real benediction of the spiritual blessing, and a great opportunity for the development of Teachers, through these sessions.
With Bahai Love,
In His Service,
(Signed) Leroy[28]

The idea of developing the Bahá'í school into a permanent "summer teaching Institute" is further explored in the following letter from Leroy Ioas. It is clear that an institute need not be a place or a building; rather, a Bahá'í institute is any effort where the participants are united in learning how to apply the Bahá'í teachings in carrying out a common purpose:

San Francisco, June 22, 1927
Dear Mr. and Mrs. Bosch:
Attached, marked No. 1, is suggestions of the circular which I suggest we send out immediately to the Assemblies of the Coast. The rough write-up marked No. 2, is the suggestion of Dr. Khan for the Pacific Bahai Village.
My thought is this: we were originally appointed to work out plans for a summer school, and ways and means of making that permanent, the permanent part of which we were to submit to the National Assembly. Most of the Friends on the coast know of the summer school plan all ready, and therefore, I am afraid, that if we do not send out any announcement of the summer school, but simply that of the Pacific Village idea, it will be confusing to them, and may harm this summer school in August. Now what I think is, that we send out the announcement of the summer teaching Institute, which indicates we wish to discuss making it permanent; then later, we write each Secretary of the Local Assemblies about the Pacific Village idea, in accordance with Dr. Khan's inspired suggestion, and ask them to try to be officially

represented at the Conference, so our plan may have the approval of all the Assemblies. This will also give us opportunity to inform the National Assembly fully and secure their approval. What do you think?

If the circular meets with your approval, and you will send word quickly by letter or wire, I will have it gotten out immediately, and thus the work will be under way. Then we can go ahead and supplement it, with the added plan for making the Teaching Institute permanent and developed into the Pacific Bahai Village Idea. It occurs to me this is the most forceful way to do it. Just like it grew on us, first to just have the Teaching Classes, then to make it permanent, and now to create the first Bahai Village. So let us have the idea grow on the rest of the Bahais. Further, there are many details for us to decide upon before we announce the Village idea, which Dr. Khan touches in his suggested circular. We should have these matters concluded before we announce too much.

The letters you addressed to 46th Street came to us all right, and I delivered the one to Dr. Kahn last night, which made him very happy and pleased with your kind words. The one to Mr. Linfoot we have forwarded. The telegram came and you will note we included in the circular this information.

Did I leave a note book of mine in your car, and if so, may I ask if you will send it to me.

With deep Bahai love,

(Signed) Leroy[29]

The notion of a "Bahá'í Village" may have been inspired by news of such a village being formed in Daidanow, Burma at the time. There, the Burmese friends lived in a village compound they called 'Abdu'l-Bahá's Village. That village proved a safe-haven for Bahá'ís in Burma who were otherwise religiously ostracized. Despite the success of such a village in Burma, John and Louise had the wisdom to recognize the pitfalls of communal living and warned against it, as they felt it might detract from the purpose of the Geyserville Summer School becoming a training ground for teachers of the Cause. Louise Bosch wrote in a letter of John's concern that some Bahá'ís might confuse the laws of Bahá'u'lláh with their own whims and desires when attending the summer school. In addition to expressing her husband's opinion on the matter, Louise's own practical and dispassionate sentiment is heard loud and clear by understanding the difference between and a community and a colony:

My husband said that a settlement like this place was intended to be a <u>Community</u> and not a Colony. That the Laws of Baha'u'llah, interpreted by 'Abdu'l-Baha, directed and guided and presided over by Shoghi Effendi, would be the management. For instance: whoever works for the National Spiritual Assembly is a steward for the <u>Cause</u>, not for the people.

"Nobody can live in a Colony successfully," he [John Bosch] said, "because in a Colony there is always one man or another, who by love of leadership will want to run things his own way. But in a <u>Community</u> everyone has his own things, and waits upon himself, and pays his own way. In a Community no one will sit at another man's table unless invited."

All of the Colonies so far have failed because the principle of authority in them was wrong. The management of them was wrong.

In this Baha'i Community the Laws of Baha'u'llah must be carried out. The members of that Community, who want to do things their own way, will automatically drop out of the Community (or else will do what is right). The Laws of Baha'u'llah alone can be the governing Power, John said.

(Signed) Louise Bosch
Geyserville, California
June 12, 1928[30]

By July of 1927, the Pacific Coast Summer School Committee had outlined plans for its first summer session, to take place in the next month, August of 1927. Aside from the details about practical matters such as room size, the following letter gives insight into how John Bosch and the committee made sure that the school would "be conducted as a purely Bahá'í institution." It is interesting to note that more than two decades later, the Guardian affirmed that the participants of the summer school must concentrate on "deepening their grasp of the Teachings" and cautioned against courses that were "not sufficiently Bahá'í in nature"[31] John Bosch, Leroy Ioas, and George Latimer had such a clear vision regarding the way in which the institution of a Bahá'í summer school would evolve in the future:

> Consideration was given to various locations: Santa Barbara, California; St. Helena, California; Los Gatos, California; and the location selected, Geyserville, California. In arriving at a conclusion as to best location, such items as accessibility, economic stability, equipment, and above all, whether the facilities offered would permit [us to] conduct the School as planned, from an entirely and purely Bahai standpoint.
>
> At Geyserville, Mr. and Mrs. Bosch have very kindly offered their property for the School. There are a number of buildings on the property, the largest of which is a building containing ten rooms. The Bosches are now having this building remodeled, etc, which will make an ideal headquarters for the school and the classes. The large living room on the main floor will seat 65 people. The property is right at hand to the railroad station, the auto highway skirts the land, and it is right near the heart of Geyserville.
>
> Moderately priced hotels and eating houses are located at Geyserville, while better accommodations can be had at Healdsburg, just 15 minutes ride by auto.
>
> The land has already become a center of attraction to the Bahais of California each year, the various assemblies hold a Unity Feast there on August 1st.

Being situated on Bahai property already owned by a Bahai Family, the School can be conducted as a purely Bahai institution, under the direction of the National Assembly, through the appointed Committee.

The specific plan of teaching for the first year will be, first, to prepare all those who are anxious to teach, so they may become experienced teachers; second, a source of Bahai study for the children and young peoples; third, would [sic] out a plan of conduct and study for the Gardens, which will be helpful to those engaged in this commendable work to each Assembly, and to stimulate interest in it.

After the course of study and practice as Teachers is outlined, it is the intention to have the different Teachers, already appointed as such, to take charge of the instructional work, during whatever period is necessary. It is hoped Mr. George Latimer will be able to spend the entire period of the sessions, to be in general charge and control of the teaching work.

The first year will naturally be one of experiment, to a certain extent, in developing the work, and it is thought best not to attempt to make any permanent organization at this time. With the names suggested added to the Executive Committee, as outlined above, giving representation to the different sections of the Pacific Coast, and being those who are most deeply interested in the plan, it is felt the best results will be attained. As the work develops the Committee can then offer recommendations as to permanent organization to handle the Summer School.

It is the hope and prayer of the Committee that if best God will confirm this attempt to increase the Unity of the Friends, by drawing them together for study of His Word and preparation for the diffusion of His Fragrances. The drawing together for the Friends who are anxious to serve will prove a magnet of the Spirit which will increase the potency of the Cause in this territory, and make possible the attraction of new souls to the Beloved Cause.

(Signed) Leroy Ioas (and on behalf of John Bosch and George Latimer)[32]

John and Louise's mature experience in the teaching field is evident in the types of courses planned for the summer session—courses aimed at strengthening the participant's spiritual foundation in the Cause so that he or she would become better equipped to teach others about the Cause. In dozens of letters written on his behalf, the Guardian made clear that he felt that "the most important thing for the Bahá'í Schools all over the world at present to do is to strongly impress upon the Bahá'í attendants the urgency of arising, not only to fulfil pioneer goals and to consolidate the work on the home front, which is getting weaker every year instead of stronger, but also to bring home to the friends the necessity of dispersing.[33] It was important to John that the courses planned for the summer school be aimed at developing future traveling teachers of the Cause. This meant not only learning the fundamental teachings of Bahá'u'lláh, but also practicing how to convey those teachings to others in their purest form.

With the opening of its first summer session in August of 1927, an information flyer was prepared for circulation among the Bahá'ís of the Pacific Coast of the Western States. John and Louise must have felt like youth setting out on their first great teaching adventure, and ready to send out invitations for others to join the summer school campaign:

July 1st, 1927
Dear Leroy Ioas,
How fast the time is flying and the great day is rapidly approaching. We are anxiously awaiting the circular letter to be mailed to the friends as soon as it is printed, especially for those in Portland. Hoping you will return safe and sound from Los Angeles, we are ever yours,
John and Louise

Information Flyer:
Course of Study
Bahai Summer School
Geyserville, California

Session 1: August 1–14 1927
Courses given by Leroy Ioas, Howard Hurlbut, and Frederick D'Evelyn

Aug 1: 10:00am: Proofs of the Existence of God
2:00pm: Relation of God and Man
Aug 2: 10am: Evolution of Man
2:00pm: Immortality
Aug 3: 10am: Need of a Manifestation
2:00pm: Station of the Manifestation
Aug 4: 10am: Continuity of Manifestations
2:00pm: Resume and Discussion
Aug 5: 10am: The Holy Spirit
2pm: The "Word"
Aug 6: 10am: Open for Special Subject
2pm: Open for Special Subject
Aug 7: Special Sunday Public Meeting
Aug 8: 8:10am: Bahai History and Manifestations
2pm: The Covenant of God and its Continuous Preservation of the Bahai Cause
Aug 9: 10am: Prophetic Proofs of the Cause
2pm: Explanation of Christian Parables
Aug 10: 10am: Bahai Principles
2pm: Bahai Principles, continued
Aug 11: 10am: Bahai Institutions: Temple, Organization, Unified Plan, Hokuk*

---

* The word *Hokuk* likely refers to the Law of Ḥuqúqu'lláh, which would not have been binding on the Western believers at the time but was studied at the Geyserville Bahá'í School.

2pm: Intimate touches of Lives of Bab,
Baha'Ullah, and Abdul Baha
Aug 12: 10am: Prayer
2:00pm: Spiritual Healing: Bahai Teachings in
comparison with New Thought Movements
Aug 13: 10am: Open for Special Subjects
2:00pm: Open for Special Subjects
Aug 14: Sunday, Special Public Meeting

Session II: Courses conducted by Sophronia Aoki, Gladys Aoki, Charles Bishop, Louise Caswell, Ella Goodall Cooper, Nellie French, Shanaz Waite, Marion Yazdi, and Leroy Ioas.

Aug 15: 10am: Oneness of Mankind, Foundation of Religion
is One, Independent Investigation of Truth
2:30pm: Public Speaking class
Aug 16: 10am: Equality of Man and Woman, Solution of
Economic Problems, Universal Education
2:30pm: Public Speaking Class
Aug 17: 10am: Resume and Discussion
2:30pm: Public Speaking Class
Aug 18: 10am: Proof of the Existence of God,
Man's Relationship to God
2:30pm: Public Speaking class
Aug 19: 10am: Evolution of Man, Immortality, Religion
and Science
2:30pm: The Holy Spirit and "The Word"
Aug 20: 10am: Pilgrimage to the Holy Land, My Visit
to Abdul Baha (Mrs. Ella Goodall Cooper)
2:30pm: Bahai History and Manifestations,
The Most Great Infallibility
Aug 21: Sunday: Prayer as Spiritual Healing

Aug 22: 10am: The Covenant of God and its Continuous
Preservation of the Bahai Cause
2:30pm: Continuity of Manifestations
Aug 23: 10am: Spiritual Progress
2:30pm: Spiritual Healing in Acca (Mrs. Cooper)
Aug 24: 10am: The Need of a Manifestation
2:30pm: Living the Bahai Life
Aug 25: 10am: Will and Testament of Abdul Baha[34]

At the conclusion of its first session, Leroy wrote that "the Committee felt that if only a few—perhaps nine at most—could attend the sessions the first year their efforts would be rewarded, but the expectations were more than fulfilled, for there was an attendance, during the month, of forty confirmed believers, including fifteen young and enthusiastic souls."[35] How satisfying it must have been for John Bosch, who had written to 'Abdu'l-Bahá in 1919 asking His advice on how to use his property at Geyserville "for the preparation of a Baha'i School or College for teaching [. . .] the pure teachings of Baha Ullah."* All shared in John and Louise's joy, as this letter from Ali and Marion Yazdi attests:

1175 Arch Street
Berkeley, California
August 22, 1927
Dear Louise and John and all:
After soaring with such joy and exhilaration in the spiritual atmosphere for eleven happy days, it seems a little difficult to get adjusted to walking in the earth realm again. We were very happy at Geyserville. We cannot thank you enough for the hospitality and comforts you gave us. The beauty of Abha was seen in all

---

* See Chapter 5 for the full transcript of Bosch's letter to the Master.

your tireless service. You were an inspiring example to us all and we will always be better for having been with you.

Every day of the Summer School seemed to fulfill the verse in the Koran which says: "A Day will come wherein the lights of unity will enlighten all the world. The earth will be irradiated with the light of God. That light is the light of unity. There is no God but God."

Next year Ali and I shall arrange to have our vacation at the time of the Summer School [. . .].

Ali and Marion Yazdi[36]

Together, John Bosch, Leroy Ioas, and George Latimer had succeeded in originating a Bahá'í school for the Pacific Coast region devoted to the training of Bahá'í teachers. The committee's vision for the school was that it become a "structure of spiritual impetus for the Cause," and by spring of the next year, the committee sought the consultation of the summer school attendees in order to make effective plans for the next summer:

Report of the Bahai Summer School Committee
March 6, 1928
(To the attendees of the first summer school in 1927)
Dear friends:

The Bahai Summer School has now become a definite institution amongst the Bahai's of the West. The success of the session last year was due to the free and open consultation and cooperation of its enthusiastic and ardent supporters. This letter is addressed to those who attended the classes last year, who are in reality a consulting committee for the furtherance of the work before us. In laying plans for the coming year, your advice and consultation is desired, that the foundations already laid, may grow into a structure of spiritual impetus for the Cause on the Coast [. . .].

Let us hope that the work which is done this year will redound very fully in bringing new life to the Cause and more channels for its spread, and this build up the structure of Universal Brotherhood as quickly as possible.
In His Service,
Bahá'í Summer School Committee[37]

With a second world war looming on the horizon of the decade to come, the Cause of Bahá'u'lláh would attract an ever-growing interest in the tenets of His Faith from citizens of the world seeking answers to global problems. The aftermath of the first world war could not have been far from the minds of the members of the Pacific Coast Summer School Committee. In a particularly cruel irony of the era, after the first world war, African-American servicemen who fought to liberate Europe from tyranny returned to the United States to face a tyranny far more insidious in the 1919 "Red Summer" of racial violence in post-World War II America. In a letter dated August 5, 1932, written on his behalf, the Guardian made clear the spiritual necessity of the summer school: "He sincerely trusts that these summer courses will serve to deepen the knowledge and the understanding of the friends and enable them to diffuse the teachings of the Faith to the struggling and almost hopeless world." Therefore, the participants in the Geyserville Bahá'í School would not only have to prove through words their commitment to the expansion of the Bahá'í Faith in America and throughout the world, the participants would have to demonstrate through deeds the power of the oneness of humanity.[38]

9 / Not Alone of the Mind, but of the Depths of the Heart

In the spring of 1926, Louis Gregory attended the National Bahá'í Convention, which was held that year in San Francisco. It had been nearly five years since the passing of 'Abdu'l-Bahá, and the American Bahá'í community was striving to advance its goals of increasing its membership and widening the geographic distribution of its adherents. Louis Gregory's biographer, Gayle Morrison, describes this period of transition in the years after the ascension of 'Abdu'l-Bahá:

> In the first five years of the Guardian's ministry, the community had responded to a different challenge, that of accepting a new focus of authority. Although few may have recognized the extent of the change at the time, it now seems clear that, as Louis Gregory and others journeyed to San Francisco to attend the Eighteenth Annual Convention in April 1926, a profound transformation had already occurred in the American Bahá'í community.
> Indeed, the convention itself symbolized a break from the past. The number of delegates and visitors from the old established centers in the eastern and midwestern states was much lower than in previous years, but the total attendance was greater than ever; the halls were filled with new faces from the West.[1]

Morrison's mention of a "break from the past" alludes to the decades of challenges faced by the American Bahá'í community in its struggle to foster social equality as much as spiritual equality. The believers accepted the spiritual principle of human equality, but Bahá'í community life did not reflect the application of this principle, particularly in the years between 1914 and 1916, when Bahá'í meetings in Louis Gregory's community in Washington DC were segregated. In the decade leading up to the San Francisco Convention of 1926, Louis Gregory worked to raise the consciousness of race unity in the American Bahá'í community. Five years prior, in 1921, Louis Gregory assisted in the promotion of the first Race Amity Convention in the United States—a convention that was requested by 'Abdu'l-Bahá of Mrs. Agnes Parsons, a Bahá'í with far-reaching social influence in Washington DC. The success of the conference surpassed all expectations, with notable speakers that included Louis Gregory, Alain Locke, and Coralie Franklin Cook.[2]

Louis Gregory's biographer Gayle Morrison notes that 'Abdu'l-Bahá expressed "extraordinary expectations regarding Louis Gregory's singular role in race relations" as evidenced in the following excerpt of a Tablet from 'Abdu'l-Bahá to Louis Gregory written in 1909:

"I hope that thou mayest become . . . the means whereby the white and colored people shall close their eyes to racial differences and behold the reality of humanity, and that is the universal unity which is the oneness of the kingdom of the human race, the basic harmony of the world and the appearance of the bounty of the Almighty. [. . .]. Rely as much as thou canst upon the True One, and be thou resigned to the Will of God, so that like unto a candle thou mayest be enkindled in the world of humanity and like unto a star thou mayest shine and gleam from the Horizon of Reality and become the cause of the guidance of both races."[3]

At the 1926 Bahá'í National Convention in San Francisco, Louis Gregory was asked to address the assembled delegates and visitors.

Inspired by a force that he once characterized as "the instruction and stimulus that have flowed from Haifa," Louis Gregory spoke on "The Oneness of Mankind," and among his hearers was John Bosch. One can only imagine John Bosch sitting in rapt and undivided attention as Louis Gregory spoke of the most vital principle of God's will for His creation. At the conclusion of his talk, Louis Gregory used the analogy of the lever of Archimedes in order to illustrate the magnitude of the kind of racial unity called for by Bahá'u'lláh and the effort required of the Bahá'ís in order to realize this transformation: "Among the different races and groups and classes of people in the world, the ideal of today is co-operation, mutuality, service. If one wants to distinguish himself let him become distinguished in service to humanity. (Applause). Let him stand upon this principle of the oneness of God and the oneness of the entire human race. Who-ever stands upon this exalted principle will never be shaken by the shifting sands of time; who-ever stands upon this exalted principle, like the lever of Archimedes, will move the world."[4]

To appreciate Louis Gregory's reference to the Greek physicist, it is useful to imagine the illustration: The lever can be pictured as a long plank resting on a fulcrum. On one end of the plank sits a seemingly immovable object—a heavy globe that must be moved. If the fulcrum is placed close to the heavy globe and a lesser force is applied from the other end, the principle demonstrates that a small force can move a seemingly immovable object due to the multiplication of the power of the lesser force. By this analogy, the small body of believers can move the world as long as they distinguish themselves from that world and as long as their work is leveraged upon the principle of the oneness of humanity.

In the United States, the question of how to achieve greater unity, harmony, and oneness had long been on the minds of the believers. Mrs. Keith Ransom-Kehler, who was on pilgrimage in Haifa at the time of the 1926 Bahá'í National Convention in San Francisco, wrote a letter to the convention explaining that "On the eve of my departure from Haifa, our Guardian, Shoghi Effendi, said that it would be well if I wrote the delegates and friends a message from him." She explained that the Guardian emphasized the vital importance of the friends' spontaneous and whole-hearted support of the Spiritual Assemblies, because such earnest support, given without reservation or misgiving, constitutes a safeguard of the Cause. Mrs. Keith Ransom-Kehler's letter continued by saying that the Guardian had indicated that the most essential thing in all matters would be for the friends to work in harmony. If they did not work together, there was nothing to teach. What was needed was not so much devotion to the Cause but rather love for God, for the Master, and for the Cause that needed to be translated into love for one another. After all, the Cause could not be expected to unite the world if it could not even unite two individuals.[5]

John Bosch would have been well aware of the unity to which the believers had been called to achieve, especially in the years following the passing of 'Abdu'l-Bahá. The Master's Will and Testament makes clear that self-renunciation is essential in bringing about spiritual and social unity—and that such renunciation would take time and effort on behalf of the believers. As well-intentioned as they were, early Bahá'ís in the United States, like John Bosch, had limited experience in how to bring about spiritual and social unity. It would not be until 1938 that Shoghi Effendi would outline for every member of the American Bahá'í Community "those essential virtues of self-renunciation, of moral rectitude, of chastity, of indiscriminating fellowship, of holy discipline, and of spiritual insight that will fit them for the preponderating share they will have in calling into being that World Order and that World Civilization of which their country, no less than the entire human race, stands in desperate need." In that same letter, the Guardian made clear that the people of America are "prey to one of the most virulent and long-standing forms of racial prejudice," and while he made this observation in 1938, his use of the word "virulent" alludes to the centuries-old malignancy of the social disease of racism.[6]

From an historical standpoint, one can appreciate the kind of person who, in the early 1900s, recognized in the teachings of Bahá'u'lláh that the oneness of humanity is God's most immediate commandment for His creation in this day. Yet, it was a kind of spiritual paradox for many of the early American believers who, on one hand, embraced the principle of oneness as a spiritual reality, and on the other hand, lived in a racially segregated society in the United States. For some early believers, therefore, the oneness of mankind remained merely a pious hope rather than a working reality. Shoghi Effendi warned that the principle of the Oneness of Mankind must be founded on something greater:

> Let there be no mistake. The principle of the Oneness of Mankind—the pivot round which all the teachings of Bahá'u'lláh revolve—is no mere outburst of ignorant emotionalism or an expression of vague and pious hope. Its appeal is not to be merely identified with a reawakening of the spirit of brotherhood and good-will among men, nor does it aim solely at the fostering of harmonious coöperation among individual peoples and nations. Its implications are deeper, its claims greater than any which the Prophets of old were allowed to advance. Its message is applicable not only to the individual, but concerns itself primarily with the nature of those essential relationships that must bind all the states and nations as members of one human family. It does not constitute merely the enunciation of an ideal, but stands inseparably associated with an institution adequate to embody its truth, demonstrate its validity, and perpetuate its influence. It implies an organic change in the structure of present-day society, a change such as the world has not yet experienced. It constitutes a challenge, at once bold and universal, to outworn shibboleths of national creeds—creeds that have had their day and which must, in the ordinary course of events as shaped and controlled by Providence, give way to a new gospel, fundamentally different from, and infinitely superior to, what the world has already conceived. It calls for no less than the reconstruction and the demilitariza-

tion of the whole civilized world—a world organically unified in all the essential aspects of its life, its political machinery, its spiritual aspiration, its trade and finance, its script and language, and yet infinite in the diversity of the national characteristics of its federated units.[7]

Fostering interracial fellowship—no matter the degree to which an individual has advanced toward oneness—within the Bahá'í community is a fundamental requisite for every follower of Bahá'u'lláh. After all, when a person accepts Bahá'u'lláh as the Messenger of God for this day, he or she begins the lifelong work of "striving every day to bring our behavior more into accordance with the high standards that are set forth in the Teachings." When John Bosch wrote his declaration to 'Abdu'l-Bahá of his acceptance of these Bahá'í teachings, he wrote that his "watchword would be Justice," and on that day John Bosch's social relations were about to become more diverse than he ever imagined. He worked all his life to practice justice, fairness, and equity, owing much to his first Bahá'í teacher, Mrs. Beckwith, who warned him that "to hear of this [Message] is the greatest privilege, but it will be followed up by the greatest obligations and better not know it if you cannot follow it."[8]

The first African-American believer was Mr. Robert Turner, and he is best remembered as the one to whom 'Abdu'l-Bahá promised that "'if he remained firm and steadfast until the end, he would be a door through which a whole race would enter the Kingdom.'"[9] Louis Gregory wrote,

Robert Turner was the butler of Mrs. Phoebe Hearst [in California], early Bahá'í and mother of the well-known publisher of that name. Robert Turner's post was one of unusual responsibility, carrying with it largely the stewardship of his wealthy and socially prominent employer [. . .]. When Mrs. Hearst was given the Bahá'í message by Mrs. Getsinger, Robert Turner, from the vantage ground of his service station, listened with eager interest to words not addressed to himself. He sought opportunities to know more about so wonderful a Faith, was taught and became a firm believer.10

In December of 1898, Phoebe Hearst organized a group to travel to the Holy Land to meet 'Abdu'l-Bahá, and the group included Robert Turner, Lua Getsinger, and May Bolles. Robert Turner was much beloved by 'Abdu'l-Bahá and when he passed away in 1909 after an illness, 'Abdu'l-Bahá wrote a Tablet wherein He supplicated God to "Glorify the precious Robert in Thy Kingdom and in the garden of the Paradise of Abha. Bring him in[to] intimate association with the birds of the celestial meadow."[11]

John Bosch was a frequent participant in the Bahá'í meetings at the home of Mrs. Helen Goodall in San Francisco before the passing of Robert Turner, and since it was from her that 'Abdu'l-Bahá received communication about the passing of Robert Turner, it is very likely that John Bosch knew Robert Turner. Therefore, it is likely that John Bosch was aware of 'Abdu'l-Bahá's words concerning the station of Robert Turner as "a door" through which African Americans would enter the Cause of God. After Robert Turner's passing, it would be the opportunity of every member of the Bahá'í community to find ways of keeping the door open very wide for the welcoming of African Americans into the forefront of the community of the Most Great Name.

The National Spiritual Assembly elected at the 1926 Convention in San Francisco confronted a full agenda for the year ahead. In its annual report in April 1927, the National Spiritual Assembly outlined three areas requiring its attention, the third of which "consisted in the development of methods and policies capable of conveying the spirit and teachings of the Cause to the surrounding public."[12] In addition, the National Spiritual Assembly gave special attention to the subject of race unity in its Annual Report of 1927:

One of the recently appointed national committees is engaged in work of such fundamental importance that its plans should be mentioned somewhat in detail. We refer to the committee on inter-racial amity which is endeavoring to carry out that program of spiritual reconciliation which 'Abdu'l-Bahá so emphatically declared to be essential to the well-being, perhaps even to the safety of the American people. In requesting Mr. Louis Gregory to serve as executive secretary of this committee, the National Spiritual Assembly considered that this true servant of Bahá'u'lláh would surely find in this field a task worthy of his ideals and attainments. The friends are requested to give particular attention to the plans of the committee on inter-racial amity, in order that as soon as possible racial amity meetings may be held in cities throughout the country.[13]

In addition to Louis Gregory, the members of that committee were Mrs. Agnes S. Parsons, Mrs. Louise D. Boyle, Mrs. Coralie F. Cook, Mrs. Mariam Haney, Mr. Alain Locke, Dr. Zia M. Bagdádí. After the committee's first meeting, it stated that the "plans suggested cannot bring forth the desired results until every believer purifies his heart from any trace of race prejudice." The National Spiritual Assembly responded to the committee's suggestion by publishing a letter in the March 1927 issue of the *Bahá'í News Letter* stressing that "the efforts by Bahá'ís to heal this spiritual sickness afflicting the body of humanity depends upon each worker purifying his own heart from all trace of racial prejudice."[14]

John Bosch stayed informed of all issues concerning the progress of the American Bahá'í community. Not only would he have read the annual report of the National Spiritual Assembly, but he also kept abreast of the continual guidance from the Guardian. A few months before Geyserville's first summer school session in 1927, the Guardian wrote to the American Bahá'í community regarding the urgency of race unity studies at the summer schools. Louis Gregory's biographer, Gayle

Morrison, wrote, "Never since the days of the Master had the Bahá'í principles of interracial equality been stated in such terms. Indeed, Shoghi Effendi's 1927 message on race is perhaps his most urgent and forceful assessment of any specific problem confronting the American Bahá'ís up to that time."[15] Shoghi Effendi's letter was directed specifically to Green Acre, but to John Bosch, the letter must have felt like a clear directive to the Geyserville Bahá'í Summer School Committee:

> It is my earnest hope and prayer that the forthcoming gathering at Green Acre, the program for which has been so carefully and judiciously prepared, may serve as a testing ground for the application of those ideals and standards that are the distinguishing features of the Revelation of Bahá'u'lláh. May the assembled believers—now but a tiny nucleus of the Bahá'í Commonwealth of the future—so exemplify that spirit of universal love and fellowship as to evoke in the minds of their associates the vision of that future City of God which the almighty arm of Bahá'u'lláh can alone establish.
>
> Not by merely imitating the excesses and laxity of the extravagant age they live in; not by the idle neglect of the sacred responsibilities it is their privilege to shoulder; not by the silent compromise of the principles dearly cherished by 'Abdu'l-Bahá; not by their fear of unpopularity or their dread of censure can they hope to rouse society from its spiritual lethargy, and serve as a model to a civilization the foundations of which the corrosion of prejudice has well-nigh undermined. By the sublimity of their principles, the warmth of their love, the spotless purity of their character, and the depth of their devoutness and piety, let them demonstrate to their fellow-countrymen the ennobling reality of a power that shall weld a disrupted world.
>
> We can prove ourselves worthy of our Cause only if in our individual conduct and corporate life we sedulously imitate the example of our beloved Master, Whom the terrors of tyranny,

the storms of incessant abuse, the oppressiveness of humiliation, never caused to deviate a hair's breadth from the revealed Law of Bahá'u'lláh.

Such is the path of servitude, such is the way of holiness He chose to tread to the very end of His life. Nothing short of the strictest adherence to His glorious example can safely steer our course amid the pitfalls of this perilous age and lead us on to fulfill our high destiny.

Your true brother,

SHOGHI.

Haifa, Palestine

April 12, 1927[16]

As planners of the summer school program, John Bosch, Leroy Ioas, and George Latimer made certain that each program placed an emphasis on the Guardian's directive that the school be "a testing ground for the application of those ideals and standards that are the distinguishing features of the Revelation of Bahá'u'lláh." A survey of the programs offered at Geyserville from 1927 and beyond demonstrates that commitment. For instance, "The Oneness of Mankind" was a course offered during its first summer in 1927 and repeated again in 1928. In 1929, the course delved into the sociology of racism. In 1930, a course on "Inter-racial Harmony" was offered, followed by a course on "The Abolition of Racial Barriers" in 1931.

In 1932, Louis Gregory was both a member of the National Spiritual Assembly and Secretary of the National Race Amity Committee. John and Louise invited Louis Gregory to the Geyserville Summer School in 1932, adding that they would adjust the summer school calendar to fit his schedule. Here is Louis Gregory's response to their invitation:

I am still hoping to be with you in July for your summer school and present indications are, God willing, that it will work out. Matters will be perhaps entirely clear following the annual convention. I think that it is far better in any event for you to have your meetings at the usual time rather than in June. People who have the vacation habit will be more likely to come at the usual time.

Please let me know what is expected of me. Presume that you want some talks on Racial amity and related subjects. Shall try to help in whatever way under consultation and guidance are thought best.

Please also pardon my ignorance of California geography. On what railroad is Geyserville and how is it approached from the East? Does one have to go first to San Francisco?

With Abha greetings and best wishes to your household and friends,

Your brother in service,

Louis G Gregory[17]

As it turned out, Louis Gregory was needed at Green Acre that summer, but John Bosch kept the Geyserville program as planned had Louis Gregory been able to come. The theme of the Geyserville Summer School in 1932 was "Universal Peace—The Goal of a New World Order" with a variety of courses offered, such as "Oneness of Humanity—the Consummation of Human Evolution," "The Nobility of Man," "Unity in Diversity," "Unity in a Common Faith," and "World Citizenship." In effect, all of the courses that would have been taught by Louis Gregory were now being taught by other teachers, and as a result, the human resources who could serve in the capacity of promoting the Bahá'í teachings on race unity increased.

Another influence in the shaping of Geyserville Bahá'í School's first summer session in 1927 was an unprecedented talk given by Mrs. Sadie Oglesby at the 1927 Bahá'í National Convention that was held just months before Geyserville's first summer session. Sadie Oglesby was the first African American woman to make a pilgrimage to Haifa, where she stayed twenty days in March of 1927.[18] Upon her return, she traveled from Boston to the Bahá'í National Convention for the United States and Canada, which was held in Montreal that year. Here, in part, are the recorded minutes of Sadie Oglesby's sincere, loving, and frank address to the Convention. It should be noted that while Sadie quotes the words of Shoghi Effendi, her recollections are merely pilgrims' notes and do not represent the actual words of the Guardian:

> Since going to the Holy Land, we have been coming into a deeper realization, over here, of the tremendous spiritual forces that are ready to be released in the world [. . .]. We had a most glorious visit with Shoghi Effendi, and I can never express it to you. Of course, those of you who have visited that Holy Shrine know that it is beyond my power to describe it. We are not the same people we were before we went away; we don't feel the same about anything—and that is very natural. Since I have so few minutes to spare, and there are many things to tell you, I will have to go at it.
> Shoghi Effendi asked me many questions about this Colored Problem, and always, it seems as though he was trying to find why there were not more Colored believers. We have beautiful reports—he reads them and finds what we are doing, but he asks, "How many Colored believers are in this centre, or the other centre?" and "Why is it they are not there? Is it because they don't feel welcome—because they are not kindly received?"
> I said, "Shoghi Effendi, we have felt hurt, for many years, and we are a sensitive people; we approach the Cause looking for trouble; we are looking to find flaws—that seems natural, because all the churches stand for universal brotherhood; this is proclaimed in every church, and the Christian world stands for universal brotherhood, and yet, the colored group has knocked at so many doors to try and find the spirit of universal brotherhood. They hear another call, and listen, and they are looking to see it in practice [. . .]. It appears to me, and has for some years, that these two groups, the White and the Black races, are the outer ends

of the great circle that is coming together, and, if we could join these two groups, all the other groups would come in."

He said, "Just so—you have analyzed it perfectly. When these two groups join hands, the circle is rounded and everything will adjust itself [. . .]. No doubt the white people of America are watching to see what the Baha'is are doing with the colored people, and, when they see the white Baha'is accepting the colored people as brothers, in every sense of the word, it will give them confidence in your religion, and they will join with you, helping to establish universal brotherhood [. . .]. The world is looking to see what the Baha'is of America are going to do for the colored man, and the peace and tranquility of the world depend on that one thing. In this great hour of turmoil, when everybody and every group of people are talking about universal brotherhood and justice, we Baha'is must be that centre that is not living in the realm of thinking about it, but the ones who actually have it in practice."[19]

Later in her address, Mrs. Oglesby explained how the Guardian discussed the importance of having at least one person of color on every committee, even if it meant having the same person of color serving on several committees, because, he said, "[the Whites] don't know the Colored Man's problems." Sadie explained further:

I said, "But, Shoghi Effendi, when we get together to elect these members, we assemble in prayer, seeking Divine Guidance, and we cast our votes, and we try to follow and obey—what else can we do?"

He said, "Study the needs of the Cause, and then you will know that the need of the Cause is that the Negro be represented, that he might express his viewpoint, that you might understand his position; that we might reach across this chasm and study it and know the needs—don't go at things blindly."[20]

Sadie Oglesby said that the Guardian seemed to want to talk of nothing else during her time in the Holy Land and that he encouraged her to be bold in her assertion of the vital importance of opening the doors of the Cause to people of color:

> Shoghi Effendi says it is his conviction that, once the doors are open—once the hearts of the friends yearn for the spirit of the Colored Man in these groups, they will flock to you. I said, "I have tried to go among the Baha'is and manifest love, obedience, forgiveness and charity, that we might see that it is possible for us to live together, because I have read the words of the Master, when he said we must even give up the right and accept the wrong, for the sake of harmony," and he said, "Yes, that is right, but this is a different time; this is a vital moment, and the issue is to bring the White and Colored people together in heart, that they might pulsate as one and know themselves as absolute brothers."[21]

At the height of her address—an address that so deeply captivated the hearts of the delegates that they voted unanimously to send a transcript of her talk to every Local Spiritual Assembly in the United States and Canada—Mrs. Oglesby addressed the importance of racial diversity in all aspects of Bahá'í life, including its administrative bodies: "In this day, the Colored Man wants to have something to say about his problems, and, when he finds he can come and talk to you about his problems, then, and only then, will you be able to adjust them." And, referring to the assembled delegates at the National Convention, Mrs. Oglesby said, "As I looked around today, knowing that this group represents all the Baha'i Centres over the United States and Canada, I see just about one drop of Negro blood." Then she explained how she and her husband became Bahá'ís through Harlan and Grace Ober:[22]

> If it had not been through the divine gift of God through Mr. and Mrs. Ober, our spiritual teachers—if it had been that I found them off duty once, we would have turned our faces in another

direction; we were guilty of looking for shortcomings, but we have never seen them off duty with us, or with anybody else, at any time. If they had not remained in Boston until my husband and myself were strong enough to turn our eyes towards God, I assure you, dear souls, we still would have been looking in the dark. So, it comes down to this, we have to hold the light up; we have to hold it high, and if they see you off duty a minute, they will go another way.[23]

Sadie Oglesby's insights served as a timely reminder of Bahá'u'lláh's injunction to humanity to let "deeds, not words, be your adorning."[24] Her courage to take action at the Bahá'í National Convention was certainly a milestone—one that had its inspiration from the honest discourse on race unity fostered by Louis Gregory at former National Conventions. Furthermore, Sadie Oglesby's contribution to the consultation at the Convention in 1927 is confirmed in the words of Shoghi Effendi, who wrote to the U.S. National Spiritual Assembly in April, 1927, one month after Sadie Oglesby's pilgrimage to Haifa. In that letter, Shoghi Effendi makes an appeal to the National Spiritual Assembly to advance interracial amity with boldness, decisiveness, and wisdom:

As this problem, in the inevitable course of events, grows in acuteness and complexity, and as the number of the faithful from both races multiplies, it will become increasingly evident that the future growth and prestige of the Cause are bound to be influenced to a very considerable degree by the manner in which the adherents of the Bahá'í Faith carry out, first among themselves and in their relations with their fellow-men, those high standards of inter-racial amity so widely proclaimed and so fearlessly exemplified to the American people by our Master 'Abdu'l-Bahá.

I direct my appeal with all the earnestness and urgency that this pressing problem calls for to every conscientious upholder of the universal principles of Bahá'u'lláh to face this extremely delicate situation with the boldness, the decisiveness and wisdom it demands. I cannot believe that those whose hearts have been touched by the regenerating influence of God's creative Faith in His day will find it difficult to cleanse their souls from every lingering trace of racial animosity so subversive of the Faith they profess. How can hearts that throb with the love of God fail to respond to all the implications of this supreme injunction of Bahá'u'lláh, the unreserved acceptance, of which, under the circumstances now prevailing in America, constitutes the hall-mark of a true Bahá'í character?[25]

The first session of the Geyserville Bahá'í Summer School took place three months after the 1927 National Convention, and the Guardian's appeal to the American believers could not have been more immediate on the minds of John and Louise as they opened their home that summer to Bahá'ís and to seekers interested in learning about the teachings of Bahá'u'lláh. Two of the attendees at the school were Helen and Charles Bishop of Oregon. While sleeping in one of the rooms at Geyserville, Charles had a dream about Louis Gregory, and Helen wrote to Mr. Gregory about the dream:

> Just before Charles wakened in the morning, he was amazed to see you walking through the air, high in the clouds, with a banner which now unfurled to the breeze. He cried out to you in sheer astonishment, "Louis, you are walking in the air!" but you were wholly unconscious of your lofty height and went serenely on oblivious of the fact that you were in this unique station.
>
> Then he observed that you had come out of the west to the east; you were turned to attention and then faced the South and continued your course with the banner high and shining.
>
> Then he observed that there was a "fleet" of airships in the North, hundreds of them filling the sky.
>
> Dear Louis—you can interpret this as it appears to you, but the reality which came to Charles through (and in) the dream

was this: you had transcended all earthly limitations, had attained an ethereal consciousness and alone (this impressed him) with an unfaltering purpose and a steady pace would in time of crisis carry the banner of Baha'u'llah to spiritual victory.[26]

Charles Bishop's high regard for Louis Gregory seems to be a confirmation of the Guardian's characterization of those Bahá'ís "whose hearts have been touched by the regenerating influence of God's creative Faith" and who use the Bahá'í summer school as a "a testing ground for the application of those ideals and standards that are the distinguishing features of the Revelation of Bahá'u'lláh."

Over time, racial diversity became more visible in the Bahá'í communities on the Pacific Coast of California. Mrs. Rosa Shaw became a Bahá'í in 1915 and served on three committees in the San Francisco Bahá'í community. Her husband, John Shaw, became a Bahá'í in 1918 and served on the Local Spiritual Assembly of San Francisco in 1927, 1931, and 1934. John Shaw's talk at Geyserville, titled "The Negro as World Citizen" was published in the African-American based newspaper *The Peoples Advocate* in January of 1944. The Shaws pioneered to Haiti for one year in 1939, which was one year after the Gregorys' teaching trip to Haiti. In 1944, Rosa Shaw devoted a year of travel-teaching in Halifax, Nova Scotia, where she helped strengthen the teaching work in that city, which had the highest concentration of African Americans in Canada at that time.[27]

In San Francisco, Earleta Cranshaw (Fleming) learned of the Bahá'í Faith in 1934 when Rosa Shaw invited Earleta and her mother, Olivia Cranshaw, to tea in San Francisco. At the time, Earleta was twelve years old and had felt racially ostracized from her Church diocese. Rosa Shaw invited Earleta and her family to Geyserville, where Earleta felt the power of social and spiritual unity and soon became a deepened and confirmed believer. In 1953, Earleta and her sister Luella traveled to the Bahá'í National Convention in Chicago, where Rúhíyyih Khánum announced the goals of the Ten Year Crusade. Upon their return from the Convention, Luella McKay and Earleta Fleming decided that they would go to an African country to settle and teach the Cause. Earleta tells the story of how they made their decision: "We knew we wanted to pioneer to an African country, so my sister Luella and my husband John and I unrolled the map of Africa and spread it out on the floor, and we looked at it until our eyes gravitated toward the north of the continent. Together we pointed to Ceuta, Spanish Morocco. It is difficult to explain the feeling we had, but it felt like guidance." Luella McKay and John and Earleta Fleming arrived at their pioneering post in Ceuta, Spanish Morocco in October of 1953, one month after the passing of Earleta's Bahá'í teacher, Rosa Shaw. In doing so, they were named by the Guardian as Knights of Bahá'u'lláh to Spanish Morocco. As Earleta reflected on the days when she first learned of Bahá'u'lláh's message of the oneness of mankind and how it helped her to develop a love for all of humanity, she attributed the opening of her heart to the experiences with the Bahá'ís at Geyserville. She said, "I accepted the Faith because of Bahá'u'lláh. They [at Geyserville], too, found and accepted Bahá'u'lláh."[28]

While Earleta was attracted to the Bahá'í Faith because she felt racially ostracized from her Church, Cynthia Barnes Slater explained that her attraction to the Cause was due, in part, to the fact that she wanted to build upon her spiritual roots: "My parents instilled in me a firm belief in a Supreme Being, and knowledge and pride in my African ancestry. My family gave me the ability to discern and to rise above the unique challenges I faced being 'young, gifted and Black.' Yet, the church I grew up in expected allegiance without discernment, obedience without questions. I sought a spiritual community that guided my spiritual path and valued critical thinking. While my parents were devout Christians, they wisely encouraged all six of their children in their chosen spiritual paths. As the oldest, I led the way in questioning my spiritual roots."[29]

During the summer break from studying political science at Cornell University, Cynthia began attending Bahá'í meetings in San Francisco and the summer school sessions at Geyserville. She explained that her investigation of the Faith carried her through her college years. After her graduation from Cornell in 1974, she returned to San Francisco and declared herself a believer in Bahá'u'lláh. That year, she was appointed to the first Bosch Bahá'í School Council, which facilitated the transition of the Geyserville Bahá'í School to its new location in Santa Cruz, California. Cynthia has lived a life shaped by her practice of the teachings of Bahá'u'lláh, both at home in the United States and overseas in Africa. She pioneered to the Togolese Republic in West Africa for three years from 1981 to 1984, where she earned a living as an English teacher and volunteered as an assistant to Dr. Thelma Khelghati, who was a Continental Counselor for the Bahá'ís of western Africa at that time. In summing up her experience as a Bahá'í, Cynthia wrote, "All in all, reflecting on those years and experiences, I think the spiritual companionship, plus the love of Bahá'u'lláh and His Writings, nurtured at Geyserville (and in San Francisco) reinforced and sustained my commitment to being active in the Faith."[30]

Elaine West (Leo), who was a Bahá'í youth living in East Palo Alto, California, had a similar response when asked to describe the feeling of unity she felt at Geyserville. As a youth, Elaine worked as registrar at the Geyserville Bahá'í Summer School for six weeks one summer in 1971. She, like most African Americans, felt that society was still working to catch up with the Civil Rights Act of 1964; however, she felt that the Bahá'ís at Geyserville had caught up already, and she observed, "They were woke, if you know what I mean." She said that her days at Geyserville were the best days of her life, adding, "If I had to describe it, it would be heaven. I felt safe and protected. Because everything had a spiritual component, there was a standard to which all had to attain. The Bahá'ís there were special people—all of them—and they were unique simply because they were Bahá'ís."[31]

Another Bahá'í whose service to the Cause had its beginnings at Geyserville was Adrienne Ellis (Reeves). Adrienne had been living with her family in Phoenix, Arizona, where she attended Bahá'í meetings at the home of Zahrah Schoeny in 1939. Having felt the sting of racial prejudice in other settings, Adrienne was attracted to the genuine friendliness and warmth at the Schoeny's home. After Adrienne had attended Bahá'í meetings for almost a year, Mrs. Schoeny asked, "Don't you want to join us and be a Bahá'í?" and Adrienne said, "Yes." That next summer, in 1940, Adrienne attended the Geyserville Bahá'í Summer School, a place she described as a "living laboratory" for the believers to "live and study the Faith in unity."[32] Adrienne Ellis (Reeves) and her friend Eva Flack (McAllister) were soon inspired to homefront pioneer for the Cause, and Adrienne shared her pioneering plans with John and Louise:

137 No. Occidental Blvd
Los Angeles, California
September 30, 1942
My blessed dears,
    I write to you from the depths of an overflowing heart. In three days I shall embark on this great adventure, this marvelous mission the significance and results of which will be incomprehensible to man. For when one takes one step toward the Blessed Beauty, He takes two toward them. I have taken my first step in offering my services as a pioneer in His Cause—each confirmation, each test successfully passed will be another step. My steps will be faltering and weak, but His are mighty and world-shaking and the power released thereby is overwhelming.
    How have things been with you since Summer School? I hope you both have been well and happy. You are constantly in my thoughts and prayers. Summer School had a new meaning for me this year because I saw you two a great deal. In previous years, I have never had the privilege of seeing you so often and talking to you so frequently. [Our discussion] was very sweet and very helpful and I shall not soon forget it. I often think of what you and Louise told me about the necessity of keeping one's self in a prayerful attitude in order to successfully pray.

NOT ALONE OF THE MIND, BUT OF THE DEPTHS OF THE HEART

I know you greatly enjoyed the visits of the Gails and of Marion Holley [Hofman] and Mildred Nichols. Eva and I visited Marion and Mildred on our way home from Geyserville and it was a fitting climax to Summer School. We enjoyed every minute of it, especially at bedtime when the four of us had prayers together. We got to see Mark Tobey too, which was a treat. Eva had never met him so she was very pleased. Now, to make things better, we are going to visit them again on our way to North Carolina. Isn't it wonderful to have such a blessing and inspiration to begin this mission? God is so good to these unworthy mortals.

We have had a wonderful time since July here in Los Angeles together working, studying, seeing a lot of Baha'is. Everyone has been so kind to us, showering us with gifts of clothing, books and money. In the home where Eva has been working, the lady (Mrs. Anderson) asked her about her religion. Eva told her something about it, then she asked for some literature. Eva gave her three books which she stayed up nights to read and then asked for the Baha'i World which she had seen Eva reading. She read from it until Eva stopped working there and said she wanted to buy more Baha'i books to read. So Eva referred her to a Baha'i who lives just across the street. We are elated because Mrs. Anderson is so interested—she is already a Baha'i in action if not in thought. Her husband is also interested.

We shall have some stopovers on our way to North Carolina first in San Francisco to see Marion [Holley Hofman] and Mildred [Nichols], in Laramie to see Val Thornton, in Chicago to see the Temple, and in Washington DC to see Jessie Perry, Ruth and Heshmat Ala'i.

How I wish we could see you enroute but that, I suppose, is improbable, we shall be near you, both physically and spiritually while we are in San Francisco, for when we are with Marion, we are with you. Isn't it marvelous that she lives with someone like Mildred! Mildred is just the sort of an individual who is best for

Marion and they love each other so devotedly that it is a pleasure to see them together. We have loved Marion before knowing Mildred, have learned to love Mildred almost as well.

Again, accept my gratitude for the many kindnesses you showed us this summer. The gift of money you gave us shall be a gift to the Temple when we visit it.

I shall write you after our arrival and give our address. Eva sends tenderest love and greeting, as do I.

Ever yours,
Adrienne[33]

Adrienne's nephew, Mr. Robert C. Henderson, said that Adrienne was his family's "first point of contact with the Revelation of Bahá'u'lláh" and that his aunt's relationship with John and Louise Bosch was "the closest that Adrienne could get to being in the presence of 'Abdu'l-Bahá, because Adrienne knew that John and Louise had the special privilege of being present at the Ascension of 'Abdu'l-Bahá."[34]

Adrienne Ellis was one of those believers who, upon becoming a Bahá'í in 1939, would have been influenced by Bahá'u'lláh's summons to all of humanity to "Be anxiously concerned with the needs of the age ye live in, and center your deliberations on its exigencies and requirements." In 1942, she decided to take "one step toward the Blessed Beauty" and arose to pioneer. By this time, the believers in North America would have already received the Guardian's seminal letter addressed to the Bahá'ís of the United States and Canada. The letter, called *The Advent of Divine Justice*, outlined the spiritual requisites which were "indispensable to the spiritual triumph of the American believers" in advancing the Cause of Bahá'u'lláh in North America. In this letter, the Guardian also identified racial prejudice as "the most vital and challenging issue confronting the Bahá'í community." Written in December of 1938, twenty-six years after 'Abdu'l-Bahá's visit to the United States, it is likely that *The Advent of Divine Justice* was the most widely discussed guidance among the North American Bahá'ís at that time. Furthermore, many of those same believers, including John Bosch, would have witnessed 'Abdu'l-Bahá's visit to America in 1912 and would have been greatly influenced by His example. Therefore, to John Bosch, it must have felt as though the Guardian was speaking directly to him in the *Advent of Divine Justice* when he wrote:[35]

> Let them call to mind, fearlessly and determinedly, the example and conduct of 'Abdu'l-Bahá while in their midst. Let them remember His courage, His genuine love, His informal and indiscriminating fellowship, His contempt for and impatience of criticism, tempered by His tact and wisdom. Let them revive and perpetuate the memory of those unforgettable and historic episodes and occasions on which He so strikingly demonstrated His keen sense of justice, His spontaneous sympathy for the downtrodden, His ever-abiding sense of the oneness of the human race, His overflowing love for its members, and His displeasure with those who dared to flout His wishes, to deride His methods, to challenge His principles, or to nullify His acts.[36]

No wonder then, that John and Louise Bosch could gain the trust of seekers such as Adrienne Ellis, for they put into practice the lessons learned from 'Abdu'l-Bahá. John and Louise Bosch had wholeheartedly embraced the Faith of Bahá'u'lláh Whose teachings are for all of humanity. Bahá'u'lláh wrote:

> Let truthfulness and courtesy be your adorning. Suffer not yourselves to be deprived of the robe of forbearance and justice, that the sweet savors of holiness may be wafted from your hearts upon all created things. Say: Beware, O people of Bahá, lest ye walk in the ways of them whose words differ from their deeds. Strive that ye may be enabled to manifest to the peoples of the earth the signs of God, and to mirror forth His commandments. Let your acts be a guide unto all mankind, for the professions of most men,

be they high or low, differ from their conduct. It is through your deeds that ye can distinguish yourselves from others. Through them the brightness of your light can be shed upon the whole earth. Happy is the man that heedeth My counsel, and keepeth the precepts prescribed by Him Who is the All-Knowing, the All-Wise.[37]

John had a manner so gentle, so genuine, and so giving that a person could not help but be touched by his truthfulness, his courtesy, and his hospitality. For example, in the following letter, a friend of John's, Mr. Park Demmey, wrote to John regarding agricultural subjects, but the letter also expressed how pleased Mr. Demmey was at being treated as an equal in a discussion about race at the second annual Geyserville Bahá'í Summer School session in 1928:

August 11, 1928
1111 Russell Street
Oakland, California
My dear Mr. Bosch,
　We arrived in the city early this week and have been continually reviewing the Saturday afternoon and Sunday spent in Geyserville. To say we enjoyed it would be stating it in very mild terms. We regret [. . .] that the time was so brief as to prevent the completing of a most interesting discussion on Racial peculiarities, impressions, conventionalities and movements, with Helen and Charles Bishop.*

---

* A few years after her time at Geyserville, Helen Bishop was appointed by the Guardian to serve at the International Bahá'í Bureau in Geneva, where she acted as liaison with the League of Nations and other international organizations in the 1930s. See *Encyclopedia of Women and Religion in North America*, vol. 2 by Rosemary Skinner Keller and Rosemary Radford Ruether, 786.

Time passed so rapidly that I was unable to clearly put over my point which no doubt differs somewhat from impressions given by some others, white and colored. [. . .] I am going to write them [Helen and Charles Bishop] in detail giving my point of view on some of the topics which we discussed and on which they questioned me at dinner Sunday afternoon, for it is the view of an element of colored people with which they may not have had close contact, and an element which [. . .] represents the backbone of the race. For this reason I would thank you for their address.

[. . .] Thanking you and your wife for your hospitality and most of all for a lasting impression of good will which is necessary continually in my position seeking something above that which is generally considered a colored man's position, common labor.

Gratefully yours,
Park Demmey[38]

Mr. Demmey's experience at Geyserville suggests that he felt free to speak his mind and share his insights in an environment where the participants set aside any feelings of superiority and suspicion and regarded one another as equals in this Great Cause of Bahá'u'lláh.

John and Louise's efforts to promote the oneness of humanity at the Geyserville Bahá'í Summer School were advanced even further with the arrival of three Persian Bahá'í youth from Tehran. They were Firuz Kazemzadeh (age twenty), Amin Banani (age eighteen), and Shidan Fathe-Aazam (age seventeen) and were part of a group of nine Bahá'í youth who were given permission by Shoghi Effendi to study in the United States. They arrived by ship at California's San Pedro Harbor in February 1944, and five months later, they were guests at the home of John and Louise Bosch. Their arrival in Geyserville was reported in the local newspaper on July 27, 1944: "Among the enrollees of the Geyserville Baha'i school are three young men who with six others, all from eminent families of Iran, arrived in the United States after a three months' land and sea journey across Iran and India and the war areas of the Pacific, to continue their education in America, to associate with Baha'is, and to visit the temple at Wilmette, Illinois. Wondering what western Baha'is would be like, they soon discovered that they were true brothers and sisters, motivated by the same spiritual force which stirs the hearts and molds the lives of the Baha'is of Iran. Their greeting, "Alla'o'Abha" (glory be to God), is repeated on every hand, and it sounds like home to them."[39] In another article in that same newspaper, Firuz Kazemzadeh's impressions of the Geyserville Bahá'í school were published:

> The first Baha'i summer schools were established by the American Baha'is and we [in Iran] patterned from them. My friends and I are happy to be with our American brothers and sisters in Geyserville Baha'i school. Once more we will have the privilege to be in a society which is a pattern for the future. When one considers the distraction and horror which have overtaken the world, when one considers the human communities which have lost their way and are enemies to each other and to themselves, one cannot help being proud of our Baha'i community. How many problems that seemed to be unsolvable we Baha'is have solved! And with great satisfaction we turn to our summer schools where we see how our new society works. For us, Iranians, the American Baha'i summer schools are of an especial significance. We have traveled many thousands of miles and on the opposite side of the earth we have found people inspired by the same high ideals of the Baha'i faith. We have a common goal: the happiness of the whole of humanity, and in our summer schools in America, in Iran, in England, in India and in Australia, we try to learn how this happiness can be achieved.
>
> This year in summer school we will have the privilege of studying the new book written by our guardian, Shoghi Effendi, which he entitled *God Passes By*. This, in my opinion, gives the summer

school a special interest. I wish more Iranian Baha'is could come to American summer schools and I also wish American Baha'is might be in our summer schools. It is impossible now, but in the years to come those schools will provide universal contacts among the Baha'is of different countries.[40]

Amin Banani's wife, Sheila Banani, explained that the arrival of these nine Persian Bahá'í youth was unprecedented. It was the first time that the Guardian approved the transfer of Persian Bahá'í youth to study in the United States. Firuz Kazemzadeh and Amin Banani enrolled at Stanford University to study history, and Shidan Fathe-Aazam enrolled at the University of California, Davis to study agriculture. Firuz married Wilma Ellis (the sister of Adrienne Reeves) and, in addition to becoming professor emeritus at Yale University, led a life of remarkable service to the Cause, most notably during his service of thirty-seven years as member of the United States National Spiritual Assembly and his diplomacy in presenting the plight of the persecuted Bahá'ís of Iran to the attention of the U.S. Congress. Amin married Sheila Wolcott, and together they were honored by Shoghi Effendi as Knights of Bahá'u'lláh for their role in establishing a Bahá'í community in Greece from 1953 to 1958. Upon their return to the United States, Amin taught history at various universities, including Stanford and Harvard, until he was invited to the University of California, Los Angeles to start a program in Iranian history and literature. Shidan remained closest to the Bosches, and during his years in college, he would spend his summer vacations helping the Bosches in their orchards. Shidan married Florence Piepenburg, and together they fulfilled a goal of the Ten Year Crusade by pioneering to Africa in 1953. Upon their departure for Africa, Shidan wrote to the friends gathered at the Geyserville Bahá'í school that summer: "I am writing this, dear friends, so to make you realize what an opportunity you and every one of you have for spreading and serving the Cause. And how much the world needs well-grounded, faithful, and devoted soldiers—who are well-equipped from every point of view to carry on the Message of Bahá'u'lláh. There is no place for quick preparation and the quick making of a pioneer than where you are now—in Bahá'í summer school."[41]

'Abdu'l-Bahá wrote that "This is the day of union, the day of the ingathering of all mankind," and to John Bosch that "ingathering" transcended time and space. As John viewed it, the teaching work was universal, and the army of God was united on all planes, for "Verily God loveth those who, as though they were a solid wall, do battle for His Cause in serried lines." Although John did not consider himself a prolific public speaker on Bahá'í subjects, he was a master communicator. He maintained a correspondence with some of the most active Bahá'í teachers of his day and used the power of correspondence to communicate that feeling of standing in "serried lines" ready to do battle for the Cause "with pure intent, with righteous motives, with counsels helpful and effective, with godly attributes, with deeds pleasing to the Almighty, with the qualities of heaven."[42]

Mr. Roy Williams was one of those who "did battle" for the Cause, and Roy corresponded with John Bosch as a brother. They would have known one another from their attendance at the Bahá'í National Convention where Roy gave reports on the success of the teaching work in the Southern States. Roy Williams was born in Washington DC in 1888, and he became a Bahá'í in New York City in 1918. He was present at the Eleventh Annual Convention in 1919 when 'Abdu'l-Bahá's Divine Plan for the Southern States was read aloud to those present at the Convention. Along with Louis Gregory, Roy responded immediately by arising to serve as a full-time traveling teacher to the Southern states. In fact, Louis Gregory's biographer noted that Roy Williams' "successful teaching efforts in the South in the early years ranked second only to those of Louis Gregory himself." In a Tablet to Louis Gregory, 'Abdu'l-Bahá wrote, "Convey on my behalf to thy fellow-traveler, Mr. Roy Williams, the utmost kindness. I am greatly pleased with him and my hope is that in the future he may be greatly confirmed." In his "Bahá'í Historical Record" card of 1935, Roy Williams wrote, "I have served the Cause as a credited traveling teacher for a period of years—covering an aggregate approximate mileage of over 50,000 miles from the Gulf to Maine all east of the Mississippi and speaking to approximately 60,000 persons. I have received directly several Tablets from 'Abdu'l-Bahá and [I am] mentioned in others [Tablets] commending and approving my teaching work."[43]

'Abdu'l-Bahá kept His hand on the pulse of the development of the Faith in the United States, and He guided certain souls to be an inspiration to others. After the success of the First Race Amity Convention in 1921, Roy Williams received a Tablet from 'Abdu'l-Bahá instructing him on how to consolidate his efforts in the race amity work. The effect of this Tablet proved portentous of the vital urgency to spread the teachings of Bahá'u'lláh. Mr. Williams shared the Tablet at the Bahá'í National Convention the following year in 1922—which was the Convention that John Bosch attended after returning from Haifa in the wake of the Ascension of 'Abdu'l-Bahá. Here is the Tablet, in part:

> To his honor, Mr. Roy Williams, unto him be the Glory of God, the Most Glorious!
> He is the Most Glorious!
> O thou heavenly personage!
> Thy letter was received. The contents indicated that this year the [Race Amity] convention ended with utmost joy and love. This news became the cause of great happiness. The tiding that the Mashreq-ul-Azkar is in the process of construction with utmost perseverance will surely impart greater happiness.
> [. . .] The glad tidings of the progress of the Cause of God in that country is the cause of happiness. I hope the Congress of the White and Coloured that was instituted will have great influence on the inhabitants of America, so that everyone may confess and bring witness that the teachers of His Holiness Baha'Ullah assembles the White, the Coloured, the Yellow, the Red and the Brown

under the shade of the pavilion of the Oneness of the World of Humanity; and that if the teachings of His Holiness, Baha'Ullah be not enforced, the antagonism between the Coloured and the White in America will give rise to great calamities. The ointment for this world and the remedy for this disease is only the Holy Breaths. If the hearts be attracted to the Heavenly Bounties, surely will the White and the Coloured in a short time, according to the teachings of Baha'Ullah, put away hatred and animosity in perfect love and fellowship.

Unto thee be the Glory of Abha!
(signed) abdul Baha abbas.
Haifa. August 2, 1921
Translated by: Touhi M. Afnan, Haifa, Palestine.[44]

Later that year, John Bosch and Roy Williams began a correspondence. In the following letter, Roy wrote to John and Louise Bosch about using correspondence as a way of having a visit "by pen." Here is his letter, in part:

New York City
September 25, 1922
117 East 55th Street
Ya Baha el Abha.
Revered and beloved brother and sister,

Praise be to God, the Generous, the Bountiful, that we attained to this beautiful visit. How charming it was to speak with you, to feel the merciful emotions of your hearts and to inhale the fragrances of your pure, selfless lives while I read your letter. Now we are no longer far from each other and may visit and speak as often as we wish. The Master so wished to have a constant intercommunication, both between the individuals of the Cause and between the groups or Assemblies; both by visits physically and by visits by pen. We all know how the letters carry such fragrances and make such real visits and carry such subtle messages and greetings, revealing of ourselves more than we realize by a chance physical meeting.

[. . .] Truly my poor heart leaps with joy at such evidences of His attracting Power that makes the world but a little room across which we chat and visit. I am also sure that if all [of] us could carry on and do much good by our correspondence [. . .] that a great unity would prevail all over the Baha'i world and a real affection predominate.

[. . .] It is my utmost hope that some day I may be enabled to journey thru the West and diffuse the fragrances of God and meet and associate with those wonderful friends of God who live there. I shall never forget either of you and as you hope, I too hope, we may know each other ever better and better and live closer together eternally. [. . .]. With greetings to each of you and to every one of the beloved of God,

I am your humble servant,
Roy Williams[45]

One of the spiritual qualities so apparent in the personality of John Bosch is that he thought in terms of universal realities rather than in the finite circle of material existence. When one recalls that upon becoming a Bahá'í he wrote to the Master asking that his name be entered in the Great Book of this Universal Life, one is reminded of how deeply John recognized the proof of the continuance of spiritual evolution in the Revelation of Bahá'u'lláh. Every aspect, action, and attribute of John's life was in harmony with God's Plan for this Day. In the first nine years of the Geyserville Bahá'í Summer School, from 1927 through 1936, that spiritual evolution led to the shape of greater and greater expansion of the Cause throughout the United States. Preserving a unity of thought regarding the direction of the school was never far from John's mind. In a letter to Leroy Ioas in 1928, John wrote, "The reports you mailed are splendid . . . However I think that the heading should read 'Pacific Coast Bahá'í Summer School Committee'—the word Bahá'í should be in."⁴⁶

John and Louise's vision for the Geyserville Bahá'í Summer School was, first and foremost, that the school should be a place where Bahá'ís would build capacity to teach the Cause. Secondly, the school would be open to anyone wishing to find a path of service in the Cause. Finally, the school would be a place to further deepen one's understanding of the Covenant of Bahá'u'lláh. A decade later, the Guardian himself appealed to every American believer to make teaching "the all-pervading concern of his life." Much later, in 1954, the Guardian wrote that "the Bahá'ís must realize that they belong to a world-wide Order, and not an American civilization. They must try and introduce the Bahá'í atmosphere of life and thought into their Summer Schools, rather than making the Summer School an episode and a pleasant vacation period, during which they learn a little more about the Faith." One cannot help but wonder at how much the experience learned from Geyserville informed the Guardian's directive for all summer schools.⁴⁷

By the time the Geyserville Bahá'í School had reached its eighth summer in 1935, its reputation as a powerful center of Bahá'í learning had become well-known. The school trained Bahá'ís of all ages, but especially youth, as demonstrated in this letter written on behalf of the Guardian to a youth:

> He [the Guardian] would advise you, however, to devote some more of your time to active teaching in public. To that end he would urge you to attend, if possible, all the sessions and meetings at the Geyserville Summer School, that you may not only deepen your knowledge of the Teachings, but also acquire the necessary training for expounding them to the public. The ambition of every young Bahá'í should be, indeed, to become a well-informed and competent teacher. For this very purpose the institution of [the] Bahá'í Summer School has been established, and its importance so strongly and repeatedly emphasized by the Guardian.⁴⁸

If the duty of every Bahá'í is to actively reform the world by teaching the Cause, then it would take a systematization of those efforts to be carried out collectively. The effective growth of the Cause throughout the world would require proper training of its teaching force so that these teachers of the Cause could demonstrate how the teachings of Bahá'u'lláh are a remedy to the social, economic, and political ills of the current world civilization. John and Louise gave special attention to the systematic preparation of teachers, and the pivotal importance of such training is confirmed in the following letter written on behalf of the Guardian, which is followed by a postscript in the Guardian's hand:

Persian colony
Haifa, Palestine
27 January 1932
Dear Mr. Bosch:
Shoghi Effendi wishes me to acknowledge the receipt of your letter dated January 3, 1932. It is true that Shoghi Effendi looks to the work of the Geyserville Summer School with great satisfaction and hope—satisfaction with the progress achieved, and hope for the wonderful work of service that lies before you. The very fact that the attendance is increasing shows that those who come there do obtain some real benefit and pleasure.

Shoghi Effendi feels that the real purpose of these Summer Schools is to deepen the knowledge of the friends. Lectures are very essential for they give a wonderful picture of the subject matter. But it is not sufficient to have a picture; the friends should deepen their knowledge and this can be achieved if together with the lectures there are study classes and seminar work carried on by the same believer.

The world is undoubtedly facing a great crisis and the social, economic and political conditions are becoming daily more complex. Should the friends desire to take the lead in reforming this world, they should start by educating themselves and understand what the troubles and problems really are which baffle the mind of man. It is in these Summer Schools that this training should be provided for the friends.

In his moments of prayer at the Shrines, Shoghi Effendi will think of you, Mrs. Bosch and the other friends that are directing the work of the School and will ask for you all divine guidance and help.

With best wishes,
Yours ever sincerely,
Ruhi Afnan

Post-script in the handwriting of the Guardian:
Dear precious co-worker,
Your constant and magnificent services to the Cause, so devoted and so unostentatiously rendered are a source of profound joy and strength to my heart. The summer school at Geyserville is the object of my constant prayers. Persevere in your exemplary endeavors and rest assured.

Your true and grateful brother,
Shoghi[49]

In the space of two words, the Guardian characterizes the essence of John's attitude toward service as "unostentatiously rendered" in a spirit free from any desire to impress or to garner attention. Perhaps this is what 'Abdu'l-Bahá meant when He said to John, "With you it is not words, or movements of or with the lips. With you it is the heart that talks."[50]

In November of 1935, John and Louise deeded their property to the National Spiritual Assembly, and the Geyserville Summer School property came under the auspices of the National Spiritual Assembly of the Bahá'ís of the United States. This transfer of ownership ensured the perpetuation of the school as a lasting instrument of service to the

Cause. Although the title of the property was conveyed to the National Spiritual Assembly, the Bosches arranged it so that they could reserve occupancy of the property for the remainder of their lives.

Two years after the Bosches deeded their property, May Maxwell wrote to Louise from Haifa about a dinner conversation she shared with her daughter, Rúhíyyih Khánum, and the Guardian, who had been praising John and Louise's efforts in establishing the Geyserville Bahá'í Summer School:

> At the time Rúhíyyih Khánum was thus speaking of you, Louise, at the Guardian's table, his face lighted with happiness and he spoke of you and John in such terms of such unqualified praise, and tender affection and abiding appreciation of your services to our Faith as I shall never forget.
>
> Again and again, while we were in Haifa, from January 12th to May 30th, he spoke of the Geyserville Summer School, holding it above all the Summer Schools of the world, the only one, he said, who had placed itself entirely under the Administrative Law, the only one in America which is an integral part of the Administrative Order, and he said that it is John and Louise Bosch who have done this, an outstanding example to all the Believers.[51]

Even though the property was deeded in 1935, the Geyserville Summer School curriculum had already been under the direction of the National Spiritual Assembly of the United States since 1926. The fact that the school was under the guidance and influence of the National Spiritual Assembly was one of its distinguishing features, as explained by Siegfried Schopflocher in this letter to the Guardian. The preface to the letter is written by Leroy Ioas to John Bosch:

San Francisco
October 17, 1936
Dear John:

As promised, I am enclosing copy of the letter Fred Schopflocher wrote to the Guardian, from Green Acre, concerning the summer school at Geyserville. I asked Fred if he would be here next summer, and he said, "try and keep me away."
(Copy of letter from Fred Schopflocher to Shoghi Effendi, August 1938):

I am in Green Acre at present, after visiting Geyserville, and attending its full session. The work done there by John and Louise Bosch, George Latimer, Leroy Ioas and others is most remarkable and the little assistance which I could give this and last year has resulted in a happiness which I only experienced in Haifa and the Communities of Egypt. Out there in California we have solved the social phase of the Cause to an extent that the friends constitute one large family. There [in Geyserville] happiness reigns supreme, where the crust and mass of fear of criticism has been replaced by mutual confidence and appreciation. The Teaching work under these conditions is making great strides forward, as speakers and new teachers are being developed there. There were 19 speakers last and more this year. There is so much harmony prevalent, so much encouragement, that even the most timid approaches the platform with assurance to give talks and lectures, the quality of spirit of which cannot be surpassed. They all leave Geyserville with this firm resolution to serve the Cause and the assurance that they can do as well in their own communities after this try-out of their unique experiences. Though I mentioned a few names, due credit should be given to every one of the 300 visitors—there is not a drone on the place, everyone is a contributor—it would not be otherwise, as the spirit would not permit.[52]

Mr. Schopflocher identified a spirit of teaching that was in the hearts of those participating in the summer school at Geyserville—a spirit fostered by the example set by John and Louise in their actions. John and Louise were deeply loved by their fellow believers; every soul was precious to them, and every person who came in contact with them received a preview of how to function in a worldwide Bahá'í commonwealth. Mrs. Keith Ransom-Kehler recognized that spirit in John and Louise and explained to Louise its effect on her own personal life:

30 January 1925
Box 283, Chicago
   Most beloved Sister—
   Your letter thrilled me beyond words! How inestimably precious every word of love and cheer is to a soul like mine that is always hungering and thirsting for the divine consummation of affection and friendliness. It was especially appreciated from you, because you stand now in a special relation to all of the Believers on account of your presence in Haifa at the time of the Ascension.
   The spontaneity and joy with which you write chastens and uplifts me with an ardent desire to attain to the glorious characteristics that you attribute to me. I was touched and moved and exalted and helped by your letter. As you suspect I came into the Cause through May [Maxwell]; but the glorious privilege of being in the Cause can only be repaid by an excess of ardor to all of our co-workers. May says that I am what Abdul Baha used to call one of the "great intoxicated lovers of the world" and certainly nothing ever makes me happier than the sort of letter that you have so generously written.
   In our love of the Master, I embrace you.
   Keith[53]

Keith Ransom-Kehler (who in less than eight years would die unexpectedly in Isfahan in service to the Cause and be named a Hand of the Cause of God and become the first American martyr of the Bahá'í Faith) writes of being chastened by Louise, in the sense of having an attitude of humility that is derived from a love for humanity rather than from a love of self. To prefer another before oneself was the guiding principle of John and Louise's life, an example demonstrated to them by 'Abdu'l-Bahá Himself.

If one were to review all the talks given by 'Abdu'l-Bahá while He traveled throughout the United States, one would say that the pivotal principle around which His talks revolved was unity. In fact, 'Abdu'l-Bahá stated that the unifying power of the teachings of Bahá'u'lláh will be such that "all men will adhere to one religion, will have one common faith, will be blended into one race, and become a single people. All will dwell in one common fatherland, which is the planet itself."[54]

To John and Louise, this love for humanity was not superficial; rather, their love for humanity manifested itself in deliberate and real action so that the pivotal principle of their Faith in Bahá'u'lláh was practiced every day of their lives. Bahá'u'lláh's teachings describe a oneness of humanity that can only be achieved through "genuine love, extreme patience, true humility, consummate tact, sound initiative, mature wisdom, and deliberate, persistent, and prayerful effort" on behalf of the believers toward one another.[55] In other words, unity takes practice, and the Bahá'í summer school was an ideal setting in which to acquire such qualities, as described here by Leroy Ioas on behalf of the Pacific Coast Bahá'í Summer School Committee:

San Francisco
December 22, 1930
Dear Horace,

Regret I have not had opportunity to respond earlier to your kind favor of October 22nd in regard to report about the Summer School.

Report was to have been written, in fact two or three of them, but none of them have materialized. Keith [Ransom-Kehler] was going to write a report for the [Bahá'í] News Letter but she started out on her teaching campaign and was kept so busy that she has not been able to do anything. In fact, in passing through San Francisco en route to Los Angeles the other day she said the busiest place in the world to serve is the West Coast.

We were in Pasadena last Saturday, the 13th, at a very wonderful interracial dinner which the Pasadena and Los Angeles friends gave. There were about 170 present and Keith was the speaker of the evening. Unfortunately she wasn't well but nevertheless gave, as usual, one of her illumined talks.

So far as the Summer School is concerned, there are one or two things which should be put into the News Letter, indicating the real success and contribution which the school has given to the Cause generally, and the West Coast in particular.

The goal of the Bahai program and the fruit of the Cause is the realization of that ideal condition, where the differing elements of the human family live together happily, peaceably and enthusiastically. Only as the Bahai community life develops into a radiant working body, meeting all the problems of life, is the Cause functioning properly. Therefore, the greatest contribution we have to offer the world is a mode of life that works at transforming the problems into stepping stones of successful endeavor and establishing that dynamic force that transcends all human limitations and reaches to the consciousness of spiritual brotherhood. In the Summer School work we have been endeavoring to develop this very thing, that is, that the spirit of unity, of fellowship and of happiness should be augmented and the resultant conscious spiritualized conduct of the friends be realized, that the hearts of all who contact this body might find doors to a new mode of life they have heretofore not known. If the spirit becomes as strong as the Master wishes, it will become an attractive power for all who come under its influence.

Indicating the spiritual fellowship which the Summer School has developed, many of the older Bahais who have visited in Haifa and at the Holy Shrine state that the spirit that is developed at the Summer School is quite similar to that which is experienced in the Holy Land.

Last year the Summer School was visited for a few days by a young doctor from Russia. His was a strong belief in brotherhood, but of a cold, logical, scientific philosophy of life, developed naturally through the communistic ideas. He came to the Summer School for a stay of a day or two. The friendship of the friends was so strong that he stayed not only throughout that week, but throughout the entire Summer School. When he left he wept, saying that never in his life had he experienced such a true oneness and harmony among people as he felt among the group at the Summer School and that he felt more intimately associated with the Bahais than with his own family.

Another young man, from Southern California, driving to the Pacific Northwest dropped in to spend the evening with one of the Bahais. He was simply going to stay overnight and then continue on his business trip. He was so touched by the kindness of the friends and the harmonious atmosphere that he decided to stay over for a day or so. This day or so stretched into the entire two weeks period and when he left he announced that he wished to join the Bahai Fellowship and become one with us in carrying on our work.

[. . .] With such a spirit and harmonious feeling as this, it will readily be realized that the Summer School is united in its activities and all of the friends revolve in harmony around one activity after another. It is a demonstration of the ability of a group of diverse peoples to live together happily and harmoniously. This is the fruit of the Summer School and the purpose of its gathering, because after all the object of all training is to learn how to live. Last year there were in attendance about 75 people from the various parts of the Pacific Coast. The meetings were devoted to the study of the all-important subject of "Man and His Universe." This course included briefly the complete range of human activity, starting with evolutionary processes of life to the early days of history up to the present period of complex existence and then most important, the future of the human family, which of course was a working out of the Bahai Program of Universal Peace. Lectures were given [. . .] by the Bahais, giving the application of the principles of Baha'U'llah to the problems of the world today and what their application will do in evolving in the world to that ideal state which the Bible promises of "the Kingdom of God on Earth."

[. . .] Greatest of all the successes of the school, perhaps, is the elevating and unifying effect it is having in the various Assemblies, where a new spirit is becoming apparent of tolerance and active cooperation.

Sincerely,

(Signed) Leroy[56]

John and Louise had established a pattern of community life that reflected the high standards of the Bahá'í teachings, and each year of the Geyserville Bahá'í Summer School was a demonstration of greater and greater evidence of putting into action the guiding principles of the Faith. This is not to say that the friends had achieved perfection; in fact, human failings and personality conflicts are integral to any human endeavor that seeks to engage large numbers of people around a central point. John Bosch had a sin-covering eye and understood that the Friends must "look upon the perfection of the Faith and not upon the imperfections of the believers."[57]

In its report to the National Spiritual Assembly, the Pacific Coast Bahá'í Summer School Committee stressed the importance of the school being a place where Bahá'ís could strive to align their personal lives with the high standards set forth in the Bahá'í teachings and could achieve a greater awareness of the spiritual aspects of fellowship. In turn, this sanctified attitude toward fellowship would influence the attitude of those serving on elected institutions of the Faith, which, in turn, would contribute to an elevated sense of holiness and chastity in one's personal life. After all, teachers who have not awakened spiritual susceptibilities in themselves may have difficulty in awakening spiritual susceptibilities in others. Not only was Geyserville Bahá'í School a training ground for teachers of the Cause, it was a place where one could practice being a Bahá'í—a place where the teachings of Bahá'u'lláh become, as Leroy Ioas expresses in the following letter, "not alone of the mind, but of the depths of the heart":

640 46th Avenue
San Francisco, California
April 9, 1933
To Mr. Horace Holley, Secretary, NSA—New York
Copy to Mr. John D. Bosch
  Dear Horace:
  Attached is annual report of the Pacific Coast Summer School Committee for the May issue of the Bahai News. It is my feeling that one of the most important elements of the Summer Schools, and indicating the degree of their development, is the harmonious and enthusiastic method of carrying on. If we cannot demonstrate in fact, the world order we stand for, then how can we induce others to try it. The efficacy of the program of Baha'Ullah is the effect it has in the lives of His followers. We feel that the real accomplishment of the Summer School at Geyserville is this very thing; and it in turn has elevated the conduct of all the Assemblies on the Coast.

Annual Report
Pacific Coast Summer School Committee
San Francisco, April 9, 1933
  The sixth annual Summer School at Geyserville, California, July 3rd to 16th, 1932, was one of the most unique sessions ever held.
  The Friends on the Pacific Coast look forward with anticipation from one Summer School to the next, as the intimate association

of the Friends and the harmony it develops, brings revivification and regeneration for the ensuing year's service to the Cause.

This year the bonds forged in previous years were welded more closely, and a sustaining atmosphere of energetic devotion displayed, notwithstanding difficulties that could have caused confusion. This demonstration among sixty or more Bahais showed that the knowledge gained from study together was not alone of the mind, but of the depths of the heart, which brings about the better way of living. Non-Bahais visiting the school comment freely at the harmonious spirit that animates these gatherings. In commenting on the Bahai Summer School at Geyserville, one of the prominent teachers at the Pacific School of Religion said he had never been in a group where there was such a complete lack of racial consciousness; where each one seemed to be anxious over the happiness of the other, and where a group of people endeavored to live up to their ideals as did the Bahais!

The Bahai lectures on the evolving factors of society, the solution of the present world problems, and the paths to Universal Peace, were in advance of the contributions offered by non-Bahai lecturers, specialists along such lines. As the world in its wanderings approaches closer to the implications of the World Order of Baha'Ullah, the Bahais will be called to leadership in directing the way to Universal Peace; as the people of the world are without vision and guidance.

The sessions opened on July 3rd, under the "Big Tree," with the Annual Unity Feast. This Feast, under the "Big Tree" has become an annual pilgrimage of the Friends, for fellowship and devotion. Complete happiness and spiritual fortitude were gained by the one hundred and forty friends in attendance, setting the basis for the enthusiasm developed during the Sessions.

The courses of study included a sociological survey of the situation of society today; the bases of its evolvement into the consciousness of the New Day; and the steps to Universal Peace; also a course on the growth of the Faith itself, from the memorable deeds of the Pioneers of the Cause, as portrayed so vividly in the Dawnbreakers, to the unfoldment of the sublime and Universal Teachings of Baha'Ullah, culminating in the perfecting of the medium through which His spiritual benedictions may be assured to posterity, namely, the Administrative Basis of the Bahai Religion.

The roundtable discussions presented an interesting feature. In the afternoons the Friends gathered in the shade of the towering Redwoods, on the slope of one of the Hills, and informally discussed the various phases of the subject matter presented in the classes in the morning, or other subjects that might require clarification or discussion. Following the creative method of discussion whereby each person presented his opinion freely, so that after the clash of differing views, the Spark of Truth might be found, a new vista of unending opportunities of true consultation was unfolded.

Four public teaching meetings were held. Great interest was displayed on the part of many new souls.

It is very encouraging to see how the alluring spirit of the Cause is attracting the orthodox people of this small community. Now they look forward to the coming of the Bahais during the summer months, whereas formerly they seemed fearful of these harbingers of a new day.

Twenty-three children, including a few of the village children attended the classes for the training of children. The excellent conduct and results were due to the untiring efforts of the Committee handling this important feature of the school life. Their plans will be further unfolded during the coming summer, under the direction of the new committee appointed by the National Assembly, on the Training and Teaching of Children.

In commenting on the program of the Summer School, Shoghi Effendi, through his secretary, stated:

"The wide range of the topics that are to be discussed and studied by the Friends, cover most of the important aspects of the Cause and such a plan will undoubtedly give them a broad and sound knowledge of the essentials of the Faith. Special stress, however, should be put on the history of the Movement, as well as on the guiding principles of Bahai Administration—for on these two points most of the believers are not adequately informed."

In compliance with these instructions, the Summer School to be held July 23rd to August 5th, 1933 will present detailed courses on the History of the Movement, and the Administration of the Faith. A special course for young people will be conducted on "The Influence of Religion on Society." With these most important subjects for consideration it is urged that everyone who possibly can attend the School this year.

Let us not overlook the fact that the love of the Cause is ever augmented through sacrifice and service. Thus, the loving association we enjoy at Geyserville is assured through the sacrifice and service of John and Louise Bosch to all the Friends. Their sincere efforts could do no other than attract the benedictions of the Holy Spirit to all the Gatherings.

Pacific Coast Summer School Committee
John D Bosch, Chairman
Leroy Ioas, Secretary[58]

Maturation of the Bahá'í community and expansion of the Cause go hand-in-hand. As a pattern of Bahá'í life begins to develop within a Bahá'í community, so does the pattern of teaching. In a letter written on behalf of the Guardian, this pattern of Bahá'í life is explained: "Until the public sees in the Bahá'í Community a true pattern, in action, of something better than it already has, it will not respond to the Faith in large numbers."[59] Indeed, the participants at Geyserville witnessed something different than what they already had, and that was the spirit of fellowship, rectitude of conduct, and sanctity in the personality and character of John and Louise. The following letters are only a sampling of dozens of such notes of gratitude received by the Bosches. One letter is from Xorol Oliver, who was a Mormon woman who saw the picture of 'Abdu'l-Bahá and recognized Him as someone extraordinary. Another letter is from Canadian believer Rowland Estall, who later served as a Continental Counselor for Central America. The third letter is from Paul Wildhofer, a seeker from nearby Los Gatos, California.

September 11, 1929
Dear friends Mr. and Mrs. Bosch,

I am still living in memory of my wonderful visit at the school. If I am not able to be there again I hope and pray that that beautiful happiness will never leave me. Life is so much easier—daily trials seem to just pass by and I thank God for the heavenly rest and the happiest time in my life for years. I wish everyone I know could know you both. Just to know you is indeed a beautiful example for one to remember and try to follow. When I think of the room on the porch, I am thrilled with thankfulness for your gift was a straight path to heaven and God. I simply cannot thank you enough.

Please feel free to ask any favor from me. In that way I can compensate for such happiness.

Loving wishes,
Xorol Oliver[60]

August 8, [no date]
Dear John and Louise,

Now that I have had time to reflect upon the many new experiences, wonderful friendships and extraordinarily unusual spirit (ever in the Cause) of Geyserville, I can write and tell you, however inadequately, of the great privilege it has been to me to be present at the Summer School this year.

Coming back to our own Community which previously seemed like a real bee-hive of useful activity in the Cause, I can see by contrast with the Summer School how much more effectively we have to display the spirit of love, of unity and true service and humility so prevalent at Geyserville and so necessary to the real progress of the Cause here and elsewhere. One cannot help but realize that if the foundation of a thing is right, the rest will be also and this is so true of Geyserville. The spirit of its founders, your own dear selves, has given to Geyserville that wonderful foundation which will make it a landmark in all future Baha'i history. Surely such a wonderful contribution as you have both made to the Cause must have a great reward.

Now that we are settled into Vancouver again, we take up the work of teaching with renewed enthusiasm. Since we returned, Molly and her fiancé and another girl have joined our Community officially. There will be many more and by the time another Summer School comes again, we expect to bring a large contingent to Geyserville.

[. . .] Let me tell you in some small way how much I appreciated your kindness and hospitality. I shall always remember this first visit to Geyserville as one of the happiest and most beautiful events in my life.

Devotedly,
Rowland Estall[61]

August 21, 1929
To: Mr. and Mrs. Bosch
Dear Friends,

I want to tell you how I appreciate your kindness that you made it able to me to come to Geyserville. Those two weeks had a great importance in my life; far greater than anybody could expect. The beautiful spirit of brotherhood, which kept you all together, caught my soul too; it changed my life. At last, after a long time of hard spiritual struggles, I found the way I could go on to find the peace of my mind, it is owing to you and to Mrs. (Helen) Bishop. May God, if one ever exists, bless you for it.

I believe in the brotherhood of all the people in betterment of life, and in helping those in need. If that is enough to be a Baha'i, then I am one of them long time ago. But I need refinement. I shall study the Baha'i scriptures. I will try to understand the many beautiful things you told me. When I shall be ready, I will let you know about it.

Yours sincerely,
Paul Wildhofer[62]

These expressions of love for John and Louise are the result of the magnetic attraction that is generated when one teaches the Cause. John and Louise never excluded themselves from the call to teach—even when carrying the responsibility of hosting the summer school each year, they continued their own teaching efforts long after the summer sessions had concluded each season. When the school was not in session, John and Louise would put into practice the skills they learned at the summer school session and travel continuously to teach the Faith. In 1933, John and Louise were seventy-eight and sixty-three years old, respectively, and maintained a rigorous teaching itinerary—and they could always be relied upon when the teaching work called for action on short notice:

640-46th Avenue
San Francisco, California
December 9, 1933
Dear John and Louise:
　　With the completion of the Dome ornamentation of the Temple, our Faith has entered an entirely new situation in America. From a struggling group endeavoring in a time of the world's greatest depression, to complete the ornamentation of the Dome of one of the world's most unique religious edifices, the Baha'i Faith has emerged a victorious Order, offering to the world that peace and unity, which the Temple is symbolic of.

Undoubtedly the completion of this first unit of the ornamentation will release powerful spiritual forces in the world, otherwise Shoghi Effendi would not have paid so much attention to its consummation in such record time. The question now before us, therefore, is whether, now that we have completed the task, we can respond to the great spiritual opportunities this victory has made possible.

It would seem that a vigorous national public effort is required to carry the Cause forward to the extent contemplated by the splendor of the Temple, and achieve the victory which Shoghi Effendi states is close at hand.

Our aim is to create a very specific public effort about the middle of January to take care of the wave of interest and enthusiasm which has developed over this country due to the completion of the Dome ornamentation. It is necessary for each and every one to arise with a renewed spirit and devotion to service during this campaign to carry the Message to all who are anxious to know and learn more of the Cause.

Cannot you and Louise undertake one of the teaching trips you previously made by machine [automobile] to the various centres. Undoubtedly a visit on your part to such points as Cloverdale and as far north as Willits, Santa Rosa, Sacramento, Fresno, Visalia thence Los Angeles and back up the Coast line would be a tremendous good. The Teaching Committee strongly hopes that you two can undertake such a trip for a few weeks bringing increasing love of the Friends to you and further helping to increase the dignity and prestige of the Cause wherever it has been known and in new centres where it may be introduced. The Teaching Committee will be glad to cooperate in every way in having Local Assemblies arrange meetings openings etc for you.

Please let me know promptly extent of trip you can make, points you can visit, etc, so that we may start the ball rolling as quickly as possible.

(Signed) Leroy[63]

By 1934, John and Louise were approaching the seventh season of the summer school on their Geyserville property. John was seventy-nine, and Louise was sixty-four. More than 150 people attended the sessions each season. Some of the guests stayed in lodging on the Bosch property, some stayed at auto camps (campgrounds) nearby, and others camped in various other places in the vicinity. Expansion of the school lodging facilities was an inevitable necessity, as noted in this letter written by Leroy Ioas on behalf of the Pacific Coast Bahá'í Summer School Committee:

June 25, 1934
Mr. John D. Bosch
Mrs. E Goodall Cooper
Mr. George Latimer
Mrs. Amelia Collins
Dear Friends,

When at Geyserville last Sunday checking up all of the details for the Summer School I found that up to Sunday there were 87 registrants for the Summer School, and plans being made by about 25 more to attend. It appears, therefore, that we shall have about 100 people attending the School from out of town, which in addition to the local people at Geyserville, will make a very stupendous School this year. It is evident that we must immediately take into consideration some plan for enlarging the facilities at Geyserville, and also to relieve Louise from the intense work of attempting to house all of those people.

The Guardian has recently sent word and written that all of the Baha'is should attend these Summer Schools and that if necessary the Summer School should be held at different times, so that those who cannot attend at one time could attend at another time. And further that the Summer School should be so arranged and conducted that interested people can attend and become confirmed at the sessions.

It is interesting that amongst those 87 there are perhaps more non-Baha'is than we have ever had before, and I find that particularly around the Bay region there are many people who are interested in the Cause who would like to attend the Summer School. Therefore, if we would clear the situation, as the Guardian apparently wants it done, we could make the Summer School a real institution of learning for both Baha'is and interested people.

It seems to me we must face, and very definitely, the necessity of building some type of dormitory facilities at Geyserville, or, encourage various Baha'i families in the Bay region to build small places in which they can live themselves, leaving the accommodations which the Bosches are so generously making available to the believers open to the newly attracted ones. We have discussed this before and there had always been the ever-present question of finances, particularly at a time when every penny was needed for the Temple. Forsythe Ward[64] is building a small place at Geyserville which I understand he is financing by means of one of the Federal Housing Act loans.

I called at the Bank today and learned that under this Federal House Act, individuals can secure money for the building of small summer places, and that the loans are payable over a period of either three or five years. Therefore, if a person were to build a small place at a cost of say $500, and use the 5-year plan of payment, it would mean a monthly payment for the 5-year period of a few cents over $10. Mr. Linfoot says he can build a pretty nice little place for $500. My thought is that we might let it be known and the result may be the building of half a dozen such places by next year.

Another thought is that a dormitory capable of housing a maximum of twenty people could be built for about $1,000 and it might be worth while for this Committee to consider having this done under the Federal Housing Act and working out some scheme of payment. I doubt if the national Assembly would undertake at this time any such construction work, but if the Committee members wish to do something specific along this line it might be a gift which the Committee could make to the Summer School and which, of course, they would have to stand responsible for over a period of years. Perhaps we can have an opportunity to review this pretty carefully during the early part of the Summer School this year so that we could have something definite in mind for next year.

As a matter of information, the Auto Camp at Geyserville has leased to some of the Baha'is and only two remaining cabins which they had not promised to others. Louise has arranged to take care of quite a number of people at the farmhouses in town. There are also quite a number who will be camping on the grounds.

Leroy[65]

As the work of the committee expanded over the years, the success of the summer school was due, in large part, to the spirit of love and unity shared by its earliest committee members, George Latimer, Leroy Ioas, and John Bosch. Leroy's wife, Sylvia Ioas, used to joke that they were like the Three Musketeers who were all for one and one for all.[66] Although the following guidance from Shoghi Effendi concerns the functioning of the Local Spiritual Assembly, it is relevant to the work carried out by the members of the Pacific Coast Summer School Committee:

The maintenance of a climate of love and unity depends largely upon the feeling among the individuals composing the community that the Assembly is a part of themselves, that their cooperative interactions with that divinely ordained body allow them a fair latitude for initiative and that the quality of their relationships with both the institution and their fellow believers encourages a spirit of enterprise invigorated by an awareness of the revolutionizing purpose of Bahá'u'lláh's Revelation, by a consciousness of the high privilege of their being associated with efforts to realize that purpose, and by a consequent, ever-present sense of joy. In such a climate, the community is transformed from being the mere sum of its parts to assuming a wholly new personality as an entity in which its members blend without losing their individual uniqueness.[67]

To advance the Committee's vision of expansion required the help of someone with "individual uniqueness"—a fairy-god mother of sorts—and Mrs. Amelia Collins would fit the bill just right.

10 / Your Milly

Mrs. Amelia Collins is perhaps best known for the "Collins Gate" that stands at the headway of the main path that leads to the holy Shrine of Bahá'u'lláh in Bahjí. The gate was named for her by Shoghi Effendi, the Guardian of the Bahá'í Faith, as a loving remembrance of Amelia Collins' singlehearted devotion to doing whatever she could to ease the great burden placed on Shoghi Effendi as Guardian of the Cause of God.[1]

During the Guardian's ministry, ten individuals were posthumously elevated to the rank of Hand of the Cause of God. The Guardian gave Amelia Collins a special recognition that distinguished her from other Bahá'ís, however, by naming her as the first living person since the time of Bahá'u'lláh to be elevated to the rank of Hand of the Cause of God. Although he did not announce his first contingent of Hands until December of 1951, Shoghi Effendi personally appointed Amelia Collins in 1946 in a letter to her wherein he wrote, "the high rank you now occupy and which no Bahá'í has ever held in his own lifetime has been conferred solely in recognition of the manifold services you have already rendered." The Guardian went on to explain the unique duty conferred upon her as Hand of the Cause: "Indeed the character of this latest and highly significant service you have rendered places you in the category of the Chosen Nine which, unlike the other Hands of the Cause, are to be associated directly and intimately with the cares and responsibilities of the Guardian of the Faith."[2]

Born in 1873, Amelia Engelder Collins was a contemporary of May Maxwell, Lua Getsinger, and Louise Bosch. She preferred the name "Milly," signing all her letters that way, and closing one of her letters to John and Louise with "Your Milly—not Amelia." She had a sense of humor about her insistence on the informal use of her name, and in one of her letters to the Bosches, she used letterhead with the name "Amelia Earhart" printed across the top of the page, as a humorous nod to the famous flyer who was known for insisting on being called Amelia.

After the death of Milly's husband Thomas Collins in 1937, she represented the Faith both at home and abroad until she was called to the Holy Land in 1951 to serve as vice president of the International Bahá'í Council. After the passing of Shoghi Effendi in 1957, she remained in Haifa and served as Custodian with her fellow Hands of the Cause of God in the Holy Land.

The Guardian called her the "outstanding benefactress of the Faith" because of her "munificent contributions" toward purchase of important properties. These contributions included donations toward the building of the Western Pilgrim House, the superstructure of the Shrine of the Báb, the International Archives, embellishments around the Shrine of Bahá'u'lláh in Bahjí, and the entire purchase of land for the future Temple site on Mount Carmel. She also contributed toward endowments for the building of Bahá'í Houses of Worship in Europe, Australia, and Africa.[3]

Milly described her feelings toward the Guardian as analogous to the "yearning of a mother's heart." Having had no children of her own, she viewed the Guardian as her own precious care, in the same sense that a mother instinctively wishes to protect her precious child. After the passing of 'Abdu'l-Bahá, when the provisions of His Will and Testament had become known, Milly said that her "whole heart and soul turned to that youthful Branch, [Shoghi Effendi], appointed by Him to watch over and guide the Faith of Bahá'u'lláh. How I prayed that God would help me to make him happy!"[4]

Amelia Collins became a close confidant of Rúhíyyih Khánum, especially after the passing of Rúhíyyih Khánum's mother, May Maxwell, in 1942. Of Amelia Collins, Rúhíyyih Khánum wrote:

[To be appointed Hand of the Cause of God] was the highest honour [the Guardian] could confer on a believer, living or dead, and he so named many Bahá'ís, East and West, after their death; the most outstanding of these was Martha Root whom he characterized as the foremost Hand raised up in the first century of the Faith since the inception of its Formative Age. The one exception was Amelia Collins. He cabled her on 22 November 1946: "Your magnificent international services exemplary devotion and now this signal service impel me inform you your elevation rank Hand Cause Bahá'u'lláh. You are first be told this honour in lifetime. As to time announcement leave it my discretion."[5]

Milly became a Bahá'í in 1919. She and her husband, Thomas Collins, lived in Pacific Palisades, California, and although her husband was not a declared Bahá'í, he supported the work of the Cause through Milly. Her husband accompanied her on her first pilgrimage to the Holy Land in 1923, where she met Shoghi Effendi. Both of them traveled again to the Holy Land in 1937, and upon their return passage, Thomas died unexpectedly on the ship while it was still at sea. As a confirmation of Thomas Collins' great contributions to the advancement of the Cause, the Guardian wrote to Milly after his passing: "How pleased the Beloved must be: how proud He must feel of your truly great achievements! The soul of dear Mr. Collins must exult and rejoice in the Abbá Kingdom. Persevere and be happy."[6]

While Amelia Collins was on pilgrimage in 1923, the Guardian shared with her the contents of a letter that would become an early blueprint for the administration of Bahá'í affairs. The letter, dated March 12, 1923, and addressed to the Bahá'ís of America and other countries, gave guidance related to the election and duties of Local and National Spiritual Assemblies and the establishment of the Bahá'í Fund. The overarching theme throughout the letter is twofold: the Guardian calls upon every believer, to first deepen himself in the Spirit of the teachings, and "labor incessantly to exemplify in all our dealings with our fellow-men that noble Spirit of which His beloved Son 'Abdu'l-Bahá has been all the days of His life a true and unique exponent" and secondly, to not neglect "the essential, the most urgent of all our obligations, namely, to bury our cares and teach the Cause, delivering far and wide this Message of Salvation to a sorely-stricken world."[7]

Upon her return from Haifa, Milly attended the Bahá'í National Convention and was asked to read the Guardian's letter to the Convention. She explained that after that Convention, "wherever I went, I found that the friends had received that same letter, and that they and the members of the Spiritual Assemblies were busily engaged in discussing it."[8] The following year, in 1924, Amelia Collins was elected to the National Spiritual Assembly of the Bahá'ís of the United States and Canada. It is important to note that Louis Gregory, Mariam Haney, and Albert Vail were also elected that year, and all three had been actively involved in the Race Amity work called for by 'Abdu'l-Bahá. Furthermore, the Guardian's injunction that the friends "bury their cares and teach the Cause" would have been very much on the mind of every member of the National Spiritual Assembly. In fact, it was Louis Gregory who summarized the mood of the 1924 Bahá'í Convention in this way:

> The Bahá'í message heralds this new spiritual consciousness, the spirit of the new age that floods the world with ideals of unity. Its motion attracts people of every race and nation, every religion and creed, as the one solution of social reconstruction and world unity. Within this movement science finds its freedom to advance, religion finds the love-power to unite, and society finds a world program of family life in the oneness of God and the one-

ness of humanity. These are but impressions, imperfect in their expression, feeble and shadowy as reflections of truth. Yet may they not convey the hope that this convention was the beginning of a great awakening throughout the western world?[9]

Milly served on the National Spiritual Assembly each year from 1924 through 1933 (and again in 1938 through 1951), and she would have been very much aware of the Geyserville Bahá'í Summer School's impact in deepening the believers and in raising up teachers of the Cause. Attendance at Geyserville was growing every year, with as many as three hundred people attending each summer. Expansion of the school's facilities was inevitable, and with the help of Milly Collins the expansion became possible.

In 1936, John and Louise deeded their property to the National Spiritual Assembly, and in that same year, Milly paid for the construction of Geyserville's meeting hall. She was generous and practical when it came to the needs of the Cause, remarking in a letter to the Bosches that "Waiting is not in my make up." Hand of the Cause Mr. Faizi wrote that "When Milly would offer a contribution at a meeting of the Hands of the Cause, she would urge us to keep it confidential. 'Just send the money,' she would say; 'don't mention my name.'"[10] John Bosch seemed to understand Milly's unvarnished approach to accomplishing tasks, as illustrated in this letter from him to her:

Geyserville, February 16, 1936
Dear Milly,
Your letter and the architect's sketch and design received. I went at once to the Stevens Lumber Company at Healdsburg and today have received their prices of material and of estimate of cost of such a Hall as designed by Mr. Sullwold.
Mr. Stevens said that this design was wonderful for detail and for beauty, that it was a big building, that there was no questioning of its being well designed and very beautiful, for acoustics

perfect, etc. But that the cost of construction, as detailed in the design, would take the best part of $4,000. However, he said with another roof construction, and with the height of walls reduced, the price would come down considerably.

The biggest expense would be the tile roof he said, but a good grade of Asphalt Shingles could be substituted. This would reduce the roof-sheathing from 2" thick to 1" thick—as you know a tile roof has to have a roof underneath it.

Regarding the floor—a saving could be effected by having a hard-wood floor instead of a cement one as it would save the covering of linoleum that would be needed over the cement floor, the price of difference between a cement versa hard wood floor to be very little—20 cents a square foot for hard-wood flooring. But I believe that it is even as your architect says and as you quote in your letter: "The most practical and cheapest floor will be to pour cement same as foundation is made," —providing the linoleum is not too high in price.

Will say here that I never thought about it at the meeting that the new place suggested for the construction would be hidden behind the tree instead of being in clear view of the highway as a beacon for all passers by to see [. . .].

With these reductions the price would naturally drop about $1,000 from the aforesaid $4,000. But, says Mr. Stevens "If the cost were no object, the plans as drawn are very beautiful and would make a perfect building" [. . .].

Am hastening to send on to you this report by air-mail but hope you both may come here as talking is so much easier than writing.

Am returning the architect's sketch and design as you may want it, but Louise wants it too, for framing [. . .].

We are thinking how wonderful it really would be to have such a hall here and how this would be the fulfillment of Shoghi's hopes and desires for this place!

With much love,
Yours,
John D. Bosch[11]

As was often the case with Milly when it came to funding building projects for the Cause, cost was not an object, as the following letter demonstrates. It is also interesting to note that Milly was sixty-three years old at this time, and John was eighty-one, yet they managed the details of the building project with a youthfulness that speaks of their tireless service. Milly always respected John in this regard because he never complained of the work, while Milly did complain, if only in a lighthearted manner. Some years later, after serving in Haifa for a time and exhausted from her labors, she would often say that she wished someone would tell the Guardian how old she was.[12] Perseverance was second nature to Milly.

14954 Corona Del Mar
Pacific Palisades, CA
April 5, 1936
Dear John,
    I have just written to the Geyserville Bank, depositing 4,000 dollars and instructing them that you and Leroy can both draw on it.
    I went to the place in San Francisco that Mr. Stevens recommended for finish and they sent me to the Fuller place Paints. They have given me a material for outside finish and also the color for inside—the wholesale houses did not have the suitable fixtures—am getting a design, will bring it up when I come next.
    Be sure to have the furnace pit well cemented so that it will be O.K. when a furnace goes in.
    The chairs are a problem. We looked and looked. Leroy and I thought it might be nice to have 125 of one kind and about 25 easy armchairs. What do you and Louise think about it? Please let

me know what you think of 100 like those that are in Old Fellows Hall (in Geyserville), only the seat a bit wider. I can get them here for $2.25 each stained, all chairs in S.F. were $3.00 but one place and they were not so good looking. I would like a chair that looks cozy. Please give estimate without exterior or interior stain or finish. Use Oregon Pine (not knotty) for wainscoting in Hall. Board three widths, instead of all one width. What would it cost to have dressing rooms and lavatories finished with the pine right to the ceiling? Use redwood shingles, like sample. Electric wiring to have a three-pronged switch, so that we can switch light low, medium, high. Tell me frankly.

I cannot get my mind on anything but this Hall, for after all, it is not such a small undertaking and is Bahá'u'lláh's Hall and must look good.

Dear Louise. Imagine me leaving my shoes in wood box for you to care for. And I am worried about my valuable diamond brooch. Hope it is safe on my blouse that I left behind. Please drop me a line saying it is there. I should not take anything but a toothbrush with me for my mind is not on my things.

I was so weary when I got back here I hardly knew my name [. . .] I was so happy with you two saints. May I abide there always one day.

Much love and thousand thanks and I wish it were not so necessary to put so much on your shoulders. Tom says if John bosses the job he knows it will be the best ever. I told Tom that Frye (the builder) was told that John was appointed official fault-finder!

No more now. I am with you today in print for the public meeting and for the dedication of the breaking of the ground. Always when there are lectures, ceremonies—even weddings, I am to be elsewhere. Never mind. It is Baha'u'llah's plan for me.

Always your
Milly[13]

Milly referred to the fact that she and her husband could not be present at the formal dedication of the meeting hall, as they were traveling abroad in Germany at the time. Construction of the hall began on April 8, 1936, and was completed and dedicated that summer on July 12, 1936. The dedication opened with the words of Shoghi Effendi, received by cablegram: "HEARTILY JOIN CELEBRATION OPENING AUDITORIUM GENEROUSLY FUNDED BY WELL BELOVED DISTINGUISHED FRIENDS MR AND MRS COLLINS. ASSURE THEM PROFOUND ABIDING GRATITUDE. LOVE ASSEMBLED FRIENDS."[14] Talks were given by Leroy Ioas and Louise Bosch, followed by the official turning over of the property to George Latimer, who acted as chairman and received the property on behalf of the Bosch Trustees for the National Spiritual Assembly.

The Bahá'í Summer School Committee wished to name the meeting hall "Collins Hall," but Milly would have none of that and sent a telegram on July 1st, 1936 to John Bosch that read "NAME BAHAI HALL INSTEAD OF COLLINS." John Bosch must have agreed to her request; he named it "Bahá'í Hall," and a week later Milly wrote to John Bosch: "Utmost gratitude for the name [Bahá'í] that has taught us there are no separations."[15]

By the next summer, Milly also funded and guided to completion a dormitory on the Geyserville campus that could accommodate as many as fifty guests. Her generosity had no bounds, owing to her love of the place and of John and Louise themselves. After one of her visits to the school, she wrote, "I have a short list of magic names—the list headed of course by Shoghi Effendi. John and Louise—also magic names for me! Never has Geyserville, you, the hills, every inch of it meant so much to me."[16]

Milly regarded the Geyserville Bahá'í School as a paradise that was second only to the paradise of being in Haifa. Geyserville was her heaven, and being with John and Louise was her home. As part of the gift of the property to the National Spiritual Assembly, John and Louise arranged their trust in such a way that guaranteed that they could live on the property until their deaths—and this arrangement included Milly:

> May 20, 1939
> Dear Milly,
> As you will see from the enclosed letter we have been again to see Lawyer Swartfager regarding the deeding over of our portion of the Nurani Hill Property to you. We were once before to his office for this purpose but were unable to see him that time. The wording of the enclosed letter is just something preliminary, just the way it came to him to put it to begin with and it can be changed to other wordings conveying the same idea.
> As we have trust in each other to give the whole property to the Cause after our respective deaths, the one that expires last of the three of us can dispose of it to the National Spiritual Assembly, or if the NSA would not want it, to the Summer School direct, or in any way fitted to the Cause here.
> Please add or change anything on the enclosed letter that you want to add or change. The last one, i.e. the donor, the one that gives the property away, should give it in the name of all three. Let us know, Milly, what you think of it and we will then proceed with the matter.
> Always and always yours,
> John and Louise[17]

John and Louise's death preceded Milly's, and the property went to the National Spiritual Assembly, as was the original wish of John Bosch. The school had operated for the first nine years under the direction of John and Louise. After that, from 1936 until 1973, the Geyserville Bahá'í School operated under the full auspices of the National Spiritual Assembly (which was the National Spiritual Assembly of the Bahá'ís of the United States and Canada until 1948). In those years, hundreds and hundreds of Bahá'ís and friends of the Faith attended sessions at Geyserville Bahá'í School, resulting in the raising up of ranks of capable teachers of the Cause. Some went homefront pioneering, such as the Entzminger family, who pioneered to Oklahoma after being inspired at Geyserville. Others ventured into the arena of international pioneering service, such as Virginia Orbison, who gained such confidence as a Bahá'í teacher that she pioneered to Santiago, Chile in the 1940s. Geyserville Bahá'í School inspired a spirit of service, as noted in a letter from Mariam Haney to John and Louise after Mariam's visit with her ten-year old son, Paul Haney:

Burlingame, California
September 4, 1936
My beloved Friends,
Before I leave for the East [Washington DC], I want to tell you what heavenly visit I had to your very delightful home. Indeed, I should have grieved had I not had the great privilege of seeing you, and of walking over that lovely and wonderful sacred ground. Yes, it is sacred because any place so whole-heartedly given over completely to the Baha'is for the only purpose of furthering the spread of His Most Great Cause cannot help but be sacred and holy. So I just had a perfectly marvelous time with you both, and you were so kind, and served us so graciously and with such a warmth of the Spirit, with such pure love, that our hearts were greatly touched.

It was a bounty from the Lord that He allowed us to go; and I carry with me to the Eastern friends a sweet and precious story about the Geyserville School and the two true devoted and loyal souls who made the School possible.

I shall never forget our visit. It made a profound impression upon me—the visit to the new hall, the heavenly place I felt in the home and that last little bounty the Lord allowed us in the quiet radiance of the Spirit in and amongst the redwood trees high on the hill. Ah! That was a precious time. [. . .]

And you <u>two</u> shall be known down thru the coming ages as the two lovely souls who set their hearts on real values—who were able to strike upward to unscaled heights. I really am taken out of the world of language as I try to express my deep appreciation and my lasting gratitude for your kindness to me. [. . .]

What sweet, sweet memories I will always have of my visit to you. How precious will be the story I have to tell the friends as I journey home. I hope with all my heart I shall be able to serve you. In the not too distant future, I think Paul will be prosperous, and then we shall surely give and give and give to that heavenly Bahai Center.

Yours tenderly and affectionately,
Mariam.[18]

Mariam Haney's letter highlights the "Spirit in and amongst the redwood trees high on the hill," as though she were looking for the right word to characterize the feeling she had when she walked in that redwood grove. Her conclusion of simply "Ah!" is not unlike the feelings expressed in dozens of similar letters from various friends writing to John and Louise about being among the redwoods.

The symbolic influence of Nature upon the soul is a spiritual verity that John and Louise understood as a necessary feature of the spiritual transformation that could take place at the Bahá'í school. In His writings, Bahá'u'lláh explained spiritual principles by using examples from the natural world. For example, He wrote that "Nature, in its essence, is the embodiment of My Name, the Maker, the Creator. Its manifestations are diversified by varying causes, and in this diversity there are signs for men of discernment. Nature is God's will and is its expression in and through the contingent world."[19]

To reach the redwood grove at Geyserville Bahá'í School, one had to cross a plum tree grove, then climb a gentle hill where, at the top, stood a large grove of redwood trees. It was customary for the friends to walk to the redwood grove together for devotions. If one has never entered a redwood grove, the following description by California forester F. H. Clark in 1891 captures the way in which a redwood grove makes one feel a transformation of the spirit: "Having made these noble trees an especial study during the past year, I approach them always, I may say, with reverence. As giants and patriarchs of the forest they stand alone. Nowhere throughout the world can be found living trees that are more majestic and inspiring [. . .]. The trees are grand without being oppressive; noble but not arrogant; lords of the soil that do not impoverish the land [. . .]. We seek their companionship with quiet satisfaction; for, in striking contrast with the heavy shade and gloomy depths of our great pine forests, the shadows in the densest growth of redwoods are made soft and semi-luminous by rays of sunlight piercing the feather foliage."[20]

Author John Steinbeck described the transcendence of the redwood forest region of California in this way: "The redwoods, once seen, leave a mark or create a vision that stays with you always. No one has ever successfully painted or photographed a redwood tree. The feeling they produce is not transferable. From them comes silence and awe. It's not only their unbelievable stature, nor the color which seems to shift and vary under your eyes, no, they are not like any trees we know, they are ambassadors from another time."[21]

John Bosch treasured the natural beauty of the property and described it as a place with "wooded hill land [. . .] with timber pines, manzanita trees, groups of colorful madrones, also some Laurel trees—in fact, a natural Park, a perfect ground for health walks up to the heights and most beautiful views of the mountains and valley."[22] All of this, in addition to fruit trees and a redwood grove, gave one the sense of being in paradise, as Milly Collins so often mentioned in her remembrances to John and Louise.

The coast redwood—one of the three types of sequoia tree species—is the tallest living thing on earth and can reach heights above 370 feet. This redwood can be seen as a symbolic representation of what it means to know and to love God, as the tree grows in a straight path toward the light in the forest canopy. Furthermore, the redwood tree has leaves that have evolved in such a way to collect the water from the coastal fog—similar to how a believer may gather spiritual sustenance from the "clouds of [God's] bounty." Reminiscent of those Hands of the Cause of God who are spiritual "pillars," these coast redwood trees resemble firm pillars in the forest of other trees. Symbolic of the fires of tribulation that strengthen the soul of man, redwood trees are resistant to flame, and their bark actually thickens in fire. The trees grow so tall that one might think that its weight would cause its own collapse, but the redwood tree grows in a formation of a circle with other redwood trees—usually about eight or nine—and the roots of these trees interlock with the roots of the other trees in the circle. As a result, the roots of these trees create strength in unity.[23]

In 1973, the state of California made plans to expand the Redwood Highway to run through the center of the Geyserville Bahá'í School property. As a result, the state seized the property through its eminent domain process, which forced the National Spiritual Assembly to relocate the school. Moving the location of the school was unthinkable at first. So central were the redwood trees to the spiritual atmosphere of the summer school that the thought of losing these symbols of spiritual strength was unimaginable to the Bahá'ís who knew Geyserville.

Dr. Firuz Kazemzadeh, Mr. John Kenton Allen, and Mr. John Cook were appointed by the National Spiritual Assembly to locate a new site for the school. Ideally, they hoped to find a property with plenty of trees so that the people attending the Bahá'í summer school would enjoy the inspiration of nature as the mirror of divine attributes. They searched for a new site in the foothills above Santa Cruz, California, where acres and acres of coast redwood trees grow.

One of the members of that committee, John Kenton Allen, said that he was looking for a site that was remote yet accessible, that would provide enough space to conduct a school, and that would be inexpensive enough to be purchased from the funds available from the sale of the Geyserville property. Most importantly, he felt that the new site had to have a spiritual atmosphere befitting of a Bahá'í school. When John Kenton Allen and his teenage son Andrew drove onto the property that is now Bosch Bahá'í School, they knew they had found the ideal substitute for the Geyserville property.[24]

The property was previously an equestrian camp, and its owner was losing money on the venture and was motivated to sell. The campus is comprised of sixty-eight acres in all, and most of it redwood forest. The site also has a swimming pool, a dozen cabins, a meeting hall, dining hall, and a small house. The Martha Root Meeting Hall and adjoining classrooms were not built until decades later. In July of 1974, Bosch Bahá'í School was inaugurated, and the spirit of the original Geyserville property flourished in its new surroundings of redwood trees.

The concern over losing the redwood grove at Geyserville was assuaged after the discovery of a circular grove of redwood trees on the Santa Cruz campus that lies within the larger forest of redwood trees on the property. This small grove was spared when, after the San Francisco earthquake of 1906, the redwood forest area above Santa Cruz was logged for rebuilding the city of San Francisco. But this singular grove on the property must have been too small to cut in 1906, however. As a result, what remains is a clerestory of redwood trees standing taller than the eye can see, and when one looks upward, one has the feeling of standing in a Bahá'í House of Worship, with the redwood tree canopy above as the high ceiling and the trees themselves as the walls.

The redwood grove at the old Geyserville campus was called "Ioas Grove" and was marked by a plaque on a jasper stone in honor of Hand of the Cause Leroy Ioas. When the smaller grove of redwood trees was discovered on the new Bosch Bahá'í School campus, the jasper stone was relocated to the new grove in memory of Leroy Ioas and his unfailing dedication to the establishment of a permanent Bahá'í school on the western coast. The placement of the jasper stone in its new grove appears as though it always belonged there.

Louise, ever insightful, must have had a premonition that the school would change location. Of the Geyserville campus, Louise described its mysterious influence on the soul: "'The school is not just a physical property—its name and geographic location may change in response to circumstance. Rather, the school is a vision, an idea, a workshop, a laboratory, an example. Its foundation is spiritual and that which is spiritual is impervious to the changes and chances of the temporal world. It is a precursor of the kind of world Bahá'ís are building, a glimpse of the society to which the teachings of Bahá'u'lláh will give rise.'"25

The Bosch property at Geyserville embodied the serene presence of John and Louise—their generous nature, their gentle manner. When Milly Collins referred to Geyserville as paradise, heaven, and home, she was describing how she felt about John and Louise. To be near them was to be in paradise. To know them was to be in heaven. To be loved by them was to be home. Once when Milly had been traveling from Geyserville to a National Teaching Committee meeting, one of the friends asked her where she had arrived from, and Milly replied, "From heaven." She had a love for John and Louise she described as "a love that cannot be measured." In another letter to them, she wrote, "I can hardly wait to be in that home of yours John and Louise, which is the nearest to Haifa for me" and "how tenderly I think of your dear and your blessed care of us all. Future ages will speak of it in befitting language."26

Perhaps that "befitting language" is heard in the Guardian's words regarding Bahá'í summer schools. These words were written in 1938 to describe the American Bahá'í community, but one cannot help thinking how these observations also characterize the tireless devotion of John and Louise Bosch, the financial support of Milly Collins, and the sacrifices of so many of the heroes, martyrs, and saints of the Cause who arose from the community of The Most Great Name: "What other community has shown the foresight, the organizing ability, the enthusiastic eagerness, that have been responsible for the establishment and multiplication, throughout its territory, of those initial schools which, as time goes by, will, on the one hand, evolve into powerful centers of Bahá'í learning, and, on the other, provide a fertile recruiting ground for the enrichment and consolidation of its teaching force?"[27]

11 / Saints

John Bosch lived to see the conclusion of the first Bahá'í century. He passed away in July of 1946, one month before his ninety-second birthday. The first session of the Geyserville Bahá'í Summer School had been held during the summer of 1927—an undertaking that John had begun at the age of seventy-one. It gives one pause to consider how much can be achieved when one is at the prime of life—and how much more may be achieved in old age. On the subject of living a Bahá'í life, the Guardian wrote, "There are two kinds of Bahá'ís, one might say: those whose religion is Bahá'í and those who live for the Faith. Needless to say if we can belong to the latter category, if we can be in the vanguard of heroes, martyrs and saints, it is more praiseworthy in the sight of God."[1] John and Louise lived for the Faith. Their marriage was characterized by their unity of purpose in all things, particularly in their service to the Cause. Every aspect of their life together was in the interest of promoting the Message of Bahá'u'lláh.

Some of the greatest Bahá'í teachers of the first Bahá'í century passed through their lives in one way or another. Helen Goodall, a Disciple of 'Abdu'l-Bahá and remembered as the "shepherd" of 'Abdu'l-Bahá's flock of followers in the West, was the one who confirmed John Bosch in the Covenant. Thornton Chase, also a Disciple of 'Abdu'l-Bahá and the first American believer, was the one with whom John Bosch studied the history of the Cause and with whom he shared a spiritual brotherhood. Keith Ransom-Kehler, who was named martyr and a

Hand of the Cause of God and remembered as the "valiant emancipator of her Persian brethren," collaborated with John and Louise on the Pacific Coast teaching campaigns. Lua Getsinger, also a Disciple of 'Abdu'l-Bahá and remembered as the "mother teacher of the West," was instrumental in bringing about the marriage of John and Louise. Martha Root, who was posthumously named a Hand of the Cause of God and remembered as the "finest fruit of the Formative Age" of the Faith, stayed with John and Louise at Geyserville as a respite from her continuous international teaching work. May Maxwell, named a martyr and the "spiritual mother" of Canada, Europe, and Latin America, was one of the closest confidants of Louise Bosch. Others who shaped John and Louise's lives were Hand of the Cause of God Louis Gregory, Mrs. Mariam Haney, and Mrs. Sadie Oglesby, who inspired John and Louise's efforts to advance the Bahá'í principle of race unity. Still others with whom John and Louise shared a life of service were Hand of the Cause of God Leroy Ioas, "the Guardian's Hercules," George Latimer, the "firm pillar of the American Bahá'í community," and Hand of the Cause of God Amelia Collins, the "outstanding benefactress of the Faith." All became central to the lives of John and Louise Bosch.[2]

In surveying the Guardian's writings, one finds only a handful of instances where he attributes the epithet of saintliness to an individual serving in the Formative Age of the Faith. Martha Root, for instance, is described as saintly, in addition to being described as the "FOREMOST HAND WHICH 'ABDU'L-BAHÁ'S WILL HAS RAISED UP IN FIRST BAHÁ'Í CENTURY."[3] Other individuals to whom the epithet of "saintly" is attributed by the Guardian are Hand of the Cause of God William Sutherland Maxwell, Hand of the Cause of God Roy Wilhelm, and John Bosch.*

William Sutherland Maxwell's saintliness became apparent the moment he accepted Bahá'u'lláh as the Manifestation of God. He

---

* The idea that these three Bahá'ís are referred to as saints by the Guardian was first suggested to the author by Mr. Hooper Dunbar at a session at Bosch Bahá'í School in 2012.

and May Bolles Maxwell were on pilgrimage to Haifa in 1909, and they had invited Louise Stapfer (Bosch) to accompany them. It was a special pilgrimage for May and Louise, as they had been the closest of friends, and since Louise had just recently become a Bahá'í, being together in the presence of the Master had a special significance for them both. Sutherland was not a declared believer at the time, but an encounter with the Master would reorient Sutherland's relationship to his Creator:

> One day at table, [Sutherland] said to 'Abdu'l-Bahá, "The Christians worship God through Christ; my wife worships God through You; but I worship Him direct."
> 'Abdu'l-Bahá smiled and said, "Where is He?"
> "Why, God is everywhere," replied Sutherland.
> "Everywhere is nowhere," said 'Abdu'l-Bahá. He then went on to demonstrate that such worship was worship of a figment of the imagination and had no reality; we must worship God through something tangible and real to us, hence the role of the Manifestations.
> Sutherland bowed his head in acceptance. The real seed of his faith germinated from that hour.[4]

In the biography *The Maxwells of Montreal*, Violette Nakhjavání noted, "the Guardian gave May [Maxwell] the rare accolade of a martyr after her death but he called Sutherland 'saintly.'"[5] Sutherland Maxwell's saintly life was recounted by his daughter, Rúhíyyih Khánum, as she reflected on two Bahá'ís, Martha Root and Sutherland Maxwell, whose service to the Cause meant so much to the Guardian:

> It seems to me, in looking back on Shoghi Effendi's life, that aside from the great sweep of the Faith, whose victories meant so much to him, Martha Root in one way and Sutherland Maxwell in another brought him more deep personal satisfaction than any

other believers. They were very much alike in some ways, saintly and modest souls who adored Shoghi Effendi and gladly gave him the best they had in service and loyalty. Though Martha's services were far more important for the Cause, the talents of Sutherland became a medium through which Shoghi Effendi could express at last with ease the great creative and artistic side of his own nature and this gave him both satisfaction and happiness.[6]

Toward the end of Sutherland Maxwell's life, the Guardian appointed him Hand of the Cause of God in the following cable that was sent on December 23, 1951, and arrived in Montreal on December 25th. It read:

> MOVED CONVEY GLAD TIDING YOUR ELEVATION RANK HAND CAUSE STOP APPOINTMENT OFFICIALLY ANNOUNCED PUBLIC MESSAGE ADDRESSED ALL NATIONAL ASSEMBLIES STOP MAY SACRED FUNCTION ENABLE YOU ENRICH RECORD SERVICES ALREADY RENDERED FAITH BAHA'U'LLAH[7]

Mr. Sutherland Maxwell had been ill and was convalescing in Montreal when he received the cable. His caretaker, Rosemary Sala, wrote to Rúhíyyih Khánum describing the moment when Sutherland received the telegram: "'Your father read it slowly aloud. Then it was so beautiful to see the light and life come into his tired face, yet such a touching humility. He sat silent a moment then said, "But I didn't do it all alone. There were so many others to help me!" We felt so blessed and privileged to be with him at that moment.'"[8] Upon the passing of Sutherland Maxwell, the Guardian sent a message to the Bahá'í world—a message that identifies the nature of Sutherland Maxwell's saintly life. Here is the message, in part:

> WITH SORROWFUL HEART ANNOUNCE THROUGH NATIONAL ASSEMBLIES THAT HAND OF CAUSE OF BAHÁ'U'LLÁH, HIGHLY ESTEEMED,

DEARLY BELOVED SUTHERLAND MAXWELL, HAS BEEN GATHERED INTO THE GLORY OF THE ABHÁ KINGDOM. HIS SAINTLY LIFE, EXTENDING WELL NIGH FOUR SCORE YEARS, ENRICHED DURING THE COURSE OF 'ABDU'L-BAHÁ'S MINISTRY BY SERVICES IN THE DOMINION OF CANADA, ENNOBLED DURING FORMATIVE AGE OF FAITH BY DECADE OF SERVICES IN HOLY LAND, DURING DARKEST DAYS OF MY LIFE, DOUBLY HONORED THROUGH ASSOCIATION WITH THE CROWN OF MARTYRDOM WON BY MAY MAXWELL AND INCOMPARABLE HONOR BESTOWED UPON HIS DAUGHTER, ATTAINED CONSUMMATION THROUGH HIS APPOINTMENT AS ARCHITECT OF THE ARCADE AND SUPERSTRUCTURE OF THE BÁB'S SEPULCHER AS WELL AS ELEVATION TO THE FRONT RANK OF THE HANDS OF CAUSE OF GOD.[9]

A few months before Sutherland's death, Roy Wilhelm passed away on November 24, 1951. Like Sutherland Maxwell, Roy Wilhelm's saintliness was awakened by 'Abdu'l-Bahá—a saintliness recognized later by the Guardian, as the following cable makes clear:

HEART FILLED SORROW LOSS GREATLY PRIZED, MUCH LOVED, HIGHLY ADMIRED HERALD BAHÁ'U'LLÁH'S COVENANT, ROY WILHELM. DISTINGUISHED CAREER ENRICHED ANNALS CONCLUDING YEARS HEROIC OPENING YEARS FORMATIVE AGE FAITH. STERLING QUALITIES ENDEARED HIM HIS BELOVED MASTER, 'ABDU'L-BAHÁ. HIS SAINTLINESS, INDOMITABLE FAITH, OUTSTANDING SERVICES LOCAL, NATIONAL, INTERNATIONAL, EXEMPLARY DEVOTION, QUALIFY HIM JOIN RANKS HANDS CAUSE, INSURE HIM EVERLASTING REWARD ABHÁ KINGDOM. ADVISE HOLD MEMORIAL GATHERING TEMPLE BEFITTING HIS UNFORGETTABLE SERVICES LOFTY RANK.[10]

Roy Wilhelm was a millionaire businessman in New York City, where he managed a successful import firm. Roy's mother accepted Bahá'u'lláh in 1898, and although Roy received a Tablet from 'Abdu'l-

Bahá in 1904 wherein the Master acknowledged Roy as a Bahá'í, it was Roy's pilgrimage to 'Akká in 1907 that consecrated his Faith. Upon meeting the Master face-to-face, Roy Wilhelm was entirely transformed, as though he had been remade by the reality of the pure teachings of God. He returned from the Holy Land so devoted to the Cause and to the Center of the Covenant that the Master relied on him as a confidant regarding the steadfastness of the American friends.[11]

Both Roy Wilhelm and John Bosch shared a common link with the final days of the Master's earthly life: It was to Roy Wilhelm that the Master sent His last communication to the United States, and it was in the hands of John Bosch that a portion of the Master's Will and Testament would be delivered to the United States. Together, John Bosch and Roy Wilhelm stood sentry for the protection of the Master's Will, with John in Haifa at the reading of the Master's Will and Testament, and Roy in the United States at a time of great tests for the American Bahá'í community. It was a tenuous period, to say the least, and the Master relied on Roy Wilhelm to be a trusted correspondent, as Rúhíyyih Khánum described here in this excerpt from *The Priceless Pearl*:

> It must not be thought, however, that the act of promulgating the Master's Will solved all problems and ushered in a new era in the Cause with the greatest of ease. Far from it. Before Shoghi Effendi reached Haifa the Greatest Holy Leaf had been obliged to cable America on 14 December: "Now is period of great tests. The friends should be firm and united in defending the Cause. Nakeseens [Covenant-breakers] starting activities through press other channels all over world. Select committee of wise cool heads to handle press propaganda in America." Grave as the events indicated in this cable were, they cannot be considered apart from the serious situation which existed in America when 'Abdu'l-Bahá died. He had been deeply concerned over Covenant-breaking in that country for some time, even having predicted in a letter writ-

ten some years before that a storm would arise after His passing and praying for the protection of the believers. On 8 November 1921 He cabled Roy Wilhelm, His trusted correspondent, "How is situation and health friends?" to which Mr. Wilhelm, the next day, was obliged to reply: "Chicago, Washington, Philadelphia agitating violation centering Fernald, Dyer, Watson. New York, Boston refused join, standing solidly constructive policy." An immediate reply was cabled back by 'Abdu'l-Bahá on 12 November, in the strongest language, and clearly indicating His distress: "*He who sits with leper catches leprosy. He who is with Christ shuns Pharisees and abhors Judas Iscariot. Certainly shun violators. Inform Goodall, [Edna] True and [Agnes] Parsons telegraphically.*" That same day the Master in a second cable to Roy Wilhelm said: "*I implore health from divine bounty.*" These were the last messages America ever received from Him.[12]

Both Roy Wilhelm and William Sutherland Maxwell figured intimately into the story of John and Louise Bosch. Although John Bosch would have known Sutherland Maxwell due to May Maxwell's closeness to Louise, it was Roy Wilhelm in whom John found a sense of brotherhood he had not felt since the passing of Thornton Chase. Roy first learned about John from fellow New Jersey Bahá'í and Disciple of 'Abdu'l-Bahá, Isabella Brittingham. Roy was unable to attend the Convention in 1909, and he wrote to John to convey his regrets at not having been able to meet him at the Convention. Thus began a friendship that lasted the remainder of their lives. In 1910 Roy Wilhelm was elected to the Bahá'í Temple Unity Executive Board and served on that administrative body each year through 1913. Roy was then elected to the National Spiritual Assembly in 1925 and in every year until 1946, except for one year due to illness. As part of Roy's personal teaching efforts, he funded the printing of thousands and thousands of Bahá'í pamphlets, which he whimsically called "Big Bens" and "Little Bens."

Roy was always looking for ways to distribute Bahá'í literature, and in John's friendship Roy found a very capable distributor, as John was never without a book or a pamphlet on the Bahá'í Faith:

Sunday, April 4th, 1910
My dear Bahai Brother:
I was pleased to receive your welcome letter of sometime since and to know that your efforts are bearing fruit. Mrs. Brittingham had written me of you and I was disappointed at having missed you last Spring. It was my intention to cover the ground again this Spring, as the business results from former round had been very satisfactory, but at the eleventh hour a certain office complications came up which prevented—I hope to go next year so that perhaps it is only a pleasure deferred.

I know your earnest face, as have had it before me daily in the group [photograph] made upon Mrs. True's steps, which is on my *chiffoneir*. I certainly hope you will again come East to the Convention, and that I shall have the pleasure of meeting you there. I reached Chicago some sixty days after the Convention last year, but several members were still in the city, and do you know it seemed to me that the spirit was still very strong there. I am not of the emotional kind, rather too matter-of-fact, I guess, but at that Sunday meeting several of the visitors spoke, and to my astonishment I was so overcome that my feelings nearly swamped me—an entirely new experience for me.

I am mailing you a little package of printed matter which you may be able to find use for. With kindest greetings to you and to all the friends of GOD, I remain,
Sincerely, your brother,
Roy Wilhelm[13]

Although John and Louise spent a great deal of their time teaching the Faith, they had their leisure time, too. Louise was a great reader, and she enjoyed walking the grounds of their Geyserville home. John's time outside of Bahá'í activities was taken up with caring for his orchards, canning prunes, and raising goats. And like any good friend to another, John tried to persuade Roy that raising goats could be good for Roy's health in every way—not only for the nutritional value of goat's milk and goat's cheese, but for the qualities that are fostered in a human being when tending to and caring for animals. Roy was resistant to the idea at first. He cited the demands of his business as an excuse and joked that being a bachelor, he did not see himself as the shepherd of "kiddies." Despite Roy's resistance, John did his best to convince Roy of the benefits of raising goats, and the idea began to grow on Roy's mind:

June 16, 1915
My dear Brother Bosch:
    I have been thinking of you too, and almost sent you a postcard the other day, but have been so blooming busy haven't been able to carry out half that I had wanted to.
    [. . .] I am sure you have been having a very enjoyable time while the friends have been visiting you. Wish I could have just dropped in too: believe I could even have stimulated an additional caper in your festive goat family. I found plenty to do when returned, and am not <u>out</u> <u>from</u> <u>under</u> yet.
    Kindest remembrance to the good wife, and greetings to inquiring friends, I remain,
    Yours sincerely,
    Roy
P.S.: What a shame the trolleys don't connect little old NY and Geyserville![14]

As John Bosch and Roy Wilhelm's friendship grew, their jovial affection for one another also grew. Roy's witty sense of humor in his letters to John and Louise showed not only his love for them, but also his unpretentious manner in expressing that love: "Dear Fellows, I love you and wish I could at this very moment walk right into your midst and give you both a good hug. I would love to see John wiggle his mustache like he did years ago."[15] John was humored by Roy's lack of self-importance and did not seem to mind it when Roy addressed John as "Uncle Johnny Dee" or "Johnnie Dee"—a nod to the millionaire businessman and philanthropist John D. Rockefeller. The joke is that John Bosch always signed his name "John D. Bosch" but only because there was another John Bosch living in the same county and he did not wish his mail to be sent to the wrong person. In the following letter, Roy Wilhelm—a millionaire philanthropist himself—played upon the fame of the name "John D" by addressing John Bosch with a wink of his pen: "My dear Uncle Johnny Dee." It is also worth noting that this letter alludes to Louise's visit in 1919 to see May Maxwell in Green Acre, where Louise found the book on Tahiti called *Le Mariage de Loti*. It was also the time when John was alone in Geyserville and wrote to 'Abdu'l-Bahá about wishing to offer his property as a school. After writing his letter to the Master, John wrote a second letter to his closest friend, Roy Wilhelm, to ask if he had seen Louise at Green Acre, to report to him of his use of the "Big Bens" teaching pamphlets, and to send him a contribution to the Temple. If John had been feeling lonely, Roy's brotherly affection in the following letter must have filled the void left by Louise's short absence:

August 21st, 1919
My very dear Uncle Johnny Dee:
  Well it does seem good to hear from you again! Indeed I saw Sister Louise about a week ago at Green Acre, we had dinner together (during which she gave more attention to providing for me than to looking out for herself) and as I told her, the big fly in the ointment was that Uncle Johnny could not be with us too.
  Glad you have found the Big Bens of service to you among enquirers, and only wish it were possible to include in the list of

addresses all places where there are assemblies—obviously that is not possible where the space [on the Big Bens] is so limited, the best we could do was to squeeze in just the leading cities, most of which have a population of more than a quarter million. Many of the smaller places have inserted a leaflet of their own, giving local address with announcement as to where and when meetings are held—some being just labels an inch or so in length and gummed at one end [. . .].

Geyserville has certainly set a very pretty pattern in her liberal subscription to the Mashrakel-Azkar. While I have no doubt as to where the bulk of that contribution came from, I only wish that all of us in America could so realize the importance of this opportunity [. . .].

There has gone forward to you today 100 Big Bens. You can remit the $2.00 at your convenience.

Yours as yore,

Roy[16]

Roy continued to correspond with John and Louise while they were in Tahiti, and Roy funded Alexandre Drollet's translation of Baha'i pamphlets into Tahitian. When John and Louise returned from Tahiti, Roy wrote to them about how he hoped that the cabin he was building on his property in West Englewood, New Jersey could be used for the Faith in some way. He was also thinking seriously now about raising some "kiddies"—goats, that is—and John made sure to suggest to him what kind of goats and sent along a photograph of the goats, to which Roy replied with the following letter:

December 10th, 1920
Dear friends,
Really only had time a few days since to drop you a card. Now I must do a little better. This time of the year ever fetches a lot of extra duties, then there are ever the Committee meetings galore,

new people to meet, etc. Indeed I thought the whole blooming country knew about that Bungalow as you call it of mine, really it is a genuine Log Cabin. I began it some two and half years ago and only this present week has it been far enough advanced to have the roof placed. Up till three weeks ago I did all the work myself, father occasionally helped a little, but he is not so young as he used to be, so I have to fight him to keep off the job.

Some folk want to know why I am building it, some think when it is completed I may marry, well I do not know myself, hardly, but back tucked in my mind there is the idea of it being used as a place to hold Bahai meetings. It will have covering the veranda and all a seating capacity of 150 Persons. Two living rooms upstairs, fitted out in the cellar with toilets, two of them, do not know yet about a bath. You see Mother, Father, and I live in the house, then next to that is my garage then this Log Cabin. The wood I got right out of the woods adjoining my property, in fact from the same Estate as I secured the lots several years ago. By spring I am sure the place will be fit for a person or two to live in it. It is becoming quite the talk of the town. Must sometime have a good photo of it taken and pass one on to you—bless your hearts, thought you knew of the enterprise long ago. Of course the Cabin will have a large fire place.

The Goats. I did appreciate your long talk on them. As for the pictures, aren't they fine. Thank you a lot. I believe am not ready to talk business with you on them yet going slow these days.

Am enclosing slip showing the cost of Cable sent to Abdul Baha for you in September—I thought I could stop you asking for it, but see cannot—so here it is. No doubt Abdul Baha is writing you a Tablet, rather than cabling a reply. Aziz, the interpreter over there said in a very recent letter that he had many Tablets for the American believers, but had not the time just then to translate them, let us hope one is for you good folk. Rest assured any Tablets are rushed registered to the parties addressed.

The check of $100 as initial payment for the Tahitian B.B. [Big Bens] I endorsed right over to the printer, Walter Bowen. I also wrote your friend Mr. Drollet just what was expressed in your letter and when reply comes will let you hear. The printer, as all are, is most busy at this season of the year, I do not like to rush him, but likely proofs will come along shortly. Have not gotten the French Edition of the B.B. [Big Bens] as yet, so you see what we are in for. After first of the year things will have adjusted themselves nicely, I believe, so we will be patient a while longer.

Now for a little news from the Goodall-Cooper party. Nellie Lloyd and I have gotten mail from these dear friends speaking of their leaving Naples December 8th, from Naples, bound for home, that ship should reach this port about day or two before Christmas. Quite likely they will not remain long here but hurry to the Pacific Coast. What a wealth of news they will bring with them. Mons. and Madam Dreyfus-Barney are now at Haifa. Mr. Mountfort Mills and his wife plan to leave for Haifa January 5th, then about a month later, Mr. Louis Bourgeois and his wife sail for the same Blessed Spot. So we have ever friends either going or coming.

Lillian Capes, that dear girl who back in 1910 went to Teheran to teach in the Tarbiat School, died recently of typhus, just a week ago I got a cablegram from Dr. [Susan] Moody announcing the sad news. What a Loss! What a Loss! We shall miss her friendly letters, and as for Tarbiat School how shall they fill the gap. Some one surely must be raised to come to the assistance of the two good Doctors over there.

Well we are in the Christmas Holiday rush. Not a speck of snow, and weather most unusual, glad of it for it admits of my getting heaps of work done on the Log Cabin. You see now that you have gotten me started on the item, I keep mentioning it.

Bahai greetings . . .
Your brother,
Roy[17]

After the passing of 'Abdu'l-Bahá in November of 1921, the Guardian summoned to the Holy Land various Bahá'ís who could advise him on matters of import regarding the protection of the Cause. The two American Bahá'ís called to the Holy Land at that time were Mountfort Mills, most likely for his expertise in international law,* and Roy Wilhelm for his uncompromising loyalty to the Will of 'Abdu'l-Bahá.** The passing of the Master was a calamity, to say the least, and those Bahá'ís who assisted the Guardian through the succeeding months of darkness must surely have been transformed in ways that humbled them in the knowledge that they lifted the Guardian's burdens in some small way.

The spirit of detachment that is derived from unqualified service to the Cause can sometimes manifest itself in the way that a person values material wealth, for "this earth's happiness does not depend on wealth" and "material advantages do not elevate the spirit of man." Echoes of these words from 'Abdu'l-Bahá' can be heard in these words from Roy to John in a postcard he sent John in 1935: "As we accumulate summers and winters some things come along I suppose to make us cling less tenaciously to 'this dust bin of strife.'"[18]

In 1922, a year after the passing of 'Abdu'l-Bahá, Roy Wilhelm was a member of the Bahá'í Temple Unity Executive Board and at the helm of the promotion of the Temple Fund, to which John and Louise contributed generously. In the following letter, Roy alludes to the unifying efforts of people like John and Louse in contrast to the disunifying mischief of the Covenant-breakers. Recalling that 'Abdu'l-Bahá cabled Roy that the American believers should "Certainly shun violators" of

---

* For Shoghi Effendi's commendation of Mountfort Mills's expertise in law, see Shoghi Effendi, *Bahá'í Administration*, 180.

** Note: The reason for Roy Wilhelm's presence is a surmise gleaned from Rúhíyyih Khánum's explanation in *The Priceless Pearl* that in the early months of Shoghi Effendi's ministry as Guardian of the Cause, he "felt the need for support and consultation," and Roy Wilhelm was one of the many Bahá'ís called to Haifa to assist the Guardian in March, 1922. See Rúhíyyih Khánum, *The Priceless Pearl*, 55.

the Covenant, Roy felt a responsibility to guide the American believers away from misunderstandings and misinterpretations of the Master's Will and Testament. So great must have been Roy's anxiety over this burden that he often concealed it behind the veil of humor.

October 2nd, 1922
My dear John and Louise:
Every time I receive one of your good letters it changes me into a high-stepper for that day. The spiritual ozone you inject, as well as the material good feeling is just a pattern of what we as a body at large should be accomplishing in this harassed world of ours. So I vote you that we all take a good substantial lesson from dear Johnnie Dee and Louise.
First I will tell you about poor father whose physical condition has improved a trifle so that it seems now he may recover if no other complications ensue, but still five weeks have passed and he does not recognize us yet. He of course is confined in bed under the constant supervision of nurses night and day. I think I sent you a little acknowledgment of those wonderful prunes you so kindly sent, the finest fruit I ever saw. I have carefully preserved the seed in the hope that they might grow here but I would appreciate a tip from you as to whether they should best be planted in the Spring or in the Fall. All of your other trouble for us too is greatly appreciated. Whenever the crop is right just ship along what you can spare to West Englewood, N.J. as heretofore. During his former illness the only thing that father really enjoyed was your prunes. While I did no small nibbling on my own account, he was in reality the <u>big elephant</u> that made the largest hole in our supply.
My hands are so full that I cannot write much more now except to send my love and tell you how much I think of you and appreciate what you are doing constantly. If I could whisper a little in your personal ear I would tell you some things which it is wiser

not to express upon paper, though I will say, not to be misled by any misunderstanding or misinterpretations which may reach your ear from very sincere people as to recent occurrences in the Cause; half information and misinformation is responsible for a great deal of trouble now as heretofore, and if we do not look out we will smother the Cause and keep it from influencing broad, progressive minds just the same as has been the case to this point in orthodox Christianity.
With Abha greetings, I remain
Yours ever,
Roy[19]

It was Roy Wilhelm who funded much of Martha Root's worldwide teaching efforts, and it was through Roy that she first learned of the Cause of Bahá'u'lláh. Like so many early believers, however, Martha Root was truly confirmed through 'Abdu'l-Bahá's visit to the United States. She attended as many of His talks as possible, and the most memorable one for her was the Unity Feast hosted by 'Abdu'l-Bahá Himself at Roy Wilhelm's West Englewood property on June 29, 1912. (As a fulfillment of the Master's wish, that Unity Feast—called the Souvenir Picnic—is commemorated every year on the Wilhelm property in West Englewood.)

The death of Roy's father coincided with the death of Martha Root's father, and the fact that Roy was moved to write to John and Louise about both occurrences is telling of the depth of the friendship shared by John Bosch and Roy Wilhelm:

November 6, 1922
Dear John and Louise:
Your welcome letter and the seven lovely boxes have been received. No doubt you will have heard that after sixty-three days of unconsciousness father died a week ago today and the service was held at home last Thursday afternoon. During his long ill-

ness this Spring the only thing he really enjoyed was your prunes and when he got better he seemed to have more fun gnawing on them than anything else he ate. So you see, that gives one more accumulated thought of thankfulness to dear Johnnie Dee and Louise.

I intended enclosing a letter that you might see what others thought of the service, but I am afraid in the large accumulation it either got lost or destroyed. At any rate, we tried to have a freedom from that deep sense of gloom which is so often present at funerals, and several have since remarked that it really seemed more like a beautiful spiritual wedding, or words to that effect. The music was by Italian Harp, beautifully played, and the service was held by the Reverend Dr. Weir of the Unity Church of Montclair, where Abdul Baha spoke, and by Mountfort Mills. At the grave the brief burial service was recited by Dr. Manuel Bolden, the colored minister from Harlem of whom you may have heard and who by the way, lost his wife about a month ago. Mountfort also read a prayer. It is pretty hard to adjust to a loss like this which, from a human standpoint seems irreparable; yet, mother and I do not grieve and feel we have many, many bounties; one of them is that had father recovered physically the doctors tell us he would not have been in possession of his mental faculties, and so we know that, all things considered, his taking in this way and without suffering is really pure mercy.

Last night I opened three of the boxes [of prunes] and found them in perfect condition. I will keep a close eye on them and make very certain that none are lost in the way you feared. These were to be sent upon <u>a business basis</u> so please let me have your memorandum that I may send you a check for the money part. [. . .]. I wish you would make a little Parcel Post package Louise, and send along to me any of your knives and scissors that need sharpening. I can do it all at home in a jiffy, I have a motor grinder. Just put a cork over the points and wrap them well. It

wouldn't cost much in postage and I would be so glad to have a chance to do this for you.
Mother I know would wish to join in love.
P.S. Martha Root's father died last Friday . . . she was with us the day father was stricken. Probably she will go to China now.
Yours,
Roy[20]

John and Louise archived the letters they received from friends, of which there were dozens and dozens. Each letter closed with a valediction that praised the character of John and Louise—and of all those valedictions, the most metaphorically accurate is this one from Roy, where he drew an analogy between the love kneaded into the fruits of John's orchards and the love kneaded into the hearts of the Friends: "Many, many thanks for the love you have kneaded in [my heart] as well as [in] the lovely fruits themselves."[21] In a postcard dated 1935, Roy characterized this love further, and he associated it with his enthusiasm for Martha Root's teaching work and the teaching work being undertaken by John and Louise at Geyserville Bahá'í School:

New York, September 25, 1935
Your welcome letter of lovely sentiments sets a wee mark for me to shoot at, distant tho' it seems. I will thank you in advance for the prunies, and especially your very kind thought, but I hope you are not taking too great trouble.

Continually I hear of your good works . . . as to rest: that you'll have in heaven. Martha writes most enthusiastically of the Icelanders—a very superior people. Helsingfors, Finland is her address for next 2 or 3 weeks.

I'm enclosing two good stout hugs—say ouch when they hurt.

Could you use "Some Answered Questions" in your Summer School library?
Roy[22]

John and Louise attended many Bahá'í National Conventions in Chicago. Being present at Convention gave them a chance to participate in consultation with Bahá'ís from all parts of the United States. With regard to the purpose of the Bahá'í Convention, Shoghi Effendi points to "the unique functions it fulfils in promoting harmony and goodwill, in removing misunderstandings and in enhancing the prestige of the Cause." He draws attention to the "tremendous impetus" in the execution of the plans of the Faith that results from the "consultation and mingling of the friends" at Convention, and to the valuable role of the delegates in carrying back to their fellow-believers "a very real awareness of the work in hand and the needs of the hour."[23] Since John and Roy's friendship was a long-distance one, Roy's happiness in hearing that John planned to attend the Convention in 1931 is shown in his humorous reference to their decades-long friendship. Nevertheless, behind Roy's humor is an unmistakable regard he had for John:

April 4, 1931
Dear old John and young Louise:
First I'll thank you on behalf of the National for your check for which receipt is enclosed.

I am delighted that the flea jumped from the monkey onto John but am curious to know whether it camps in his whiskers or on top of his head—the latter is something it could not very well do on mine. Have you heard the little story of the two fleas which were conversing on a dog's back when one suddenly turned to the other asking pardon for breaking off the conversation, saying—"I have to leave now, here comes a dog going my way."

The best news of all is that John is coming to the Convention but I'll use my strongest influence with the doorkeep not to let him in unless he brings Louise. I can see you now in that big hat you wore at the Chicago Convention thirty, forty, or sixty years ago, when you made that lovely little talk of your visit to Haifa which was so much enjoyed. I know Curtis [Kelsey] would wish to join his love with mine if he knew that I were writing you. <u>Do</u> <u>try</u> and both of you come.

   Sincerely yours,

   Roy[24]

Roy obviously took great delight in cajoling John, and perhaps it was because Roy saw in John Bosch a bit of himself. John was gentle yet uncompromising; he was wise yet humble; he was selfless yet forthright, especially in matters of business. In the letter that follows, John Bosch was sending a fiscal report to the Treasurer's Office of the National Spiritual Assembly and outlining the costs of the Geyserville Bahá'í Summer School to be included in the annual report at the National Convention. The brevity of John's report is an inspiration in itself:

April 9, 1932
Geyserville, California
Treasurer of N.S.A.
Evergreen Cabin
West Englewood, N.J.

   Of the N.S.A. account we had the amount of $24.16 on hand and this sum was used up to pay a speaker. All other expenses have been paid by the Summer School.

   At the Summer School meeting in San Francisco on March 13th, 1932 with all of the Committee present—Mrs. Cooper, George Latimer, Leroy Ioas, Mrs. A. Collins, JD Bosch—as questions of finances were discussed, it was decided that if a budget is authorized by the N.S.A. for the year 1932–1933 for the Summer School, that it should be accepted.

   Very truly yours,

   John D. Bosch[25]

It is difficult to know whether or not John was being witty in the brevity of his report or whether it was natural in him to make the complicated simple. Furthermore, John addressed the letter to the "Treasurer of the NSA" rather than to Roy, suggesting a formality that was not necessary for Roy. Regardless of what John meant by the formality, John's economy of language was not lost on Roy Wilhelm:

April 18, 1932
Dear John:
Your NSA letter of April 9th with the information about all the wealth you have on hand as well as the credit of having a lot more for which you had everything but the money itself, is received. Why, John, you could have a fine old *Soiree* on $24.16 unless, of course, you wanted to have a real party with a lot of canaries etc. Anyway, I do not blame you for wishing to have this matter set straight, and I will give the National a poke on it at the forthcoming meeting, as well as call their attention to the correction in name.
What you really should have written was that you and LOUISE were coming this year. I strongly advise that Louise herself come for reasons which I will not explain here. If you fellers will just behave and come, I will buy you the biggest bootleg of soda water I can find in the Gold Coast region which I believe is what they call the Wilmette-Evanston district. Do try and come!
Much love to you both.
Sincerely yours,
Roy[26]

Business aside, spiritual matters were at the heart of John and Roy's friendship. In 1932, Roy Wilhelm and his mother hosted their annual "Souvenir Picnic" in commemoration of the picnic and Unity Feast given at their home by 'Abdu'l-Bahá. At that picnic in 1912, 'Abdu'l-Bahá said that "Hundreds of thousands of meetings shall be held to commemorate this occasion; and the very words I speak to you today shall be repeated in them for ages to come." The Master exhorted the friends to "become of one heart, one spirit and one susceptibility" and that the friends must "be exceedingly kind and loving toward each other, willing to forfeit life in the pathway of another's happiness."[27] John and Louise were unable to attend the twentieth annual commemoration and Louise sent this note of regret to Roy:

Dear Roy,
To your twentieth annual meeting and Feast in memory of the visit of Abdul Baha we send you greetings and Love.
How much we wish to be with you on this memorial occasion. "Yes," we will be with you in spirit of the beloved Cause and that the Western & Pacific spirit will always be Ever-Green in your beautiful Cabin.
Louise and John[28]

As treasurer of the National Spiritual Assembly, Roy was responsible for receiving the contributions to the Temple Fund, but more importantly, he was responsible for raising the friends' awareness of the spiritual bounties of giving to the various funds of the Faith. After all, only enrolled believers may contribute to these funds, which makes such contributions a precious honor indeed. The Guardian explained that "the progress and extension of spiritual activities is dependent and conditioned upon material means" and that giving to the Bahá'í Fund is "a practical and effective way whereby every believer can test the measure and character of his Faith, and to prove in deeds the intensity of his devotion and attachment to the Cause."[29] Roy knew how deeply John and Louise understood this principle:

December 2, 1935
Dear John and Louise:
I wish the whole country would take a lesson in constancy from Geyserville and two or three similar Assemblies. This last month we again had nineteen blanks, Assemblies who have not sent in anything at all. This is about the average number of silent

ones. How in the world can we expect to get electricity if we do not connect with the Power House. I enclose one of the cards we passed around at the Temple gathering in October—got a smile out of them by saying I was giving them a card containing "beauty hints."

[We] are still enjoying your lovely prunies but they take second place when it comes to your card and letters on "Goatology" and I note what you say, John, about goats wanting to be loved, so since I have had no luck in getting a wife, that gives an additional reason for wanting a goat. Thanks for your suggestion as to the breed and also for that splendid suggestion about trying a goat first. I supposed all their milk tasted alike but evidently there is considerable variation in its goatiness [. . .].

You will find a statement in Baha'i News which certainly ought to awaken these sleeping communities.

With Abha love!
Sincerely
Roy, Treasurer[30]

John recommended the Alpine goat, which was surely a choice influenced by his Swiss roots. It was not long before Roy imported goats from Switzerland and began breeding a flock on his property on Speckled Mountain in Lovell, Maine where he kept a winter cabin retreat.[31]

Roy knew how to strike a balance between the material aspect of giving and the spiritual rewards of it. By 1940 John was in his eighty-fifth year and Roy was in his sixty-fifth. Both were as busy in their Bahá'í activities as ever—John with the Geyserville Bahá'í Summer School and Roy in his thirtieth year of service on the National Spiritual Assembly. Both men were vigilant about the needs of the Faith—especially the financial needs of the Faith—and they continually encouraged one another regarding the Fund. When Roy received the following cable from the Guardian dated February 16, 1933, he directed the National Treasurer's office to forward a copy of the cable to John:

REPEATED EVIDENCES AMERICAN BELIEVERS' SLEEPLESS VIGILANCE COURAGEOUS LOYALTY EXEMPLARY SELF-SACRIFICE ESTABLISHED THEM IN EVERY BAHÁ'Í HEART AS CHAMPION-BUILDERS WORLD ORDER BAHÁ'U'LLÁH. FOUNDER OF OUR FAITH WELL PLEASED TOKENS THEIR WISE STEWARDSHIP 'ABDU'L-BAHÁ PROUD OF THEIR VALOR GREATEST HOLY LEAF RADIANT WITH JOY AT THEIR FIDELITY.[32]

The concern over the funds necessary for the completion of the Temple and the continuation of the teaching work was ever on the minds of John and Roy. Their shared hobby of raising goats must have served as temperance to their anxious concern over the sacrificial efforts required—and unparalleled bounty—of completing the House of Worship. In the following letter, written on his return from a meeting of the National Spiritual Assembly in Chicago, Roy playfully refers to his "Camp" at Speckled Mountain where he kept his flock of "kids":

New York Central Railroad, enroute home
April 30, 1940
Dear John and Louise:
Pretty jiggly but want to get this started before I get back into the rush. Took your letter to Chicago hoping to get a chance, but things kept us spinning like a top, days and late nights.

Wish you could have been [at Convention], our largest, most harmonious and most progressive Convention . . . stretched the capacity of Foundation Hall. You'd hardly know the grounds since we've gotten thousands of yards of fill.

Your continued sacrifice I'm sure will bring to you and the friends bountiful rewards one way or another—probably even in this world.

As to getting old—huh! Why 'Abdu'l-Bahá told us some fruits do not even attain a ripeness until after they leave the tree! I'm not exactly a spring capon myself, but I'm having the busiest, happiest and I hope most fruitful time of my life. As to our dear

John and Louise—well, I only wish my chances were a fraction as secure.

Going back to Camp next week to see our nearly 140 kids—most lovable little knaves and scoundrels. They all try to climb over me at once. And the credit of this new life, improved health, etc. belongs <u>largely</u> to you who, first set me to thinking about Goats.

Was fine to have George [Latimer] with us. He's doing a splendid job in organizing our properties, etc.

Abha love to you and greetings to the friends,

Roy[33]

Raising goats may have been in the interests of Roy's health, but both John and Roy took delight in the greater outcome: thousands of people came to inquire about the goats, and as a result, were given some literature on the Bahá'í Faith. Here is a letter from Roy written from his other cabin in Maine, also called Evergreen Cabin, where he is enjoying an unexpected benefit of raising goats. It is perhaps worth noting that the letterhead was inscribed with Roy's unpretentious wit: "Evergreen Alpine Herd: The Aristocrats of the Goat World":

November 4, 1940
North Lovell, Maine
Dear John and Louise:

Bertha [Roy's secretary] has forwarded your letter with receipt from Wilmette and I have the pleasure of a little one-sided chat between jumps—trying to get things ready to leave for the winter quarters and grub for nearly 200 always hungry Goats—migosh! I have to buy nearly a hundred tons of hay besides what we raise, and two hundred more kids due in the spring—Now John and Louise, you're the fello's got me into all this <u>busy happy business</u>. Well it's greatly improving my health and I only wish you were near so you could make me a visit and see what I'm up to.

Incidentally, they [the goats] help advertise what we're really trying to accomplish—with over 3,300 callers this year, many of whom know we are interested in some strange thing, and ask for literature. They come from nearly every State, and some "furrin parts."

The other day the Ladies Club, about 50 of our nearby farm and town women sent word and asked if they could meet here and learn about this Faith we believe in. Whoop la! And so it goes.

Well, between the whole business I hardly can find time to keep my chin smooth—and now and then have to go back to N.Y.—for a rest. Here's a little snap [photo] of me with some of my sweet hearts.

Many times through the year, dear John and Louise come into my memory. I'm sure your ears must tingle!

Cable communication at least I still open. You will soon receive, or maybe have now, a long powerful Cable from the Guardian to us in America. Surely it will stimulate our best efforts!

Dear fello's, I love you [. . .] .

Roy[34]

The "snap" to which Roy referred is a photograph of himself with his goats, and he used it as an advertisement. Roy's playful distraction with goats belies his true and single-minded devotion to every need of the Faith. He spent little money on himself and gave the majority of his wealth to the Bahá'í Fund. Often, he made donations to support projects that needed immediate funding, such as a short film of the Master that was filmed outside the Ansonia Hotel in New York in 1912—a service acknowledged by the Guardian in a letter he wrote to the National Spiritual Assembly in 1923: "Regarding the short film of the Master, for which, as well as for the record of His voice, I am deeply indebted to the selfless efforts and services of my dear brother Mr. Roy C. Wilhelm."[35] As it turns out, Roy Wilhelm was with John Bosch when this short film of 'Abdu'l-Bahá was made—and Roy reminiscences about it in the following letter to John and Louise:

"St. Patrick's" 1942
Dear John and Louise,
Was very nice to have word of you from Leroy during N.S.A. at Wilmette last week—and to know you are both going strong . . .

And know that I have this clipping—perhaps some distant "kinfolks" [referring to the advertisement of Roy with his goats.] I'll send it along as an excuse to slip in a loving remembrance [. . .].

"These Great Days are Swiftly Passing." Remember, John, the day at the Ansonia when you and I were walking outside and they came to make a moving picture of our Beloved! But that was a mere third of a century scant! What's a little thing like that between friends—huh!

Yours,
Roy[36]

Having stood together in the presence of 'Abdu'l-Bahá, on American soil, was the cement of John and Roy's friendship—a friendship that would witness the progress of the Cause in America from its earliest beginnings, through its gradual growth, and beyond the crises of two World Wars, of which Roy wrote to John in 1942, "Such a sick old world, but hardly ready yet to listen to the Remedy." Echoing his previously expressed sentiment about how "These Great Days are swiftly passing," Roy wrote a note to John to say that he hoped John would have "many more happy years of marvelous service." Roy knew that John would understand the reference to "swiftly passing days" as it comes from a passage of 'Abdu'l-Bahá quoted in *Star of the West* in 1914.[37] John and Roy had a shared understanding of this passage and it must have felt that 'Abdu'l-Bahá was addressing them personally:

These days are the days of Faith and Deeds—not the days of words and lip service: Let us arise from the sleep of negligence, and realize what a great feast is prepared for us; first eating thereof ourselves, then giving unto others who are thirsting for the Water of Knowledge, and hungering for the Bread of Life.

These Great Days are swiftly passing; and once gone they can never be recalled. So, while the Rays of the Sun of Truth are still shining and *The Center of the Covenant of* GOD is manifest, let us go forth to work."[38]

Both Roy Wilhelm and John Bosch donated their properties to the National Spiritual Assembly of the Bahá'ís of the United States. In March of 1935, Roy Wilhelm executed an Indenture of Trust under which the Evergreen Cabin in West Englewood and the two lots in the pine grove where the Unity Feast was celebrated in 1912, were transferred to the National Spiritual Assembly of the Bahá'ís of the United States, thereby securing the protection of the spot so especially blessed by the Master. Roy Wilhelm's generous gift surely caught John Bosch's attention, as he and Louise had long considered donating their property to the Cause. John wrote to George Latimer, who was a member of the National Spiritual Assembly at the time, to ask about how such an Indenture of Trust was arranged for Wilhelm's West Englewood property so that he might do the same. In the letter, John puns the name of "Roy" as "the King"—most likely a nod to Roy's kingly generosity:

Geyserville, California
July 13, 1935
Dear George,
Your letter of January 8th received, also the copy of the West Englewood transaction, which I suppose is the Evergreen Cabin property. How kind of Roy (the King) to donate this most wonderful piece of land to the N.S.A. Such a gift, where Abdul Baha himself spread the 19 day Feast in June 1912. This will be an everlasting memorial place, in fact an eternal "Shrine."[39]

By September of 1935, John and Louise finalized their arrangements to deed their property to the Cause—an arrangement that secured their life tenancy of the property. It must have been reassuring to John and Louise that both Leroy Ioas and George Latimer, with whom they served on the Pacific Coast School Committee, were serving on the National Spiritual Assembly at the time. George Latimer wrote:

September 25, 1935
Dear John and Louise:
Your letter with the enclosed Indenture to the Geyserville property duly signed and executed was most happily received on the 23rd, which happened to be my birthday and made the day all the more eventful for me.

[. . .] I feel that the [language of the Indenture] properly protects your life interest and estate in the entire property and this remarkable gift to the Cause of Baha 'U' llah will be recorded in the annals of history for all time. I am sure that this gift will rejoice the hearts of all the American believers and I think that I can speak for the National Assembly with the utmost appreciation for your generosity, devoted and loyal service to the Cause of God for these many, many years, climaxed by this glorious, selfless contribution which insures not only a place for the earnest study of the Teachings for future generations, but provides a haven of refuge for the believers in times of trials and tribulation.

The Indenture goes immediately to the National Spiritual Assembly for final approval, after which it will be returned for proper recording [. . .].

With the greatest of joy at the final consummation of this memorial to your life of devotion and service to the Cause, I am, as always,
Devotedly yours,
George[40]

Roy Wilhelm, who was also a member of the National Spiritual Assembly at the time that John and Louise deeded their property to it, added his own delightful wit upon the occasion of shared Indentures and the reminder to not rest on one's laurels as "some work of noble note, may yet be done" before crossing to the "better world":*

September 29, 1935
Very dear John and Louise:
Continually you return to my memory—happy days of yore—and now you seem to be right with me as I read the minutes of our last meeting with special reference to the "Bosch Trustees." Someone has said that all we take with us is what we give away, so John and Louise will need extra baggage arrangements in the (I hope) distant future when the time comes to cross to the better world.

The following is from a letter just received from the Guardian:
"It seems that the Faith is now well enough organized and has sufficient devoted and intelligent adherents to make a large scale contact with the public and try and bring at least a knowledge of its existence and its principles to the masses."

This will give us plenty to do and tax our wisdom, resources and tact to their utmost . . . interesting days ahead. I hope you both will live to see the fruits of your long devoted labours.

Affectionately yours,
Roy[41]

By 1945 John's health began to fail and he was confined to his bed most of the time. Despite his ill health, he continued to correspond with Shoghi Effendi about the progress of the summer school. The following letter is one of the responses from the Guardian to the Bosches,

---

* Tennyson, "Ulysses," The Norton Anthology of English Literature, 1962.

hand-written by Rúhíyyih Khánum on behalf of Shoghi Effendi, followed by a postscript from the Guardian:

Haifa
March 16th, 1945
Dear Bahá'í Friends:
Your most welcome letter of February 12th was received a few days ago by the beloved Guardian and he has instructed me to answer it on his behalf.

The illness of his dear John he was very sorry to hear of. He has been praying for him ever since he received word (through reading a report) that he was confined to bed.

Your long, selfless, loyal and devoted services can never be forgotten, and are certainly never forgotten by him! Every time he reads a word about Geyserville he remembers all you have contributed to the progress of the Cause in America through the establishment of this important institution and your generous donation of it to the American Bahá'í community.

In the years to come it will continually expand and be built up into an institute of Bahá'í learning, and the good it does multiply and perpetuate your dear memory amongst the friends. So you must both feel very happy and very content with your labours!

He assures you you are both very dear to him and remembered in his prayers, with love and esteem, in the Holy Tombs.

With warm Bahá'í love,
R. Rabbani
[Hand-written postscript from the Guardian:]
Dear beloved co-workers:
Your letter was indeed most welcome. Your historic services, your generous contributions to the Faith & to its institutions, above all the superb & exemplary spirit of devotion that animates you are assets that I greatly value and which posterity will no doubt remember & extol. You should feel happy, assured &

elated. You are often in my thoughts & prayers & my heart is full of love & gratitude for you both.
Your true brother,
Shoghi

John died on July 22, 1946, and Louise died on September 6, 1952. Nine months before John's passing, Louise had a sleepless night, and she wrote to Leroy and Sylvia Ioas about her restlessness. It is endearing to note that Louise had expected her death to coincide with John's death, and she was simply planning accordingly:

Sunday October 21, 1945
Dear Leroy and Sylvia,
I cannot help writing you some of my after-reflexions of yesterday's enterprise and perhaps you may be able to disperse my uneasiness and anxiety. I had very little sleep Saturday night and suffered most fearfully from cramps in legs and thighs from too much standing and from my temerity to take that long walk to the [redwood] grove but which is no one's fault except my own. So at dawn I arose to write you, as many thoughts crowded upon me with regards to our burial place upon the heights. First I thought of a hearse carrying either John or myself up that dangerous road. It shouldn't be done; thus the casket would have to be carried by hand up to the place and that would be too much for any pall-bearers. The road up the hill is not a good road and always needs fixing and that fixing never lasts and always has to be fixed over again as the winter rains wash it out. Also, it is such a distance for any of the friends to walk. Imagine if it should rain and be slippery on our burial day!

Also, I thought that there would be no water on that place lest it were pumped there and a tank provided for it, and pipes (to water any shrubs or plants that might be planted there.) And it would be certain that the cut-out underbrush would soon be grown over again with new wild growths; one lone caretaker on this big place would never suffice to keep order on so remote a spot.

It would cost an awful lot to develop a cemetery up there for just us two, the money is not available really. Yet, in consideration of the fact that there are about a dozen believers who have waited from the beginning on to pick their location to build themselves a cottage on the hillside, some for occupancy only during the summer time and some for occupancy for all the year around use, so I thought there would not really be much choice left where we two could be buried without coming too close to the cottages of the friends and that therefore we should go rather high up on the hill and which we have done yesterday, Saturday. But it is not the place that John has had in mind! What he had thought of is a place not that high up. But as the property is big we could make another attempt to find a spot, perhaps with easy access to water. Right here in our back yard where the woods begin would perhaps be a better place and there is water and water pipes just a little farther on. It's all National Spiritual Assembly ground there. Therefore it would be easy of access to all the friends and easy to water any flowers that may grow on the graves. And cheaper than the wilds up there so far away for a keeper to reach the place.

And now will say that in case John or I should <u>not</u> outlast the time required for arranging everything that is necessary for to bury us, then please make use of our plot on the Olive Hill Cemetery of Geyserville and bury us there. You would not need to be afraid of doing this, as our dear Guardian has not made it a binding behest for us to not be buried there; were he to know all about it he would surely say it is all right. Our burial is, after all, a very small affair compared with other things of the Cause. I thank you from the bottom of my heart for all your precious love for John and me, and am hoping to someday be able to do something for you.

In El Abha ever yours,

John and Louise[42]

As it happened, John and Louise were both buried at Olive Hill Cemetery—and Milly Collins paid for all of the funeral costs. Marzieh Gail, in her book *Summon Up Remembrance*, included a chapter on John and Louise Bosch. She wrote that John Bosch "was buried in Olive Hill cemetery, Geyserville, following a befitting memorial service held July 24 in the Bahá'í Hall, Geyserville School. Under the auspices of the National Spiritual Assembly, a memorial service was also held for him in the Bahá'í House of Worship on November 24, 1946. John's grave, a concrete tomb, is covered with a long plaque (the work of John Quinn) made of hammered bronze and bearing the Greatest Name." About a decade after John's death, the Guardian wrote further guidance regarding inscriptions on Bahá'í gravestones. In a letter written on his behalf to an individual believer, the Guardian stated, "In regard to your question regarding the use of the Greatest Name on tombstones of Bahá'ís, the Guardian considers this too sacred to be placed in such a position in general use, and the friends should not use it on their tombstones. They can use quotations from the Teachings, if they wish to, but not the Greatest Name."[43]

Since the plaque was only ornamental, it was easily moved from John Bosch's grave. At present, it is positioned upright against one of the foyer walls of Martha Root Hall at Bosch Bahá'í School in Santa Cruz, California. The plaque is an imposing size, approximately seven feet tall and three feet wide; the Greatest Name is engraved at the top. Also engraved on the plaque is a quotation from Bahá'u'lláh that reads: "Say: O ye who are as dead! The Hand of Divine bounty proffereth unto you the Water of Life. Hasten and drink your fill. Whoso hath been reborn in this Day, shall never die; whoso remaineth dead, shall never live."[44]

Two months after John's passing, Louise wrote her impressions of the funeral using unused sheets of paper from a freight train ledger, with blank lines for the car number, the net weight of the produce, the amount, and the date. One cannot know whether Louise thought the freight ledger was symbolic of a train carrying its cargo to a port of call, but the spiritual imagery of precious cargo headed to the next world touches the imagination and tugs at one's heartstrings. At the top of the ledger she wrote, in fine cursive lines, the word "Funeral," and it is dated September 12th, 1946:

> The funeral was well attended and beautiful. The flower-tribute was large and very beautiful. The music also was beautiful. In his honour the stores were closed during the 2½ hours of transition. The funeral oration became the opportunity for the giving of the Message of the Coming of Baha'u'llah. This all-important matter of the giving forth of the Message in that large hall and at that logical moment suggested itself as a very beseeming and appropriate time. Thus, the Message given was delicately but clearly interwoven with the address of the speaker Leroy Ioas and as delicately and eloquently revealed by him to a deeply silent and attentively listening assemblage of people gathered as said in the large hall of the Auditorium where the body was lying in state. Everything had been so carefully planned and so beautifully carried out that one could have thought it was a king that died. "It takes an eye that's king—discerning to recognize the king in every garb."[45] (From the Arabic.)

Upon the passing of John Bosch, the Guardian wrote this cable, dated July 29, 1946:

PROFOUNDLY GRIEVE PASSING DEARLY-BELOVED GREAT-HEARTED HIGH-MINDED DISTINGUISHED SERVANT BAHÁ'U'LLÁH JOHN BOSCH. HIS SAINTLY LIFE PIONEER SERVICES HISTORIC CONTRIBU-

TION OF INSTITUTION OF SUMMER SCHOOL ENTITLE HIM TO RANK AMONG OUTSTANDING FIGURES OF THE CLOSING YEARS HEROIC AND OPENING YEARS OF THE FORMATIVE AGE OF THE BAHÁ'Í DISPENSATION. CONCOURSE ON HIGH EXTOL HIS EXALTED SERVICES. ASSURE HIS WIFE AND VALIANT COMPANION OF MY DEEP-FELT SYMPATHY. ADVISE HOLD SPECIAL GATHERING IN TEMPLE AS TRIBUTE TO HIS IMPERISHABLE MEMORY.[46]

The accolades in this message are lofty indeed. The "concourse on high extolling his exalted services" surely must refer to all of John Bosch's services, including his part in the interment of the sacred remains of the Master. Mention of his "historic contribution" to the institution of the summer schools acknowledge the direction John Bosch set for summer schools as a training ground for teachers of the Cause. The "pioneer services" must refer to John and Louise's short-term pioneering to Tahiti and to other places in Europe as a direct response to the Master's Tablets of the Divine Plan.

In one of His talks given in Paris in 1911, 'Abdu'l-Bahá described the qualities of a saint: "Saints are men who have freed themselves from the world of matter and who have overcome sin. They live in the world but are not of it, their thoughts being continually in the world of the spirit. Their lives are spent in holiness, and their deeds show forth love, justice and godliness." When John Bosch first became a Bahá'í, he wrote to 'Abdu'l-Bahá asking that his name be entered in the "Great Book of this Universal Life" and that his watchword would be "justice."[47] One of the first Bahá'í books that John purchased after declaring himself a believer in the Cause of God was *The Hidden Words of Bahá'u'lláh*. Although he could not have known it then, the power of the revelation of these words of Bahá'u'lláh influenced every atom of creation:

O SON OF SPIRIT! The best beloved of all things in My sight is Justice; turn not away therefrom if thou desirest Me, and neglect it not that I may confide in thee. By its aid thou shalt see with thine own eyes and not through the eyes of others, and shalt know of thine own knowledge and not through the knowledge of thy neighbor. Ponder this in thy heart; how it behooveth thee to be. Verily justice is My gift to thee and the sign of My loving-kindness. Set it then before thine eyes.[48]

Notes

1 / On a Train

1. Myron H. Phelps, *The Life and Teachings of Abbas Effendi*. https://archive.org/details/lifeandteachings002925mbp. Accessed April 2, 2014.
2. John D. and Louise Bosch papers, U.S. National Bahá'í Archives.
3. Ibid.
4. Shoghi Effendi, *God Passes By*, 405–6.
5. Shoghi Effendi, "The Disciples of 'Abdu'l-Bahá," *The Bahá'í World*, vol. III (1928–1930): 85.
6. Helen Goodall and Ella Cooper, *Daily Lesson's Received in 'Akká*. http://bahai-library.com/goodall_cooper_daily_lessons; 'Abdu'l-Bahá, *Tablets of the Divine Plan*;. 'Abdu'l-Bahá, *Tablets of the Divine Plan*, 22.
7. Letter dated February 1, 1905 from Helen S. Goodall to John D. Bosch, U.S. National Bahá'í Archives.
8. Shoghi Effendi, *The World Order of Bahá'u'lláh*, 134.
9. Letter dated February 25, 1905 from Helen S. Goodall to John D. Bosch, U.S. National Bahá'í Archives.
10. Mírzá Mahmúd-i-Zarqání, *Mahmúd's Diary*, 269.
11. Letter dated December 8, 1910 from Helen S. Goodall to John D. Bosch, U.S. National Bahá'í Archives.
12. Shoghi Effendi, *The World Order of Bahá'u'lláh*, 131–32.
13. Letter dated June 20, 1907, from Helen S. Goodall to John D. Bosch, U.S. National Bahá'í Archives.
14. Letter dated May 17, 1905, from Helen S. Goodall to John D. Bosch, U.S. National Bahá'í Archives.
15. Bahá'u'lláh, *Gleanings from the Writings of Bahá'u'lláh*, no. 75.1.

16. Shoghi Effendi, *Directives from the Guardian*, 47.
17. John D. and Louise Bosch papers, U.S. National Bahá'í Archives.
18. Letter from 'Abdu'l-Bahá to John D. Bosch, translated by Mírzá Ameen Ullah Fareed, John D. and Louise Bosch papers, U.S. National Bahá'í Archives. The translation was sent to John D. Bosch along with the original Tablet.
19. Letter from John D. Bosch to 'Abdu'l-Bahá, John D. and Louise Bosch papers, U.S. National Bahá'í Archives.
20. Robert Stockman, *Thornton Chase: First American Bahá'í*, 208.

2 / Become as True Brethren

1. The Báb, *Selections of the Writings of the Báb*, no. 2:24:2.
2. Thornton Chase, quoted in Robert H. Stockman, *Thornton Chase: First American Bahá'í*, 3.
3. Shoghi Effendi, *God Passes By*, 413–14.
4. Telegram dated March 13, 1909 from Helen S. Goodall to John D. Bosch, U.S. Bahá'í Archives.
5. Shoghi Effendi, *This Decisive Hour*, no. 101.1; O. Z. Whitehead, *Some Early Bahá'ís of the West*, 111–119; Howard MacNutt, Introduction to 'Abdu'l-Bahá, *Promulgation of Universal Peace*, xix–xxv; Horace Holley, "In Memoriam: Mountfort Mills," *The Bahá'í World*, vol. XI (1946–1950): 509–511; Jesse Revell, "In Memoriam: Susan Moody," *The Bahá'í World*, vol. VI (1934–1936): 483–486; Bruce W. Whitmore, *The Dawning Place*, 23.
6. Shoghi Effendi, *God Passes By*, 436–37.
7. Letter dated July 29, 1909 from 'Abdu'l-Bahá to Corinne True, United States Bahá'í Archives. A more recent translation of this Tablet was completed by the Bahá'í World Center in 1977. The original translation from 1909 has been printed here in order to understand the story of John Bosch during his lifetime.
8. Bosch papers, U.S. Bahá'í Archives.
9. Letter dated March 24, 1909 from John D. Bosch to Helen S Goodall, U.S. Bahá'í Archives.
10. Letter dated December 12, 1908 from Helen S. Goodall to John D. Bosch, U.S. Bahá'í Archives.
11. 'Abdu'l-Bahá, *The Promulgation of Universal Peace*, 10.
12. 'Abdu'l-Bahá, *Selections from the Writings of 'Abdu'l-Bahá*, no. 15.7.

NOTES

13. Robert H. Stockman, *Thornton Chase: First American Bahá'í*, 212.
14. Adib Taherzadeh, *The Child of the Covenant*, 300.
15. Letter dated March 13, 1910 from Thornton Chase to John D. Bosch, John D. and Louise Bosch papers, U.S. National Bahá'í Archives.
16. Letter dated June 3, 1910 from Thornton Chase to John D. Bosch, John D. and Louise Bosch papers, U.S. National Bahá'í Archives. The translation was sent to John D. Bosch along with the original Tablet.
17. Letter dated June 15, 1910 from Thornton Chase to John D. Bosch, John D. and Louise Bosch papers, U.S. National Bahá'í Archives.
18. Letter dated September 10, 1910 from Thornton Chase to John D Bosch, John D. and Louise Bosch papers, U.S. National Bahá'í Archives.
19. Robert H. Stockman, *Thornton Chase: First American Bahá'í*, 265.
20. Letter dated September 21, 1910 from Thornton Chase to John D. Bosch, John D. and Louise Bosch papers, U.S. National Bahá'í Archives.
21. *The Dawn-Breakers: Nabíl's Narrative of the Early Days of the Bahá'í Revelation*, translated by Shoghi Effendi in 1932.
22. Mary Hanford Ford, *The Oriental Rose*. https://archive.org/details/orientalroseorte00fordrich (accessed April 5, 2014); Laura Clifford Barney, *God's Heroes: A Drama in Five Acts*. https://archive.org/details/godsherosplay00barnrich (accessed April 5, 2014).
23. Laura Clifford Barney. *God's Heroes: A Drama in Five Acts*, viii.
24. Letter dated October 20, 1910 from Thornton Chase to John D. Bosch, John D. and Louise Bosch papers, U.S. National Bahá'í Archives.
25. Letter dated November 29, 1910 from Thornton Chase to John D. Bosch, John D. and Louise Bosch papers, U.S. National Bahá'í Archives.
26. Letter dated December 3, 1910 from Thornton Chase to John D Bosch, John D. and Louise Bosch papers, U.S. National Bahá'í Archives.
27. Letter dated December 12, 1910 from Thornton Chase to John D Bosch, John D. and Louise Bosch papers, U.S. National Bahá'í Archives.
28. Letter dated December 24, 1910 from Thornton Chase to John D Bosch, John D. and Louise Bosch papers, U.S. National Bahá'í Archives.
29. Louise Bosch, quoted in Robert H. Stockman, *Thornton Chase: First American Bahá'í*, 266.

30. O.Z. Whitehead, *Some Early Bahá'ís of the West*, 11.
31. Letter dated March 21, 1911 from Thornton Chase to John D. Bosch, John D. and Louise Bosch papers, U.S. National Bahá'í Archives.
32. Thornton Chase, *The Bahá'í Revelation*, 46.
33. 'Abdu'l-Bahá, "Recent Tablets from 'Abdu'l-Bahá," *Star of the West*, vol. 11, nos. 7 and 8 (August 1, 1911): 11–13.
34. Letter dated July 27, 1911 from John D. Bosch to Thornton Chase, John D. and Louise Bosch papers, U.S. National Bahá'í Archives.
35. Marzieh Gail, *Dawn Over Mount Hira*, 204.
36. Luther Burbank, *New Creations in Fruits and Flowers*. Accessed October 10, 2016. https://archive.org/details/newcreationsinfr1894burb.
37. Letter dated June 23, 1912 from 'Abdu'l-Bahá to John D. Bosch and Luther Burbank, John D. and Louise Bosch papers, U.S. National Bahá'í Archives. The translation was sent to John D. Bosch and Luther Burbank along with the original Tablet.
38. Herrigel, quoted in Earl Redman, *'Abdu'l-Bahá in Their Midst*, 313; 'Abdu'l-Bahá, *Tablets of the Divine Plan*, no. 7.7; the Universal House of Justice, *Century of Light*, 66.
39. O.Z. Whitehead, *Some Early Bahá'ís of the West*, 4.
40. Letter dated July 6, 1912 from Thornton Chase to John D. Bosch, John D. and Louise Bosch papers, U.S. National Bahá'í Archives.
41. Shoghi Effendi, *The Light of Divine Guidance, Vol. 2*, (Bahá'í Publishing Trust of Germany, 1985), 80.
42. Letter dated July 26, 1912 from Thornton Chase to John D. Bosch, John D. and Louise Bosch papers, U.S. National Bahá'í Archives.
43. Thornton Chase and John Bosch, quoted in Marzieh Gail, *Dawn Over Mount Hira*, 207.
44. Letter dated August 1, 1912 from 'Abdu'l-Bahá to John D. Bosch, U.S. National Bahá'í Archives. The translation was sent to John D. Bosch along with the original Tablet.
45. Letter dated August 9, 1912 from 'Abdu'l-Bahá to John D. Bosch, U.S. Bahá'í Archives.
46. Telegram dated August 10, 1912 from John D. Bosch to 'Abdu'l-Bahá, John D. and Louise Bosch papers, U.S. National Bahá'í Archives.
47. Telegram dated August 13, 1912 from 'Abdu'l-Bahá to John D. Bosch, John D. and Louise Bosch papers, U.S. National Bahá'í Archives. The translation was sent to John D. Bosch along with the original Tablet.

48. Letter dated September 9, 1912 from Thornton Chase to John D. Bosch, John D. and Louise Bosch papers, U.S. National Bahá'í Archives.
49. 'Abdu'l-Bahá, *The Promulgation of Universal Peace*, 456.
50. Letter dated September 24, 1912 from Edna Sedge to John D. Bosch, John D. and Louise Bosch papers, U.S. National Bahá'í Archives.
51. Letter dated September 26, 1912 from Thornton Chase to John D. Bosch, John D. and Louise Bosch papers, U.S. National Bahá'í Archives.
52. Redman, *'Abdu'l-Bahá in Their Midst*, 211.
53. 'Abdu'l-Bahá, "Abdu'l-Bahá at the Grave of Thornton Chase," *Star of the West*, vol. 3, no. 13 (4 November 1912): 14.
54. Letter dated October 3, 1912 from Edna Sedge to John D. Bosch, John D. and Louise Bosch papers, U.S. National Bahá'í Archives.
55. Marzieh Gail, "For John, With Love," *Bahá'í News*, (July 1974): 9–21; Christopher Rick, *The Oxford Book of English Verse*, 399.

3 / I Have Traveled 8,000 Miles to See You

1. Letter dated July 27, 1911 from John D. Bosch to Thornton Chase, John D. and Louise Bosch papers, U.S. National Bahá'í Archives; Marzieh Gail, "For John, With Love," *Bahá'í News* (July 1974): 9–21.
2. Shoghi Effendi, *God Passes By*, xxiv–xxvi.
3. Letter dated August 10, 1910 from John D. Bosch to Ahmad Sohrab, U.S. National Bahá'í Archives.
4. 'Abdu'l-Bahá, *Tablets of the Divine Plan*, no. 12.2.
5. Letter dated July 6, 1910 from John D. Bosch to Ahmad Sohrab, John D. and Louise Bosch papers, U.S. National Bahá'í Archives.
6. Letter dated March 14, 1912 from John D. Bosch to Ahmad Sohrab, John D. and Louise Bosch papers, U.S. National Bahá'í Archives.
7. Letter dated March 20, 1912 from John D. Bosch to Ahmad Sohrab, John D. and Louise Bosch papers, U.S. National Bahá'í Archives.
8. 'Abdu'l-Bahá, "Tablets from 'Abdu'l-Bahá," *Star of the West*, vol. 2, no. 10 (1911): 4.
9. Letter dated September 20, 1911 from John D. Bosch to 'Abdu'l-Bahá, John D. and Louise Bosch papers, U.S. National Bahá'í Archives.
10. Letter dated October 23, 1931 from Ella Cooper to John Bosch, Bosch papers, U.S. National Bahá'í Archives; letter dated October 24, 1931 from John Bosch to Ella Cooper, Bosch papers, U.S. National Bahá'í Archives.

11. Letter dated October 24, 1931 from John Bosch to Ella Cooper, Bosch papers, U.S. National Bahá'í Archives.
12. John Bosch 1912 Pilgrim Notes, John D. and Louise Bosch papers, U.S. National Bahá'í Archives.
13. 'Abdu'l-Bahá, *The Promulgation of Universal Peace*, 501; Mírzá Mahmúd-i-Zarqání, *Mahmúd's Diary*, 310; 'Abdu'l-Bahá, *The Promulgation of Universal Peace*, 502.
14. John D. and Louise Bosch papers, U.S. National Bahá'í Archives.
15. Bosch papers, U.S. National Bahá'í Archives.

4 / Louise

1. Roger White, *Occasions of Grace*, 49.
2. Ibid.
3. Myrle and Irvin Somerhalder, "In Memoriam: Louise Stapfer Bosch," *The Bahá'í World*, vol. XII (1950–1954): 707–709. Note: The source of the translation of this Tablet is not noted in the "In Memoriam" article.
4. Velda Piff Metalmann, *Lua Getsinger: Herald of the Covenant*, 111.
5. Myrle and Irvin Somerhalder, "In Memoriam: Louise Stapfer Bosch," *The Bahá'í World*, vol. XII (1950–1954): 707–709.
6. Louise Stapfer, John D. and Louise Bosch papers, U.S. National Bahá'í Archives.
7. Violette Nakhjavání and Bahiyyih Nakhjavání, *The Maxwell's of Montreal, Early Years 1870–1921*, 249.
8. Shoghi Effendi, *God Passes By*, 405; Metalmann, *Lua Getsinger: Herald of the Covenant*, 118.
9. Metalmann, *Lua Getsinger: Herald of the Covenant*, 118.
10. Myrle and Irvin Somerhalder, "In Memoriam: Louise Stapfer Bosch," *The Bahá'í World*, vol. XII (1950–1954): 707–709.
11. Rúhíyyih Rabbání, *The Priceless Pearl*, 144; Shoghi Effendi, *Bahá'í Administration*, 195–96.
12. Letter dated October 18, 1932 from May Maxwell to Louise Bosch, U.S. Bahá'í Archives.
13. Marion Holley, "In Memoriam: May Ellis Maxwell," *The Bahá'í World*, vol. VIII (1938–1940): 632–642.
14. Violette Nakhjavání and Bahiyyih Nakhjavání, *The Maxwells of Montreal: Early Years 1870–1921*, 70.
15. Telegram dated May 5, 1916 from May Maxwell to John and Louise

NOTES

Bosch, May 5, 1916, John D. and Louise Bosch papers, U.S. National Bahá'í Archives.
16. Myrle and Irvin Somerhalder, "In Memoriam: Louise Stapfer Bosch," *The Bahá'í World*, vol. XII (1950–1954): 707–9.
17. Ibid. Note: The source of the translation of this Tablet is not noted in the "In Memoriam" article.
18. The source for the quotations in this and the previous paragraphs is from Marzieh Gail, "For John, With Love," *Bahá'í News*, (July 1974): 9–21.
19. Louise Stapfer Bosch, quoted in Roger White, *Occasions of Grace*, 49.
20. Letter dated September 20, 1912 from Louise Stapfer to John D. Bosch, John D. and Louise Bosch papers, U.S. National Bahá'í Archives.
21. E-mail dated November 2, 2013 written by Jean Paul Vader on behalf of Louise Semple to Angelina Allen.
22. Letter dated October 22, 1913 from Louise Stapfer to John D. Bosch, John D. and Louise Bosch papers, U.S. National Bahá'í Archives.
23. Bosch marriage certificate and announcement, John D. and Louise Bosch papers, U.S. National Bahá'í Archives.
24. Letter dated March 31, 1914 from 'Abdu'l-Bahá to John D. Bosch and Louise Bosch, John D. and Louise Bosch papers, U.S. National Bahá'í Archives. The translation was sent to John D. Bosch and Louise Bosch along with the original Tablet.

5 / Awakened by the Tablets of the Divine Plan

1. Geyserville Chamber of Commerce, "History of Geyserville." Accessed April 10, 2014. https://geyservillechamber.com/community-2/history/.
2. *Century of Light*, document prepared under the supervision of The Universal House of Justice, 31.
3. 'Abdu'l-Bahá, "Talk at All Souls Unitarian Church," *The Promulgation of Universal Peace*, 319.
4. Shoghi Effendi, *The Advent of Divine Justice*, ¶170.
5. The Tablets of the Divine Plan are one of three Bahá'í "Charters" that outline Bahá'u'lláh's framework of a future Bahá'í civilization. To John and Louise Bosch, the integration of these three Charters would have been clear to them: The first Charter is Bahá'u'lláh's Tablet of Carmel, establishing the Bahá'í World Center in Haifa as the spiritual and administrative center of the Cause; the second Charter is 'Abdu'l-

NOTES

Bahá's Will and Testament, establishing the administrative order of the Cause; and the third Charter is 'Abdu'l-Bahá's Tablets of the Divine Plan. Together they comprise the framework by which a spiritual unification of the planet would be directed by the Head of the Cause, safeguarded by the Covenant, and carried out by the believers themselves. See *Century of Light*, 36.

6. 'Abdu'l-Bahá, *Tablets of the Divine Plan*, 43.
7. "A Trumpet Call to Action," *Star of the West*, vol. 7, no 10 (September 8, 1916): 86.
8. Ella G. Cooper, "The New Work Now Before Us," *Star of the West*, vol. 7, no. 11 (September 27, 1916): 101–103.
9. Ella G. Cooper, "The New Work Now Before Us," *Star of the West*, vol. 7, no. 11 (September 27, 1916): 101–103.
10. "Tablets Revealed by 'Abdu'l-Bahá to the Bahá'ís throughout the United States and Canada," *Star of the West*, vol. 7, no. 10 (September 8, 1916): 87–91.
11. "The Teaching Campaign—A Suggestion," *Star of the West*, vol. 7, no. 12 (October 16, 1916): 112–13; "The New Work is Now Before Us," *Star of the West*, vol. 7, no. 11 (September 27, 1916): 100.
12. Letter dated December 30, 1915 from Louise Bosch to Alfred Lunt, John D. and Louise Bosch papers, U.S. National Bahá'í Archives.
13. Shoghi Effendi, "Our Dearly Beloved Fellow-Worker, Mr. Randall!" *The Bahá'í World*, Vol. III (1928–1930): 212–13.
14. Letter dated January 20, 1916, from Alfred Lunt to Louise Bosch, U.S. National Bahá'í Archives.
15. Letter dated September 18, 1919 from John D. Bosch to 'Abdu'l-Bahá, John D. and Louise Bosch papers, U.S. National Bahá'í Archives.
16. Marzieh Gail, "For John, With Love," *Bahá'í News* (July 1974): 9–21.
17. Ibid.
18. Marzieh Gail, unpublished manuscript, September 4, 1946, c/o National Spiritual Assembly of Switzerland; Shoghi Effendi, *God Passes By*, 536.

6 / Tahiti

1. Letter dated July 15, 1920 from Howard MacNutt to John and Louise Bosch, U.S. National Bahá'í Archives.
2. George Biddle, *Tahitian Journal*, http://www.worldcat.org/title/tahitian-journal/oclc/867717325 (accessed April 12, 2014), 23.

3. 'Abdu'l-Bahá, *Selections from the Writings of 'Abdu'l-Bahá*, no. 222.1; letter dated December, 2015 from the Universal House of Justice to the Continental Boards of Counselors.
4. Louise Bosch, "Activities in the American Field," *Star of the West*, vol. 11, no. 9 (August 20, 1920): 145–52.
5. Geni La France, eyewitness, "The German Attack on Tahiti," *The New York Times Current History of the European War*, vol. I, issue 4 (January 23, 1915). http://www.gutenberg.org/files/16363/16363-h/16363-h.htm (accessed April 12, 2014).
6. 'Abdu'l-Bahá, *Tablets of the Divine Plan*, nos. 8.25, 8.27, 8.33.
7. Letter dated June 11, 1920 from Alexandre Drollet to Louise Bosch, John D. and Louise Bosch papers, U.S. National Bahá'í Archives.
8. Louise Bosch, "A Trip to Tahiti," *The Bahá'í World*, vol. III (1928–1930): 368.
9. Letter dated October 27, 1920 from Alexandre Drollet to John and Louise Bosch, John D. and Louise Bosch papers, U.S. National Bahá'í Archives.
10. Letter dated December 10, 1920 from Alexandre Drollet to Louise Bosch, John D. and Louise Bosch papers, U.S. National Bahá'í Archives.
11. Bahá'u'lláh, *Prayers and Meditations*, no. 92.1.
12. Letter dated July 20, 1925 from Rene Gasse to John and Louise Bosch, John D. and Louise Bosch papers, U.S. National Bahá'í Archives.
13. Letter dated May 6, 1945 from Rene Gasse to John and Louise Bosch, John D. and Louise Bosch papers, U.S. National Bahá'í Archives.
14. Antonio Martínez Ron. Cultor College, "Il Ballo delle ombre influenza ed uso della fotografia nei dipinti di Paul Gauguin." Last modified November 3, 2010. Accessed April 20, 2014. http://www.cultorweb.com/fp/Gauguin.html.
15. Letter dated October 16, 1927 from Georges Spitz to John and Louise Bosch, John D. and Louise Bosch papers, U.S. National Bahá'í Archives.
16. Rúhíyyih Rabbáni, *The Priceless Pearl*, 102.
17. Letter dated January 6, 1926 from Georges Spitz to John and Louise Bosch, John D. and Louise Bosch papers, U.S. National Bahá'í Archives.
18. Letter dated March 7, 1927, from Georges Spitz to John and Louise Bosch, John D. and Louise Bosch papers, U.S. National Bahá'í Archives.

19. Letter dated September 19, 1927, from Georges Spitz to John and Louise Bosch, John D. and Louise Bosch papers, U.S. National Bahá'í Archives.
20. Letter dated October 16, 1927, from Georges Spitz to John and Louise Bosch, John D. and Louise Bosch papers, U.S. National Bahá'í Archives.
21. Letter dated June 28, 1926, from Georges Spitz to John and Louise Bosch, John D. and Louise Bosch papers, U.S. National Bahá'í Archives.
22. Letter dated April 29, 1928, from Georges Spitz to John and Louise Bosch, April 29, 1928, John D. and Louise Bosch papers, U.S. National Bahá'í Archives.
23. Shoghi Effendi, *The World Order of Bahá'u'lláh*, 99.
24. Letter dated January 29, 1934 from Georges Spitz to John and Louise Bosch, John D. and Louise Bosch papers, U.S. National Bahá'í Archives.
25. Bahá'u'lláh, *The Hidden Words*, Persian, no. 44.
26. Letter dated September 16, 1939, from Louise Bosch to Georges Spitz, John D. and Louise Bosch papers, U.S. National Bahá'í Archives.
27. Letter dated May 14, 1929 from Louise Bosch to Georges Spitz, John D. and Louise Bosch papers, U.S. National Bahá'í Archives.
28. See http://www.familysearch.org, Oscar Alcide Georges Tamahere Spitz, b. February 12, 1928, d. 1970; email correspondence with Farhan Yazdani of France, July, 2013.
29. Letter dated May 1, 1921 from 'Abdu'l-Bahá to John and Louise Bosch, John D. and Louise Bosch papers, U.S. National Bahá'í Archives. The translation was sent to Mr. and Mrs. John Bosch along with the original Tablet.
30. Shoghi Effendi, *Citadel of Faith*, 156.
31. Translation of *Haziratu'l-Quds* provided by Omid Ghaemmaghami, https://www.binghamton.edu/cnes/people/faculty/omid_ghaemmaghami.html.; "In Memoriam," *The Bahá'í World*, vol. XV (1968–1973): 535.
32. 'Abdu'l-Bahá, *The Tablets of the Divine Plan*, no. 7.5.
33. 'Abdu'l-Bahá. *The Promulgation of Universal Peace*, 10.
34. Louise Bosch, "A Trip to Tahiti," *The Bahá'í World*, vol. III (1928–1930): 368.

NOTES

7 / 'Abdu'l-Bahá is in the Utmost Longing to See You
1. Western Union Telegram, Bosch papers, Box 1, U.S. National Bahá'í Archives.
2. Hasan Balyuzi, *'Abdu'l-Bahá: The Centre of the Covenant of Bahá'u'lláh*, 462.
3. Marzieh Gail, *Arches of the Years*, 106.
4. Krug, "Accounts of the Passing of 'Abdu'l-Bahá" by Florian & Grace Krug, *World Order*, vol. 7, no. 2, 38–41.
5. Robert Weinberg, *Ethel Jenner Rosenberg: The Life and Times of England's Outstanding Bahá'í Pioneer Worker*, Bahá'u'lláh, *Tablets of Bahá'u'lláh*, 145; Robert Weinberg, *Ethel Jenner Rosenberg: The Life and Times of England's Outstanding Bahá'í Pioneer Worker*, 78; (Note: Robert Weinberg's biography of Ethel Rosenberg contains an authorized translation of the 'Abdu'l-Bahá's Tablet to Ethel Rosenberg).
6. Robert Weinberg, *Ethel Jenner Rosenberg: The Life and Times of England's Outstanding Bahá'í Pioneer Worker*, 177; the Universal House of Justice, *Century of Light*, 66.
7. Shoghi Effendi, *The Unfolding Destiny of the British Bahá'í Community: Messages from the Guardian of the Bahá'í Faith to the Bahá'ís of the British Isles*, 90.
8. Ali M. Yazdi, *Blessings Beyond Measure: Recollections of 'Abdu'l-Bahá and Shoghi Effendi*, 67.
9. Johanna Hauff, "Letters telling of the passing of 'Abdu'l-Bahá," translated by Audrey Kempner, *Star of the West*, vol. XII, no. 19 (March 2, 1922): 296–99.
10. Ibid.
11. Florence Mayberry, "In Memoriam: Curtis DeMude Kelsey," *The Bahá'í World*, vol. XV (1968–1973): 469.
12. Ibid.
13. Rúhíyyih Rabbání, *The Priceless Pearl*, 45.
14. Munavvar Khánum, "Letter to Ruth Wales Randall," *Star of the West*, vol. 12, no.18 (February 7, 1922): 275–76.
15. Charles Krug, quoted in Marzieh Gail, *Arches of the Years*, 107.
16. Letter dated December 5, 1921, from Louise Bosch to Ella Cooper, December 5, 1921, U.S. National Bahá'í Archives.
17. Ethel Rosenberg, "Letters telling of the passing of 'Abdu'l-Bahá," *Star of the West*, vol. XII, no. 19 (March 2, 1922): 300–301.

NOTES

18. Ahmad Tabrizi, "Letter from Ahmad Tabrizi to Dr Ziá Bagdádí," *Star of the West*, vol. 12, no.18 (February 7, 1922): 280–81.
19. Louise Bosch to Ella Cooper, "The shock of his death was indeed as an earthquake," *Star of the West*, vol. 12, no. 18 (February 7, 1922): 276–82.
20. Shoghi Effendi, *God Passes By*, 497.
21. Bosch papers, U.S. National Bahá'í Archives.
22. Louise Bosch to Ella Cooper, "The shock of his death was indeed as an earthquake," *Star of the West*, vol. 12, no. 18 (February 7, 1922): 276–82.
23. Marzieh Gail, *Dawn Over Mount Hira*, 210.
24. Letter dated May 1, 1921 from 'Abdu'l-Bahá to John and Louise Bosch, translated December 14, 1922, U.S. National Bahá'í Archives. The translation was sent to Mr. and Mrs. John Bosch along with the original Tablet.
25. Bosch papers, "John's Account," U.S. National Bahá'í Archives.
26. Ibid.
27. Bosch papers, "John's Account," U.S. National Bahá'í Archives; Johanna Hauff, "Letters telling of the passing of 'Abdu'l-Bahá," translated by Audrey Kempner, *Star of the West*, vol. 12, no. 19 (March 2, 1922): 296–99.
28. Letter dated December 5, 1921 from Louise Bosch to Ella Cooper, United States National Bahá'í Archives.
29. Anita Chapman, *Leroy Ioas, Hand of the Cause of God*, 290; Rúhíyyih Rabbání, *The Priceless Pearl*, 57.
30. Rúhíyyih Rabbání, *The Priceless Pearl*, 42.
31. Adib Taherzadeh, *The Child of the Covenant*, 275.
32. Bosch papers, "John's Account," U.S. National Bahá'í Archives.
33. 'Abdu'l-Bahá, "The Universal Language of the Spirit," transcribed by Dr. Lutfu'lláh Hakím, *Star of the West*, vol. 13, no. 7 (October 1922): 163–64.
34. Bosch papers, U.S. National Bahá'í Archives.
35. Rúhíyyih Rabbání, *The Priceless Pearl*, 48.
36. Ibid.
37. Shoghi Effendi, *God Passes By*, 515.
38. Ibid., 519.
39. Shoghi Effendi, *The World Order of Bahá'u'lláh*, 18.

NOTES

40. Ibid., 21–22.
41. Shoghi Effendi, *God Passes By*, 522
42. Bosch papers, U.S. National Bahá'í Archives; Rúhíyyih Rabbání, *The Priceless Pearl*, 153.
43. Letter dated May 26, 1937, from Rúhíyyih Rabbání to John and Louise Bosch, U.S. National Bahá'í Archives, Box 6.
44. Bahá'í World, Volume XI (946–1950): 502.
45. 'Abdu'l-Bahá, *The Promulgation of Universal Peace*, 606.
46. 'Abdu'l-Bahá, *Tablets of the Divine Plan*, nos. 7.14–15.
47. Ibid., nos. 7.7–7.8.
48. Shoghi Effendi, *The Light of Divine Guidance*, Vol. I, 15.
49. Bosch papers, U.S. National Bahá'í Archives.
50. Letter dated March 2, 1944 from Nellie French to Louise Bosch, U.S. National Bahá'í Archives.
51. "Passing of 'Abdu'l-Bahá," *The Bahá'í World*, vol. I (1925–1926): 28.
52. Shoghi Effendi, *The Light of Divine Guidance*, Vol. I, 47.
53. Mary Maxwell, "Current Bahá'í Activities," *The Bahá'í World*, vol. VII (1936–1938): 21.
54. Bosch papers, U.S. National Bahá'í Archives.
55. Rúhíyyih Rabbání, *The Priceless Pearl*, 57.
56. Letter dated May 8, 1922 from Soheil Afnan to John and Louise Bosch, U.S. National Bahá'í Archives.
57. Bosch papers, "John's Account," U.S. National Bahá'í Archives.
58. Gayle Morrison, *To Move the World*, 203.
59. Document prepared under the supervision of the Universal House of Justice, *Century of Light*, 18.
60. Bosch papers, "Bahá'í Historical Record," U.S. National Bahá'í Archives.
61. Shoghi Effendi, *God Passes By*, xxvii.
62. Shoghi Effendi, *The Advent of Divine Justice*, no. 17.

8 / An Indefatigable Trio
1. Shoghi Effendi, *The Advent of Divine Justice*, ¶37.
2. Ibid., ¶80.
3. Rúhíyyih Rabbání, *The Priceless Pearl*, 428.
4. Bosch papers, U.S. Bahá'í National Archives; 'Abdu'l-Bahá, *Will and Testament of 'Abdu'l-Bahá*, 25.

5. Letter dated October 28, 1922 from Leroy Ioas to John D. Bosch, U.S. National Bahá'í Archives.
6. Rúhíyyih Rabbání, *The Guardian of the Bahá'í Faith*, 23–24.
7. Rúhíyyih Rabbání, *The Priceless Pearl*, 429.
8. Letter dated November 4, 1922 from Leroy Ioas to John and Louise Bosch, U.S. National Bahá'í Archives.
9. E-mail dated December 8, 2013 from May Hofman to Angelina Allen.
10. Bahá'í Library Online, "Letters to Grace Holley and Visalia LSA." Accessed April 15, 2014. http://bahai-library.com/shoghieffendi_letter_grace_holley.
11. Ibid.
12. Letter dated December 16, 1943 from Marion Holley to John and Louise Bosch, U.S. National Bahá'í Archives.
13. Letter dated May 12, 1944 from Marion Holley to John and Louise Bosch, U.S. National Bahá'í Archives.
14. 'Abdu'l-Bahá, *The Will and Testament of 'Abdu'l-Bahá*, 13.
15. Letter dated August 2, 1925 from the San Francisco Bahá'í Assembly to John D. Bosch, U.S. National Bahá'í Archives.
16. Letter dated July 11, 1927 from Thursa Clark to John D. Bosch, U.S. National Bahá'í Archives.
17. Ramona Allen Brown, *Memories of 'Abdu'l-Bahá: Recollections of the Early Days of the Bahá'ís of California*, 44.
18. Allan Ward, *239 Days: 'Abdu'l-Bahá's Journey in America*, 119.
19. Horace Holley, "In Memoriam: George Orr Latimer," *The Bahá'í World*, vol. XI (1946–1950): 511–512.
20. 'Abdu'l-Bahá, "Recent Tablet Lutfu'lláh Hakím," *Star of the West*, vol. 10, no. 7 (July 13, 1919): 137.
21. Letter date April 24, 1944 from George Latimer to John and Louise Bosch, U.S. National Bahá'í Archives.
22. Letter dated July 20, 1919 from 'Abdu'l-Bahá to Mr. James and Rúhaniyyih Latimer, U.S. National Bahá'í Archives.
23. Marion Hofman, "In Memoriam: Leroy Ioas," *The Bahá'í World*, vol. XIV (1963–1968): 291–300.
24. Ibid.
25. Bosch papers, U.S. National Bahá'í Archives.
26. Letter dated May 1, 1927 from Leroy Ioas to George Latimer, U.S. National Bahá'í Archives.

27. Letter dated March 18, 1931 from George Latimer to John and Louise Bosch, Bosch papers, U.S. National Bahá'í Archives.
28. Letter dated June 20, 1927 from Leroy Ioas to John D. Bosch, U.S. National Bahá'í Archives.
29. Letter dated June 22, 1927 from Leroy Ioas to John D. Bosch, U.S. National Bahá'í Archives.
30. Bosch papers, U.S. National Bahá'í Archives.
31. *Centers of Bahá'í Learning: Extracts from the Writings of Shoghi Effendi and the Universal House of Justice,* compiled by the Universal House of Justice, #27.
32. Bosch papers, U.S. National Bahá'í Archives. Committee Report. July 1927.
33. *Centers of Bahá'í Learning: Extracts from the Writings of Shoghi Effendi and the Universal House of Justice,* compiled by the Universal House of Justice, #28.
34. Bosch papers, U.S. National Bahá'í Archives.
35. Leroy Ioas, "Current Bahá'í Activities: Geyserville Summer School," *The Bahai World,* vol. VII (1936–1938): 59.
36. Letter dated August 22, 1927 from Marion Yazdi to John and Louise Bosch, U.S. National Bahá'í Archives.
37. Bosch papers, U.S. National Bahá'í Archives.
38. Gayle Morrison, *To Move the World,* 130; *Centers of Bahá'í Learning: Extracts from the Writings of Shoghi Effendi and the Universal House of Justice,* compiled by the Universal House of Justice, #19.

9 / Not Alone of the Mind, but of the Depths of the Heart

1. Gayle Morrison, *To Move the World,* 125.
2. Ibid., 147, 164, 218.
3. 'Abdu'l-Bahá, quoted in Gayle Morrison, *To Move the World,* 7. The editor's note reads: "'Abdu'l-Bahá to Louis Gregory, trans. 17 November 1909, Tablets of 'Abdu'l-Bahá, National Bahá'í Archives, Wilmette, Ill."
4. Louis Gregory, quoted in Gayle Morrison, *To Move the World,* 229; "Eighteenth Annual Convention of the Bahá'ís of the United States and Canada, April 29–May 2, 1926. Hotel Whitcomb Roof Garden, San Francisco," 393–95.
5. Keith Ransom-Kehler, "Letter from Mrs. Keith Ransom-Kehler to the Convention," *Bahá'í News Letter* 13 (Sept. 1926): 2.

6. Shoghi Effendi, *The Advent of Divine Justice*, ¶32.
7. Shoghi Effendi, *World Order of Bahá'u'lláh*, 42–43.
8. The Universal House of Justice, "Requisites for Spiritual Growth," *Messages from the Universal House of Justice: 1963–1986*, no. 375.5; see chapter 1, notes 16 and 2.
9. 'Abdu'l-Bahá, cited in O.Z. Whitehead, *Some Early Bahais of the West*, 15.
10. Louis Gregory, *The Bahá'í World*, Vol. XII (1950–1954): 29.
11. 'Abdu'l-Bahá, quoted in Marzieh Gail, *Arches of the Years*, 60.
12. Horace Holley, "Annual Report," *Bahá'í News*, (April 1927): no. 17, 7.
13. Ibid., no. 17, 8.
14. Cited in Gayle Morrison, *To Move the World*, 165–66.
15. Gayle Morrison, *To Move the World*, 176.
16. Shoghi Effendi, *Bahá'í Administration*, 131–32.
17. Letter dated April 1, 1932 from Louis Gregory to John and Louise Bosch, U.S. National Bahá'í Archives.
18. Gayle Morrison, *To Move the World*, 206.
19. Bahá'í Temple Unity, Proceedings of the Annual Meeting, 1927, pp. 92–104, Bahá'í Temple Unity Records, U.S. National Bahá'í Archives.
20. Ibid.
21. Ibid.
22. Ibid.
23. Ibid.
24. Bahá'u'lláh, *The Hidden Words of Bahá'u'lláh*, Persian, no. 5.
25. Shoghi Effendi, *Bahá'í Administration*, 129–30.
26. Letter dated August 16, 1927 from Helen Bishop to Louis Gregory, Louis G. Gregory papers.
27. Gwendolyn Etter-Lewis and Richard Thomas, eds. *Lights of the Spirit*, 229, 153.
28. Telephone interview with Earleta Fleming, April 8, 2018.
29. Cynthia Barnes Slater, essay published on http://www.bahaiteachings.org, April 11, 2018.
30. Cynthia Barnes Slater, email communication dated April 7, 2018.
31. Phone interview between author and Elaine West (Leo), April 7, 2018.
32. Gwendolyn Etter-Lewis and Richard Thomas, eds. *Lights of the Spirit*, 273.

NOTES

33. Letter dated September 30, 1942 from Adrienne Ellis to John and Louise Bosch, U.S. National Bahá'í Archives.
34. Author's interview with Robert C. Henderson at the 110th United States Bahá'í National Convention, Bahá'í House of Worship, Wilmette, Illinois, May 26, 2018.
35. Bahá'u'lláh, *Gleanings from the Writings of Bahá'u'lláh*, no. 106.1; Shoghi Effendi, *The Advent of Divine Justice*, ¶51.
36. Shoghi Effendi, *The Advent of Divine Justice*, ¶52.
37. Bahá'u'lláh, *Gleanings from the Writings of Bahá'u'lláh*, no. 139.8.
38. Letter dated August 11, 1928 from Park Demmey to John Bosch, U.S. National Bahá'í Archives.
39. The Cloverdale Reveille, July 27, 1944.
40. Firuz Kazemzadeh, quoted in ibid.
41. E-mail from Sheila Banani to Angelina Allen, January 19, 2019; letter dated June 28, 1953 from Shidan Fathe-Aazam.to the Geyersville Bahá'í Summer School. https://bahai-library.com/aazam_letter_geyserville_school.
42. 'Abdu'l-Bahá, *Selections from the Writings of 'Abdu'l-Bahá*, no. 207.2.
43. Gayle Morrison, *To Move the World*, 100; 'Abdu'l-Bahá, "Recent Tablets to American Bahá'ís," *Star of the West*, vol. 11, no. 5 (June 5, 1920): 92; Bahá'í Historical Records Cards, U.S. National Bahá'í Archives.
44. Tablet of 'Abdu'l-Bahá dated August 2, 1921, addressed to Roy Williams, U.S. National Bahá'í Archives.
45. Letter dated September 25, 1922 from Roy Williams to John D. Bosch, U.S. National Bahá'í Archives.
46. Letter dated December 5, 1928 from John Bosch to Leroy Ioas, U.S. National Bahá'í Archives.
47. Shoghi Effendi, *The Advent of Divine Justice*, ¶80; Shoghi Effendi, *Directives from the Guardian*, 68.
48. *Centers of Bahá'í Learning: Extracts from the Writings of Shoghi Effendi and the Universal House of Justice*, compiled by the Universal House of Justice, #35.
49. Letter dated January 27, 1932 from Shoghi Effendi to John D. Bosch, U.S. National Bahá'í Archives.
50. See chapter 7.
51. Letter dated January 19, 1938 from May Maxwell to John and Louise Bosch, U.S. National Bahá'í Archives.

NOTES

52. Letter dated October 17, 1936 from Leroy Ioas to John Bosch, U.S. National Bahá'í Archives.
53. Letter dated January 30, 1925 from Keith Ransom-Kehler to Louise Bosch, U.S. National Bahá'í Archives.
54. 'Abdu'l-Bahá, *Some Answered Questions*, 95. Also see Shoghi Effendi, *The Promised Day is Come*, ¶287.
55. Shoghi Effendi, *The Advent of Divine Justice*, ¶58.
56. Letter dated December 22, 1930 from Leroy Ioas to Horace Holley, Bosch papers, U.S. National Bahá'í Archives.
57. Shoghi Effendi, *The Light of Divine Guidance*, Vol. II, 78.
58. Letter dated April 9, 1933 from Leroy Ioas to Horace Holley, Bosch papers, U.S. National Bahá'í Archives.
59. The Universal House of Justice, *Promoting Entry By Troops*, 3.
60. Letter dated September 11, 1929 from Xorol Oliver to John and Louise Bosch, Bosch papers, U.S. National Bahá'í Archives.
61. Letter dated August 8 from Rowland Estall to John and Louise Bosch, Bosch papers, U.S. National Bahá'í Archives.
62. Letter dated August 21, 1929 from Paul Wildhofer to John and Louise Bosch, Bosch papers, U.S. National Bahá'í Archives.
63. Letter dated December 9, 1933 from Leroy Ioas to John and Louise Bosch, U.S. National Bahá'í Archives.
64. Forsythe Ward and wife Janet are most remembered for their service as custodians of the Shrine of Bahá'u'lláh under the direction of the Hands of the Cause in the Holy Land, followed by the direction of the International Bahá'í Council, and finally under the direction of the Universal House of Justice, between the years 1959–1969. When Forsythe Ward died unexpectedly in 1969, the Universal House of Justice commended his services at his "exalted post" in Bahji, as well as his services to the development of the Geyserville Summer School. See Janet Ward's *In Memoriam* of Forsythe Ward, *The Bahá'í World*, vol. XV, 451–53.
65. Letter dated June 25, 1934 from Leroy Ioas to the Pacific Coast Bahá'í Summer School Committee, U.S. National Bahá'í Archives.
66. Anita Chapman, *Leroy Ioas*, 63.
67. Shoghi Effendi, quoted in *Unlocking the Power of Action: Extracts from the Writings of Bahá'u'lláh, 'Abdu'l-Bahá, Shoghi Effendi, and the Universal House of Justice*. Compiled by the Research Department of the Universal

NOTES

House of Justice, 2005, #1. Bahá'í Library Online. Accessed April 24, 2017. http://bahai-library.com/compilation_unlocking_power_action

10 / Your Milly
1. Ugo Giachery, *Shoghi Effendi*, 130.
2. Beatrice Ashton, "In Memoriam: Amelia E Collins," *The Bahá'í World*, vol. XIII (1954–1963): 834–41.
3. Ibid.
4. Ibid.
5. Rúhíyyih Rabbání, *The Priceless Pearl*, 258.
6. Abu'l-Qasim Faizi, *Milly: A Tribute to Amelia E. Collins*, 9.
7. Ibid., 5; Shoghi Effendi, *Bahá'í Administration*, 35, 42.
8. Abu'l-Qasim Faizi, *Milly: A Tribute to Amelia E. Collins*, 5.
9. Louis Gregory, "Annual Bahá'í Convention: A Brief Report," *Star of the West*, vol. 15, no 1 (April 1924): 49.
10. Abu'l-Qasim Faizi, *Milly: A Tribute to Amelia E. Collins*, 5; letter dated August 20, 1942 from Amelia Collins to John and Louise Bosch, Bosch papers, U.S. Bahá'í National Archives.
11. Letter dated February 16, 1936, from John Bosch to Amelia Collins, U.S. National Bahá'í Archives.
12. Marzieh Gail, *Arches of the Years*, 310.
13. Letter dated April 5, 1936 from Amelia Collins to John D. Bosch, U.S. National Bahá'í Archives.
14. Leroy Ioas, "Current Bahá'í Activities: Geyserville Summer School," *Bahá'í World*, vol. VII (1936–1938): 60–63.
15. Bosch papers, U.S. National Bahá'í Archives.
16. Letter (undated) from Amelia Collins to John and Louise Bosch. Bosch papers, U.S. National Bahá'í Archives.
17. Letter dated May 20, 1939 from John and Louise Bosch to Amelia Collins, U.S. National Bahá'í Archives.
18. Letter dated September 4, 1936 from Mariam Haney to John and Louise Bosch, Bosch papers, U.S. National Bahá'í Archives.
19. Bahá'u'lláh, *Tablets of Bahá'u'lláh*, 142.
20. F. H. Clark, "Annual Report of the State Board of Horticulture of the State of California, for 1891." http://books.google.com.
21. Steinbeck, *Travels with Charley: In Search of America*, 188.
22. Bosch papers, U.S. National Bahá'í Archives.

NOTES

23. 'Abdu'l-Bahá, in *Bahá'í Prayers*, 112–13; 'Abdu'l-Bahá, *Will and Testament of 'Abdu'l-Bahá*, 3.
24. John Kenton Allen, interview by Angelina Diliberto Allen, Bosch Bahá'í School, Santa Cruz, July 2013.
25. Louise Bosch, quoted in Roger White, *Occasions of Grace*, 50.
26. Bosch papers, letters from Amelia Collins, U.S. National Bahá'í Archives.
27. Shoghi Effendi, *The Advent of Divine Justice*, ¶17.

11 / Saints

1. Shoghi Effendi, *Directives from the Guardian*, 10. Also see letter dated April 16, 1950 written on behalf of the Guardian, in *Living the Bahá'í Life*.
2. "The Disciples of 'Abdu'l-Bahá," *The Bahá'í World*, vol. III (1928–1930): 85; "A Pioneer at the Golden Gate," *Star of the West*, vol. 13, no. 8 (1922): 206; Rúhíyyih Rabbání, *The Priceless Pearl*, 307; Shoghi Effendi, *God Passes By*, 405; Shoghi Effendi, *Messages to America*, 30; Violette Nakhjavání, *The Maxwells of Montreal, Late Years 1937–1952*, 361–380; Marion Hofman, "In Memoriam: Leroy Ioas," *The Bahá'í World*, vol. XIV (1963–1968): 291–300; Shoghi Effendi, *Citadel of Faith: Messages to America 1947–1957*, 166; Beatrice Ashton, "In Memoriam: Amelia E. Collins," *The Bahá'í World*, vol. XIII (1954–1963): 834–841.
3. Shoghi Effendi, *Messages to America*, 30.
4. "In Memoriam: William Sutherland Maxwell," *The Bahá'í World*, vol. XII (1950–1954): 658–64.
5. Violette Nakhjavání, *The Maxwells of Montreal*, Volume II, 78.
6. Rúhíyyih Rabbání, *The Priceless Pearl*, 238.
7. Shoghi Effendi, quoted in Violette Nakhjavání, *The Maxwells of Montreal, Volume II*, 414.
8. Rosemary Salas, quoted in Violette Nakhjavání, *The Maxwells of Montreal, Volume II*, 415.
9. Shoghi Effendi, *Messages to the Bahá'í World, 1950–1957*, 132.
10. Shoghi Effendi, quoted in Horace Holley, "In Memoriam: Roy C. Wilhelm," vol. XII (1950–1954): 664–66.
11. Ibid.; Joel S Nizin (researcher on the life of Roy Wilhelm), interview by Angelina Allen, Wilmette, Bahá'í House of Worship, April 24, 2014.

NOTES

12. Rúhíyyih Rabbání, *The Priceless Pearl*, 49.
13. Letter dated April 4, 1910 from Roy Wilhelm to John D. Bosch, U.S. National Bahá'í Archives.
14. Letter dated June 16, 1915 from Roy Wilhelm to John D. Bosch, U.S. National Bahá'í Archives.
15. Letter dated February 7, 1935 from the National Spiritual Assembly addressed to Mr. John Bosch, U.S. National Bahá'í Archives.
16. Letter dated August 21, 1919 from John D. Bosch to Roy Wilhelm, U.S. National Bahá'í Archives.
17. Letter dated December 10, 1920 from Roy Wilhelm to John Bosch, U.S. National Bahá'í Archives.
18. 'Abdu'l-Bahá, *The Promulgation of Universal Peace*, 45; 'Abdu'l-Bahá, *Paris Talks*, no. 19.3; postcard dated 1935 from Roy Wilhelm to John Bosch, Bosch papers, U.S. National Bahá'í Archives.
19. Letter dated October 2, 1922 from Roy Wilhelm to John D. Bosch, U.S. National Bahá'í Archives.
20. Letter dated November 6, 1922 from Roy Wilhelm to John D. Bosch, U.S. National Bahá'í Archives.
21. Bosch papers, U.S. National Bahá'í Archives.
22. Letter dated September 25, 1925 from Roy Wilhelm to John and Louise Bosch, U.S. National Bahá'í Archives.
23. Shoghi Effendi, *National Convention: A Compilation prepared by the Research Department of the Universal House of Justice*, 39.
24. Letter dated April 4, 1931, from Roy Wilhelm to John and Louise Bosch, U.S. National Bahá'í Archives.
25. Letter dated April 9, 1932 from John Bosch to "Treasurer of N.S.A," Bosch papers, U.S. National Bahá'í Archives.
26. Letter dated April 18, 1932 from Roy Wilhelm to John Bosch, Bosch papers, U.S. National Bahá'í Archives.
27. 'Abdu'l-Bahá, *The Promulgation of Universal Peace*, 299–300.
28. Letter from John and Louise Bosch to Roy Wilhelm, Bosch papers, U.S. National Bahá'í Archives.
29. Shoghi Effendi, *Directives from the Guardian*, 31.
30. Letter dated December 2, 1935 from Roy Wilhelm to John and Louise Bosch, U.S. National Bahá'í Archives.
31. Based on the work of Joel Nizin, a researcher on the life of Roy Wilhelm.
32. Cable dated February 16, 1933 from Shoghi Effendi to Roy Wilhelm,

Bosch papers, U.S. National Bahá'í Archives. See also Shoghi Effendi, *The Decisive Hour*, no. 6.

33. Letter dated April 30, 1940 from Roy Wilhelm to John and Louise Bosch, April 30, 1940, U.S. National Bahá'í Archives.
34. Letter dated November 4, 1940 from Roy Wilhelm to John and Louise Bosch, November 4, 1940, U.S. National Bahá'í Archives.
35. Shoghi Effendi, *Bahá'í Administration*, 55–56.
36. Letter dated March 17, 1942 from Roy Wilhelm to John and Louise Bosch, March 17, 1942, U.S. National Bahá'í Archives. It should be noted that Brent Poirier has researched the location of this film and discovered that, according the archivist at the U.S. National Bahá'í Archives, there were two films made of the Master. One was made professionally outside the Hotel Ansonia, and the Archives does not have a copy of this film. The other film, which is the held at the Archives, was made in Brooklyn at the home of Howard MacNutt.
37. Letter dated 1942 from Roy Wilhelm to John Bosch, Bosch papers, U.S. National Bahá'í Archives; postcard dated December 19, 1943 from Roy Wilhelm to John and Louise Bosch, Bosch papers, U.S. National Bahá'í Archives.
38. 'Abdu'l-Baha, *Star of the West*, vol. IV, no 19, March 2, 1914.
39. Letter dated July 13, 1935 from John Bosch to George Latimer, U.S. National Bahá'í Archives.
40. Letter dated September 25, 1935 from George Latimer to John and Louise Bosch, U.S. National Bahá'í Archives.
41. Letter dated September 29, 1935 from Roy Wilhelm to John and Louise Bosch, U.S. National Bahá'í Archives.
42. Letter dated October 21, 1945 from Louise Bosch to Leroy and Sylvia Ioas, U.S. National Bahá'í Archives.
43. Shoghi Effendi, *Directives of the Guardian*, 87.
44. Bahá'u'lláh, *Gleanings from the Writing of Bahá'u'lláh*, no. 106.3.
45. Bosch papers, U.S. National Bahá'í Archives.
46. Shoghi Effendi, *Messages to America*, 106.
47. 'Abdu'l-Bahá, *Paris Talks*, no. 18.4; Marzieh Gail, *Dawn Over Mount Hira*, 204.
48. Bahá'u'lláh, *The Hidden Words*, Arabic, no. 2.

Bibliography

Writings of Bahá'u'lláh

Gleanings from the Writings of Bahá'u'lláh. Translated by Shoghi Effendi. New ed. Wilmette, IL: Bahá'í Publishing, 2005.

The Hidden Words of Bahá'u'lláh. Translated by Shoghi Effendi. Wilmette: Bahá'í Publishing, 2002.

The Kitáb-i-Aqdas. 1st pocket-sized ed. Wilmette, IL: Bahá'í Publishing Trust, 1993.

Prayers and Meditations. Wilmette: Bahá'í Publishing Trust, 1996.

Tablets of Bahá'u'lláh Revealed after the Kitáb-i-Aqdas. Compiled by the Research Department of the Universal House of Justice and translated by Habib Taherzadeh with the assistance of a Committee at the Bahá'í World Center. Wilmette, IL: Bahá'í Publishing Trust, 1988.

Writings of the Báb

Selections from the Writings of the Báb. Compiled by the Research Department of the Universal House of Justice. Translated by Habib Taherzadeh et al. Wilmette, IL: Bahá'í Publishing Trust, 2006.

Writings of 'Abdu'l-Bahá

Paris Talks: Addresses Given by 'Abdu'l-Bahá in 1911. Wilmette, IL: Bahá'í Publishing, 2011.

Promulgation of Universal Peace: Talks Delivered by 'Abdu'l-Bahá During His Visit to the United States and Canada in 1912. Wilmette, IL: Bahá'í Publishing, 2012.

Selections from the Writings of 'Abdu'l-Bahá. Wilmette, IL: Bahá'í Publishing, 2010.
Some Answered Questions. Compiled and translated from the Persian by Laura Clifford Barney. Newly Revised by a Committee at the Bahá'í World Center. Reprinted with the permission of the Bahá'í World Center. Wilmette, IL: Bahá'í Publishing, 2014.
Tablets of the Divine Plan. Wilmette: Bahá'í Publishing Trust, 1993.
The Will and Testament of 'Abdu'l-Bahá. Wilmette: Bahá'í Publishing Trust, 1944.

Writings of Shoghi Effendi

The Advent of Divine Justice. New ed. Wilmette, IL: Bahá'í Publishing Trust, 2006.
Bahá'í Administration: Selected Messages, 1922–1932. 7th ed. Wilmette, IL: Bahá'í Publishing Trust, 1974.
Citadel of Faith. Wilmette: Bahá'í Publishing Trust, 2014.
This Decisive Hour: Messages from Shoghi Effendi to the North American Bahá'ís, 1932–1946. Wilmette, IL: Bahá'í Publishing Trust, 2002.
Directives from the Guardian. New Delhi: Bahá'í Publishing Trust, 1973.
God Passes By. Wilmette: Bahá'í Publishing Trust, 2010.
The Light of Divine Guidance, Vol. 1. Germany: Bahá'í Verlag, 1982.
The Light of Divine Guidance, Vol. 2. Germany: Bahá'í Verlag, 1985.
Messages to the Bahá'í World, 1950–1957. Wilmette: Bahá'í Publishing Trust, 1971.
National Convention: A Compilation prepared by the Research Department of the Universal House of Justice, 1995.
The Promised Day is Come. Wilmette: Bahá'í Publishing Trust, 1996.
The Unfolding Destiny of the British Bahá'í Community: Messages from the Guardian of the Bahá'í Faith to the Bahá'ís of the British Isles. London: Bahá'í Publishing Trust, 1981.
The World Order of Bahá'u'lláh. Wilmette: Bahá'í Publishing Trust, 1991.

Writings of the Universal House of Justice

Century of Light. Commissioned by the Universal House of Justice. Haifa, Israel: Bahá'í World Center, 2001.
Messages from the Universal House of Justice 1963–1986: The Third Epoch of the Formative Age. Compiled by Geoffry Marks. Wilmette, IL: Bahá'í Publishing Trust, 1996.

BIBLIOGRAPHY

Compilations

Centers of Bahá'í Learning: Extracts from the Writings of Shoghi Effendi and the Universal House of Justice, compiled by the Universal House of Justice. Compilation of Compilations, vol. 1, revised September, 1990.

Promoting Entry by Troops. Compiled by the Research Department on behalf of the Universal House of Justice. Haifa, Israel: Bahá'í World Center, 1994.

Unlocking the Power of Action: Extracts from the Writings of Bahá'u'lláh, 'Abdu'l-Bahá, Shoghi Effendi, and the Universal House of Justice. Compiled by the Research Department of the Universal House of Justice, 2005.

Other works

Balyuzi, Hasan. *'Abdu'l-Bahá: The Centre of the Covenant of Bahá'u'lláh.* Oxford: George Ronald, 1971.

Biddle, George. *Tahitian Journal.* http://www.worldcat.org/title/tahitian-journal/oclc/867717325 (accessed April 12, 2014), 23.

Brown, Ramona Allen. *Memories of 'Abdu'l-Bahá: Recollections of the Early Days of the Bahá'ís of California.* Wilmette: Bahá'í Publishing Trust, 1980.

Burbank, Luther. *New Creations in Fruits and Flowers.* Accessed October 10, 2016. https://archive.org/details/newcreationsinfr1894burb.

Chapman, Anita. *Leroy Ioas, Hand of the Cause of God.* Oxford: George Ronald, 1998.

Chase, Thornton. *The Bahá'í Revelation.* Chicago: Bahá'í Publishing Society, 1909.

Chen, Constance M. "Obituary: Marzieh Nabil Carpenter Gail (1908–1993)." *Bahá'í Studies Review*, vol. 6, 1994. http://bahai-library.com/chen_marzieh_gail_obituary.

Clifford Barney, Laura. *God's Heroes: A Drama in Five Acts.* Philadelphia: J. B. Lippincott Company, 1910.

Cooper, Ella, and Helen Goodall. *Daily Lessons Received in 'Akká.* Wilmette: Bahá'í Publishing Trust, 1979.

Etter-Lewis, Gwendolyn, and Richard Thomas, eds. *Lights of the Spirit.* Wilmette: Bahá'í Publishing, 2006.

Faizi, Abu'l-Qasim. *Milly: A Tribute to Amelia E. Collins.* New York: Howard Fertig.

Ford, Mary Hanford. *The Oriental Rose.* New York: Broadway Publishing Company, 1910.

Gail, Marzieh. *Dawn Over Mount Hira.* Oxford: George Ronald, 1976.
———. "For John, With Love." *Bahá'í News* (July 1974): 9–21.
———. *Arches of the Years.* Oxford: George Ronald, 1991.
Giachery, Ugo. *Shoghi Effendi.* Oxford: George Ronald, 1973.
Hornby, Helen Bassett, ed. *Lights of Guidance.* New Delhi: Bahá'í Publishing Trust, 1996.
La France, Geni. "The German Attack on Tahiti," *The New York Times Current History of the European War,* vol. I, issue 4 (January 23, 1915). http://www.gutenberg.org/files/16363/16363-h/16363-h.htm (accessed April 12, 2014).
MacNutt, Howard, ed. *The Promulgation of Universal Peace.* Wilmette: Bahá'í Publishing Trust, 1982.
Mahmúd-i-Zarqání, Mírzá. *Mahmúd's Diary.* Oxford: George Ronald, 1998.
Morrison, Gayle. *To Move the World.* Wilmette: Bahá'í Publishing Trust, 1982.
Nabíl-i-Zarandí. *The Dawn-Breakers: Nabíl's Narrative of the Early Days of the Bahá'í Revelation.* Translated by Shoghi Effendi. Wilmette: Bahá'í Publishing Trust, 1996.
Nakhjavání, Bahiyyih, and Violette Nakhjavání, *The Maxwell's of Montreal, Early Years 1870–1921.* Oxford: George Ronald, 2011.
Nakhjavání, Bahiyyih, and Violette Nakhjavání, *The Maxwell's of Montreal, Late Years 1937–1952.* Oxford: George Ronald, 2012.
Phelps, Myron H. *The Life and Teachings of Abbas Effendi.* Putnam's Sons, 1904.
Piff Metalmann, Velda. *Lua Getsinger: Herald of the Covenant.* Oxford: George Ronald, 1997.
Rabbáni, Rúhíyyih. *The Priceless Pearl.* London: Bahá'í Publishing Trust, 1969.
———. *The Guardian of the Bahá'í Faith.* London: Bahá'í Publishing Trust, 1988.
Redman, Earl. *'Abdu'l-Bahá in Their Midst.* Oxford: George Ronald, 2011.
Ron, Antonio Martinez. Cultor College, "Il Ballo delle ombre influenza ed uso della fotografia nei dipinti di Paul Gauguin." Last modified November 3, 2010. Accessed April 20, 2014. http://www.cultorweb.com/fp/Gauguin.html.
Steinbeck, John. *Travels with Charley: In Search of America.* New York: Penguin Books, 1980.

Stockman, Robert H. *Thornton Chase: First American Bahá'í*. Wilmette: Bahá'í Publishing Trust, 2002.
Taherzadeh, Adib. *The Child of the Covenant*. Oxford: George Ronald, 2000.
Tennsyon, Alfred. "Ulysses." The Norton Anthology of English Literature. New York: W.W. Norton and Co., 2006.
Ward, Allan. *239 Days: 'Abdu'l-Bahá's Journey in America*. Wilmette: Bahá'í Publishing Trust, 1979.
Weinberg, Robert. *Ethel Jenner Rosenberg: The Life and Times of England's Outstanding Bahá'í Pioneer Worker*. Oxford: George Ronald, 1995.
White, Roger. *Occasions of Grace*. Oxford: George Ronald, 1992.
Whitehead, O. Z. *Some Early Bahá'ís of the West*. Oxford: George Ronald, 1976.
Whitmore, Bruce W. *The Dawning Place*. Wilmette: Bahá'í Publishing Trust, 1984.
Yazdi, Ali M. *Blessings Beyond Measure: Recollections of 'Abdu'l-Bahá and Shoghi Effendi*. Wilmette: Bahá'í Publishing Trust, 1988.

Index

A
'Abdu'l-Bahá
   advice for teachers of the Cause, 200
   Center of Bahá'u'lláh's Covenant, 11
   day of union and, 248
   House of Worship and, 20, 23
   John Bosch's longing to meet, 71
   John Bosch's new name and, 53–54
   Laura Clifford Barney and, 36
   Local Spiritual Assemblies and, 67–68
   meeting with Helen Goodall, 4
   Mystery of God, 6
   passing of, 149, 156–58
   Perfect Exemplar, 46
   servant of Bahá'u'lláh, 12
   son and appointed successor of Bahá'u'lláh, 2
   station of, 6, 10–12
   Thornton Chase and, 17, 46, 53, 61, 78
Alí Kulí Khán, 103–4, 207
Allen, John, 288
American Bahá'í community, 169

B
Bagdádí, Dr. Zia, 228
Bahá'í, 14

INDEX

Bahá'í history, 181–82
Bahá'í literature, xiii, 28, 35–36, 119, 300
Bahá'u'lláh
    Covenant of, 4, 6, 252
    divine civilization of, 188
    laws of, 212, 230
    Message of, 116, 197, 248, 293
    race unity and, 223
    relationship between station and 'Abdu'l-Bahá's station, 10–12
    Revelation of, 168, 229–30, 237, 242, 251
    Shrine of, 275–76
    teachings of, 8, 130, 190, 200, 215, 224–25, 235, 239, 253, 258, 262, 290
    Tomb of, 144
Bahá'u'lláh and the New Era, 4, 128
Banani, Amin, 245
Banani, Sheila, 247
Bishop, Charles, 236–37
Bishop, Helen, 236–37
Bosch, John, 294
    accolades from Shoghi Effendi after passing of, 327–28
    Bahá'í Historical Record, 180–81
    first meeting with 'Abdu'l-Bahá, 71–78
    last meeting with 'Abdu'l-Bahá, 160–61
    marriage to Louise Stapfer, 94–95
    passing of, 324–29
    pilgrimage of, 145–82
    pioneering trip to Tahiti, 110–44
    practical suggestions of regarding the fund, 107
    recollection of 'Abdu'l-Bahá's passing, 161–62
    trips to Germany, 172–75
Boyle, Louise, 228

C
Century of Light, 51, 179

Chase, Thornton, 28, 32–35, 41–42, 46–53, 57–61, 69
    The Bahá'í Revelation, 28–29, 45
    Disciple of 'Abdu'l-Bahá, 293
    meeting with John Bosch at Temple Convention, 20
    spiritual brother to John Bosch, 19
Collins, Amelia, 275–91
Cook, Coralie, 228
Cook, John, 288

D

Daily Lessons Received in 'Akká, 1908, 4
Dawn Over Mount Hira, 49
Demney, Park, 245
Disciples of 'Abdu'l-Bahá, 3–4, 21
Dispensation of Bahá'u'lláh, The, 137

E

Ellis, Adrienne, 239–42

F

Fathe-Aazam, Shidan, 245
Fleming, Earleta, 237–38
French, Nellie, 175

G

Gail, Marzieh, 49, 89–90, 159
Getsinger, Edward, 21
Getsinger, Lua, 21, 83, 294
God Passes By, 20, 63, 181, 246
God's Heroes: A Drama in Five Acts, 36–37
Goodall, Helen, 293
    association with the early days of the Faith, 3
Greatest Holy Leaf (Bahíyyih Khánum), 86–87, 163–65, 184
Greenleaf, Charles, 21
Gregory, Louis, 221–23, 226–28, 230–31, 294

INDEX

H
Hall, Albert, 21
Haney, Mariam, 228, 285–86, 294
Hauff, Johanna, 148–49, 153, 162, 170, 176
Hearst, Phoebe, 226–27
Hidden Words, The, 140

I
Ioas, Leroy, 187, 203–11, 215, 226, 228, 258–61, 268–72, 294

K
Kazemzadeh, Dr. Firuz
  appointment of to committee to locate new site for Bosch school, 288
  impressions of Geyersville (Bosch) Bahá'í school, 246–47
  observations on history of Bosch Bahá'í School, xvii
Kelsey, Curtis, 149–52
Krug, Dr. Florian, 145–47, 153
Krug, Grace, 146

L
Lamprill, Gretta, 142
Latimer, George, 51, 198–203, 205, 209, 213–15, 219, 230, 283, 294, 320–21
Local Spiritual Assemblies, 67
Locke, Alain, 228

M
MacNutt, Howard, 21
Mashriqu'l-Adhkár (House of Worship), 22–24, 26–27, 181, 184–85, 190, 195, 200, 289, 316
Maxwell, May, 83–85, 87, 294
Mills, Mountfort, 21
Mírzá Abu'l Faḍl, 171
Mírzá Jalal, 157
Monireh Khánum, 153, 163
Montague, Fanny, 81
Moody, Susan, 22, 305
Mortensen, Fred, 21

Mount Carmel, 158–59, 276
Muhlschlegel, Adlebert, 176–77
Munavvar <u>Kh</u>ánum, 152

N
Nakhjavání, Violette, 295
Nurani (Luminous), 54, 107, 181

O
Oglesby, Sadie, 232–36, 294
Oneness of Mankind, 225

P
Parker, Gladys Irene, 142
Parsons, Agnes, 228
pioneer
    call of Shoghi Effendi for, 142
    definition of, 114
Plan of Unified Action, 189–90

R
racial diversity, 237
Randall, Harry, 105
Ransom-Kehler, Keith, 257–59, 293
Root, Martha, 294
Rosenberg, Ethel, 147–48, 153
Rúhíyyih <u>Kh</u>ánum, 152, 164, 170, 184, 188–89, 277

S
Schopflocher, Fred, 256
self-renunciation, 224
Shaw, John, 237
Shaw, Rosa, 237
Shoghi Effendi, 188, 264
    appointment as Guardian, 163, 164, 167
    elaboration on source of universal consciousness, 99
    marriage to Rúhíyyih <u>Kh</u>ánum, 169

Shrine of the Báb
    illumination of, 150–52
Slater, Cynthia Barnes, 238–39
Stapfer, Louise, 81–95
    passing of, 324–29
    recollection of 'Abdu'l-Bahá's passing, 163
    service as correspondent in Haifa to Western believers, 153
    spiritual awakening of, 109–110
suicide, 154–55
summer schools, xvi
    Bosch / Geyersville, 191, 198, 202–7, 210–20, 230–41, 293, 312
    capacity to teach the Cause and, 252
    development of, 63
    development of spiritual qualities and, 258
    Esslingen, 177
    importance of race unity studies in, 228, 232, 244
    oneness of humanity and, 232, 245
    preparation for pioneering and, 248
    Shoghi Effendi's guidance on, 183–84, 252–55, 264, 290–91
    spirit of teaching and, 256, 279
Summon Up Remembrance, 326
Sutherland Maxwell, William, 294–97

T

Tablet of Wisdom, 147
Tablets of the Divine Plan, 65, 99–102, 198
    Bahá'í Charter for the spiritual conquest of the planet, 99
Temple Unity Convention of 1909, 20, 23–24, 27, 88
Ten Year Crusade, 141–42, 237, 247
Thabit (Steadfastness), 17
The Advent of Divine Justice, 183, 243
The Child of the Covenant, 164
The Life and Teachings of Abbas Effendi, 1–2, 28
The Oriental Rose, 36–37
The Priceless Pearl, 152, 164
The Promulgation of Universal Peace, 21
Thornton Chase: First American Bahá'í, 28

INDEX

True, Corinne, 22, 23, 106
Turner, Robert, 226–27

U
Universal House of Justice
　announcement of 'Abdu'l-Bahá's permanent resting place, f158
　characterization of the world of 1914, 98
　December 2015 message to the Continental Counselors, 114

W
West, Elaine, 239
Wilhelm, Roy, 121, 294, 297–322
Will and Testament of 'Abdu'l-Bahá, 64, 178, 196–97
　Charter for a new world civilization, 168
　first reading of, 164
Williams, Roy, 248–251

Photos of John Bosch

Postcard from St Galen, Switzerland, the place of John Bosch's birth.

"No doubt, when the Cause spreads more throughout Switzerland, this fatherland of his will grow to be proud of this heroic and noble soul it produced" —Rúhíyyih Khánum, writing on behalf of Shoghi Effendi.

Marzieh Gail, outstanding literary scholar and author whose early manuscript of the life of John Bosch is the foundation of this biography.

Group picture of the delegates to the first National Bahá'í Convention, March 21, 1909. Taken at the home of Corinne True.

Upper row, left to right: Mrs. H.C. Morton, Charles Greenleaf, John C. Crowley, Thornton Chase, Corinne True, Mountfort Mills, Mr. Perry, Edward Struven

Third row, left to right: Marie Watson, Emma Foster, Mrs. A.M. Bryant, Mrs. Parry, Mr. John F. Behrens, Howard MacNutt, Leon A. Lehman, Albert Hall, Annie L. Parmerton, Della Lincoln, Marie Hopper

Second row, left to right: Mrs. John Deremo, Sophia Engelhorn, John Bosch, Harrison Mills, Bernard Jacobsen, Susan I. Moody, M. Lesley O'Keefe

Front row, left to right: Arthur Agnew, Charles Mason Remey, Charles S. Hargis, H.A. Nelson, D.D. Babcock, Benjamin Taylor, Adolf M. Dahl, Edward C. Getsinger.

Feast at the home of Helen Goodall in Oakland, October 1912. John Bosch, holding the Greatest Name, is seated at the foot of 'Abdu'l-Bahá. Helen Goodall is seated on the ground, second from left.

Studio portrait of John Bosch that he sent to Louise Stapfer.

Louise and John, Geyserville, California.

Thornton Chase in his study. To John he wrote, "It is truly not words that make one of any importance in the Kingdom but that sweet, pure, unselfish, loving, sincere nature which 'Abdu'l-Bahá perceived at once in you, and which we all perceive with you, to the degree of our enlightenment. Truly you are of the chosen, not only of the called."

John and Louise in Tahiti with Alexandre Drollet's family, 1920.

Members of the Pacific Coast Bahá'í Summer School Committee, 1926.
From left to right: George Latimer, John Bosch, Leroy Ioas.

From left to right: Shidan Fathe-Aazam, Amin Banani, John Bosch, and Firuz Kazemadeh, July 1944, Geyserville, California.

Louise G. Gregory, Hand of the Cause of God. His address on "The Oneness of Mankind" to the 1926 National Bahá'í Convention in San Francisco, California inspired John Bosch's plans for the first session of the Geyserville Bahá'í Summer School in the following summer of 1927.

Amelia "Milly" Collins, Hand of the Cause of God. Once when Milly had been traveling from Geyserville to a National Teaching Committee meeting, one of the friends asked her where she had arrived from, and Milly replied, "From heaven."

John Bosch with Roy Wilhelm.

John David Bosch, named "Nurani" ("Luminous") by 'Abdu'l-Bahá.

Of John, Louise said, "I knew immediately he was the man who would share the deepest concerns of my heart."